Job Feedback:

Giving, Seeking, and Using Feedback for Performance Improvement

Second Edition

SERIES IN APPLIED PSYCHOLOGY

Edwin A. Fleishman, George Mason University
Jeanette N. Cleveland, Pennsylvania State University
Series Editors

Manuel London
Job Feedback: Giving, Seeking, and Using Feedback for Performance Improvement, Second Edition

Manuel London
How People Evaluate Others in Organizations

Manuel London
Leadership Development: Paths to Self-Insight and Professional Growth

Robert F. Morrison and Jerome Adams
Contemporary Career Development Issues

Michael D. Mumford, Garnett Stokes, and William A. Owens
Patterns of Life History: The Ecology of Human Individuality

Kevin R. Murphy
Validity Generalization: A Critical Review

Kevin R. Murphy and Frank E. Saal
Psychology in Organizations: Integrating Science and Practice

Susan E. Murphy and Ronald E. Riggio
The Future of Leadership Development

Erich P. Prien, Jeffrey S. Schippmann and Kristin O. Prien
Individual Assessment: As Practiced in Industry and Consulting

Ned Rosen
Teamwork and the Bottom Line: Groups Make a Difference

Heinz Schuler, James L. Farr, and Mike Smith
Personnel Selection and Assessment: Individual and Organizational Perspectives

John W. Senders and Neville P. Moray
Human Error: Cause, Prediction, and Reduction

Frank J. Smith
Organizational Surveys: The Diagnosis and Betterment of Organizations Through Their Members

George C. Thornton III and Rose Mueller-Hanson
Developing Organizational Simulations: A Guide for Practitioners and Students

Yoav Vardi and Ely Weitz
Misbehavior in Organizations: Theory, Research, and Management

Job Feedback:

Giving, Seeking, and Using Feedback for Performance Improvement

Second Edition

Manuel London
State University of New York at Stony Brook

LEA

LAWRENCE ERLBAUM ASSOCIATES, PUBLISHERS

2003   Mahwah, New Jersey   London

Lawrence Erlbaum Associates, Inc., Publishers
10 Industrial Avenue
Mahwah, New Jersey 07430

Library of Congress Cataloging-in-Publication Data

London, Manuel.
    Job feedback : giving, seeking, and using feedback for performance improvement /
Manuel London.—2nd ed.
        p. cm.
    Includes bibliographical references and index.
    ISBN 0-8058-4494-5 (c : alk. paper)—ISBN 0-8058-4495-3 (pbk. : alk. paper)
    1. Employee motivation.   2. Feedback (Psychology)   3. Performance standards.
    I. Title.

    HF5549.5.M63L66   2003
    658.3'14—dc21   2002192788

Books published by Lawrence Erlbaum Associates are printed
on acid-free paper, and their bindings are chosen for strength
and durability.

Printed in the United States of America
10 9 8 7 6 5 4 3 2 1

Contents

III SUPPORTING THE USE OF FEEDBACK

IV FUTURE DIRECTIONS

Series Foreword

Series Editors
Edwin A. Fleishman
George Mason University

Jeanette N. Cleveland
Pennsylvania State University

There is a compelling need for innovative approaches to the solution of many pressing problems involving human relationships in today's society. Such approaches are more likely to be successful when they are based on sound research and applications. This Series in Applied Psychology offers publications that emphasize state-of-the-art research and its application to important issues of human behavior in a variety of social settings. The objective is to bridge both academic and applied interests.

We know from psychological research that people need knowledge of results to accomplish performance goals and improve their performance over time. Feedback generally is acknowledged as an essential component of many management functions, such as providing training and development, setting goals, building teams, and evaluating job performance. In the first edition to his book, *Job Feedback*, Dr. Manuel London described how research and experience have shown that feedback often is the weak link in the management process. Managers feel uncomfortable giving feedback, especially when it is negative. Often they do not know how to make feedback a constructive experience, how often to give feedback, or how specific to make it without sounding self-serving. Managers often worry that the person receiving the feedback will be defensive, ignore the message, or blame the messenger.

Even when feedback is positive, managers may fear that a "pat on the back" may go to a subordinate's head or antagonize the subordinate's coworkers. On the receiving end, employees often shy away from asking for feedback because they fear it will be negative, or because they think they will be perceived as looking for praise. As we pointed out in our Foreword to the first edition, such psychological and social dynamics suggest that managers need a better understanding of the importance of feedback and ways to make it constructive. Giving and receiving feedback are skills that need to be acquired and practiced. In the first edition, London described how feedback works and offered practical ideas, based on research, for improving the effectiveness of feedback in organizations.

The first edition covered the basic feedback-related processes by describing how people in organizations give, seek, and use performance feedback. Dr. London examined how givers of feedback process and evaluate information and prepare the message for delivery. He considered how the receivers of feedback react to and use the information, and showed how this happens informally during the normal course of daily events. He also showed how effective feedback processes can be incorporated into formal human resource programs, such as performance appraisal, upward and 360-degree surveys, and assessment centers. He also illustrated how feedback to groups can enhance their coordination and cooperation.

In today's world of rapid organizational change, people cannot assume that the organization will take care of their development needs. Supervisors and organizational systems may provide the resources that will enable individuals to learn how to take responsibility for their own development. However, people need to learn how to ask for feedback and use the information for self-assessment, development and career planning, and for monitoring their own progress. In his first edition, London showed how employees can get feedback not only from supervisors, but also from peers, subordinates, and customers. The manager's role is not just to give feedback, but to help the receiver make sense of the feedback in relation to other information about, for instance, changing business strategies and performance expectations. Managers and their subordinates can be held accountable for giving and using feedback.

Since the first edition of *Job Feedback* was published 6 years ago, there have been many advances in understanding how people give and receive feedback. New methods for feedback collection and delivery have been developed. Also, a number of performance management systems that incorporate feedback have been evaluated and enhanced. This second edition reports the latest job feedback research findings and program developments. It provides expanded chapters on how people evaluate themselves, relate to others who give them feedback, and process information about others. Also, there are substantially revised chapters on 360-degree feedback methods, and the volume updates research on the long-term effects of feedback on individuals and organizations. Additional new chapters examine how feedback is given and received in teams and cross-cultural organizations, and explores the impact that feedback has on changing technologies and new forms of work, such as virtual organizations. New data collection methods are described such as online survey methods and just-in-time feedback surveys customized by managers to seek the information they need to understand problem areas and track improvements in performance.

Manny London is particularly qualified to write this book. He draws on his 12-year corporate background, including his work developing human resource programs at AT&T, and his 14 years as a university professor, administrator, and consultant in performance management and career development. He has carried out research and written about career insight, management development, and 360-degree feedback programs. His research rests on social psychological principles of person perception, self-insight, and self-regulation as the foundation for organizational programs that support professional growth and performance improvement. His work demonstrates how feedback is central to continuous learning processes.

In this volume, London reports new research on the effect of feedback and executive coaching on later performance. He discusses the value of self- and peer evaluations and the relationship between personality and reactions to feedback. Highlighting self-development, the volume includes information on the development of online career resources for assessing one's own performance. The book also examines feedback methods and challenges in global, multicultural corporations. The studies described are models of how to design evaluations to assess the effects of feedback on learning and performance and how coaches help managers and executives use feedback.

This book complements the first edition of *Job Feedback* as well as the author's two other books in this Series: *Leadership Development: Paths to Self-Insight and Professional Growth*, and his edited volume, *How People Evaluate Others in Organizations*. These books may be used together by practitioners and educators for a thorough treatment of how interpersonal and self-insight can enhance developmental processes.

Fortunately, London has kept the many positive features of the first edition. He describes the processes by which givers of feedback perceive and judge performance and receivers of feedback accept and use the information over time. The volume offers useful guidelines for how to give effective feedback under different conditions and how to hold people accountable for giving feedback, emphasizing that people need to be proactive in giving and receiving feedback. The volume shows the ways to increase formal and informal feedback and how goal setting allows people to calibrate feedback about their own performance.

This book clearly demonstrates how managers can be more effective in gathering and processing performance information about subordinates and feeding back this information in ways that are nonthreatening and lead to productive behavior changes. Also, the volume shows how human resource professionals and trainers can help managers give and use feedback more effectively. Overall, the volume demonstrates how organizations can foster a feedback-oriented, continuous learning environment. London's revised and expanded second edition (the book is 50% longer than the first edition) will be valuable in helping human resource practitioners, educators, and students to understand ways to encourage feedback in organizations and incorporate feedback methods in performance improvement systems and employee development programs.

Preface

Feedback is an anomaly. People have a general sense that feedback is good to give and receive. But many people avoid it like the plague. They are uncomfortable telling others they have done well, and they feel even more uncomfortable telling others they have performed poorly. Some people would just as soon not know how they did, and they dodge evaluations of their performance and opportunities to learn how they can improve.

This is not necessarily irrational. After all, sometimes people give feedback in a dysfunctional way, for instance, to hurt others' feelings and destroy their self-confidence. Or this may be the unintentional result. Others give or request feedback to influence how people see them.

Managers in various organizational settings rarely take time to give feedback. Most managers recognize that giving feedback is an important part of the manager's role, but they do not do it! They tend to let poor performance slide by rather than nip it in the bud. They ask me in puzzlement how to cope with poorly performing subordinates and how to improve marginal performers. Their subordinates complain that their managers rarely tell them how they are doing.

I know from personal experience that managers often shy away from giving feedback and have trouble dealing with subordinates' performance problems. I learned this when I was a manager of human resource and training at AT&T and later in my current role as faculty member and administrator at the State University of New York at Stony Brook. I also found this to be true in my consulting work for large and small organizations in government and the private sector.

My interest in feedback arose from my early research on the employment interview with Milton Hakel and performance appraisal with Richard Klimoski during my days as a graduate student at Ohio State University. I especially wanted to know how people perceive and make judgments about each other. I incorporated this interest in my work on career motivation at

AT&T with Douglas Bray. We defined three components of career motivation: career insight (information about oneself and the organization), career
identity (the goals one wants to accomplish), and career resilience (ability to
overcome career barriers) (London, 1985). Feedback is an essential ingredient of an employee development program because people use information
about themselves to formulate career goals.

   Several years after studying career motivation and designing management
development programs in ways that would strengthen managers' career insight, identity, and resilience, I began work with Arthur Wohlers and James
Smither on a method to give managers information about how others see
them. Termed multisource or 360-degree feedback, this method collects ratings about managers from their subordinates, peers, supervisors, customers,
and/or suppliers. The managers also rate themselves. The technique has several goals. It is a source of information to help managers determine areas for
development. It is a way to communicate to employees what elements of
management are important, and that different constituencies have different
views of the manager's role. It contributes to a continuous learning environment. Annual (or more frequent) administrations of the survey call attention to managers' need to track their accomplishments and improvement in
areas key to effective boss–subordinate, peer–peer, and customer–supplier
relationships.

   At the State University of New York at Stony Brook, I have continued my
research on multisource feedback, applying the process in consulting
projects in different types of organizations. I also began to flesh out the
underlying psychological mechanisms and cognitive processes by which people use feedback. In a recent book, I examine interpersonal insight, showing how people evaluate and make decisions about others in organizations
(London, 2001). My model of how people process information about themselves and others suggests that some information is processed mindlessly
(London, 1995a). The information might reinforce our existing self-image,
but it does not suggest ways whereby we can change and improve. Other information is processed mindfully. For this to happen, the information must
set off an alarm in some way. This occurs when unexpected performance
results do not fit existing categories of the way we view ourselves. A process that guides or forces people to pay attention to feedback may also be a
wake-up call. As we process the information mindfully, we make attributions
about its causes and ways whereby we can control or improve our behavior.
Hopefully, this leads to constructive strategies for enhancing performance.

   As I developed theory and conducted research on self and interpersonal
insight, I realized that the concepts could be applied to improve feedback. I
wanted to make my ideas practical and accessible to human resource practitioners and training professionals as well as students in these fields. This
should be especially important in today's increasingly changing organizations in which high performance expectations and fair treatment are critical to success. In particular, I thought I could build on my work on career

motivation, multisource feedback, and self and interpersonal insight to address how people give, seek, and use feedback and how better feedback systems could be built. This is my goal in this volume. I believe that people can learn to be more insightful about themselves and better observers of others. I draw on theory and research to address issues of practical concern. In doing so, I hope to contribute to the development of sound performance feedback strategies in organizations. I examine the many ways that organizations and individuals benefit from constructive feedback. I view feedback as a key to effective performance management, and I show how feedback affects learning, motivation, and interpersonal relationships.

Six years have elapsed since the first edition of *Job Feedback* was published. During this time, considerable theory and research have been published, and new organizational performance management and employee development programs have been created. This research and practice has focused on such topics as the accuracy of feedback, the effects of feedback on performance, the measurement of contextual and task elements of performance, the unique value of peer feedback, methods for constructive feedback, coaching as a support to help managers use feedback to set goals and track progress, the use of feedback for self-development and continuous learning, personality variables (e.g., self-monitoring, conscientiousness, and emotional stability) related to seeking and using feedback, multisource feedback, and organizational factors that affect support for feedback. New methods for linking strategic planning with individual goal setting and development emphasize that feedback is not an isolated event, but part of a strategic performance management process that starts with the organization's goals and includes the evaluation of performance outcomes in relation to these goals. Other new areas pertaining to feedback involve the emergence of globalization and cross-cultural factors affecting performance evaluations and the use of technology to collect performance data.

This second edition of *Job Feedback* updates the book by reporting developments in these areas. In addition, I reorganized content and added new material. In particular, the revision includes new chapters on person perception, multisource feedback, team feedback, and feedback in multicultural organizations. I include theoretical developments in person perception and social processes that address how people make performance judgments and provide feedback, and how people welcome, accept (or reject), and use feedback. I address the development of online feedback and career resources. I report new research on the effects of feedback over time. I describe the use of coaches and psychologists to help managers and executives use feedback reports and examine feedback in global, multicultural corporations. I provide methods for encouraging continuous learning (becoming a self-developer) and creating a feedback-oriented organizational culture. I describe feedback in teams, from a facilitator or supervisor to the team as a whole as well as feedback from members to each other and the team. Other features of this new edition are new rating methods (e.g., determining the number of scale points to use) and reports of research on rater attitudes, rater similarity, and reactions to feedback (e.g., accuracy and perceptions of usefulness). This volume provides examples of just-in-time, do-it-yourself multisource surveys available through the Web and feedback to geographically dispersed "virtual" teams. I cover recent literature on topics such as the effects of feedback on performance improvement, the effectiveness of feedback and coaching, the use of coaches to deliver feedback, the value of self-evaluations, personality and feedback, the use of feedback as a method to convey valued competencies and performance expectations, and self-regulation and self-development as a basis for continuous learning.

This is a research-based textbook on the nature of feedback and feedback processes associated with performance management. As such, it is meant primarily for students in courses on human resource management, career development, management development, and industrial and organizational psychology. It is also relevant for human resource (HR) professionals, industrial and organizational psychologists, and instructional technologists/trainers to help them design and fine tune management systems and career development programs. It also is relevant for managers and employees to help them understand how feedback operates and how they can improve the ways they give and use feedback. *Job Feedback* can be used as a supplementary textbook for human resource management courses and courses on performance management systems and appraisal. It fits well with my edited volume, *How People Evaluate Others in Organizations*, published in 2001.

I am indebted to several colleagues whose work is represented here and cited at appropriate places. Edward Mone and I have written about how human resource systems can be designed to contribute to organizational change. Feedback is a central ingredient to our view of a comprehensive human performance system. I value Ed as a friend, colleague, and coauthor, and I continue to learn a great deal from his organizational insights. James Smither and I have written a number of papers on multisource ratings that have shaped my thinking about this increasingly important management tool. Jim is an innovative and careful researcher who has taught me about melding research and practice. Gerrit Wolf, my colleague at Stony Brook, continues to be an inspiration for creative ideas about management. I have benefited from his optimistic can-do philosophy. An anonymous reviewer was extremely helpful in revising this second edition. Last, but not least, I am indebted to my wife, Marilyn, and sons, David and Jared, who are never shy about giving me constructive feedback.

Manuel London

1

Introduction

Meaningful feedback is central to performance management. Feedback guides, motivates, and reinforces effective behaviors and reduces or stops ineffective behaviors. However, although feedback is an important management tool, many people feel uncomfortable giving and receiving feedback. They may give feedback as a way of reinforcing their self-image or manipulating how others see them rather than a means of improving others' or their own performance. Givers of feedback may be destructive or hurtful intentionally or unintentionally. In addition, they may be biased by factors unrelated to actual performance and, as a result, convey useless information. Receivers of feedback may be apprehensive about being evaluated, defensive in the face of negative feedback, or apt to ignore information that could improve their performance.

People often use negative terms when they observe and describe others, whereas they use positive terms to describe themselves (Langer, 1992). As a result, feedback may be disappointing and possibly detrimental. No feedback at all may be better in some cases. Feedback is not effective regardless of the content and manner in which it is given and regardless of the receiver's sensitivity to the information. Support mechanisms are needed to ensure that feedback is understood and used to set goals for improvement.

Such support mechanisms focus on the recipient's ability to comprehend the feedback, the recipient's sensitivity to feedback, the context, and accountability mechanisms. The recipient's ability to comprehend the feedback may depend on the extent to which the feedback conforms to the recipient's cognitive processing capabilities (e.g., it is not too detailed), causes the recipient to think about the task from others' perspectives, and can be applied to improve job performance. These conditions depend on the control and credibility of different sources and the clarity, reliability, and validity of the information they provide. They may also depend on the organizational standards and expectations for behaviors associated with different perspectives connoted by the information, and on the availability of coaching and role models showing how the feedback can be applied. The recipient's

1

sensitivity to feedback reflects the extent to which the recipient wants to learn and is able and motivated to process information from different sources. The context refers to what is happening in the organization and the demands and stressors experienced by those who give and receive feedback. Such conditions differentiate the recipient's role from that of others and suggest reasons (and rationalizations) for differences in perspectives. Accountability mechanisms are ways that the organization holds people responsible for giving and using feedback. These mechanisms may include requiring the recipient to explain and justify the use of feedback, encouraging employees to recognize that people may have different viewpoints about the same event, expecting raters to provide accurate and meaningful ratings, and rewarding improved performance.

In this volume, I examine how people give, seek, and use performance feedback. I describe processes by which givers of feedback perceive and judge performance, and I outline information processes by which receivers of feedback absorb (accept, deny, or ignore) and apply feedback. I consider formal sources of feedback including performance appraisal, multisource (upward and 360-degree) survey feedback methods, and assessment centers. I also examine the ways that individuals and groups receive informal feedback. This includes guidelines for how to give effective feedback under different conditions and how to hold people accountable for giving feedback.

I focus on the receiver of feedback by considering self-assessment, feedback seeking, and reactions to feedback. Several chapters provide questionnaires that employees (and readers) can use to evaluate themselves. This includes self-assessment of performance and sensitivity to feedback from others. I emphasize that individuals need to be proactive in getting feedback and show how to increase feedback. I describe how employees can draw on peers, subordinates, and other co-workers as sources of feedback in addition to information from one's supervisor. I also suggest how people can be held accountable for using feedback.

I consider ways managers become coaches and developers of their subordinates, how they establish long-term, growth-oriented relationships that enhance individual and group performance. I give special attention to ways managers use feedback to increase coordinated behavior in groups and generate win-win resolutions to conflict. I also show how goal setting permits people to get feedback about their own performance relative to their goals.

Overall, this volume demonstrates how managers can be more effective in gathering and processing performance information about subordinates, rating performance appraisals and multisource feedback surveys and feeding back this information in a way that is nonthreatening and leads to productive changes in behavior. Also, it shows how employees can gather, accept, and use meaningful performance information from appraisals, surveys, and informal discussions to change their own behavior. In doing so, the volume suggests how human resource practitioners and training professionals can help managers give and use feedback more effectively.

Because considerable work is done in teams and organizations are "going global," I examine feedback in teams and cross-cultural (multinational) organizations. Also, because advancing communications technologies make feedback and development as close, as accessible and as portable as a wireless laptop computer, I examine how technology provides new means of collecting feedback and providing developmental resources. In addition, I consider how feedback is a means of communicating changing competency requirements as the nature of work evolves. I demonstrate how feedback programs are integrated into performance management systems to promote an organizational culture that supports continuous learning.

BACKGROUND

Industrial and organizational psychologists have devoted considerable attention to studying and guiding formal performance appraisal processes, but less attention to feedback delivery and use. However, psychologists have long recognized the value of feedback to enhance job challenge, increase motivation, and facilitate learning when the information is meaningful and given in a helpful way. Knowledge of results is a critical psychological component of motivation that stems from performance feedback inherent in the task or job. Moreover, feedback is an important element of career motivation. Insight about oneself and the environment affects the stability and direction of one's career behavior. Such insight stems from performance feedback and information about potentially fruitful career directions. Also, feedback is an important element in learning. We know that people learn by modeling others, trying new behavior, and receiving feedback on how well they are doing.

That people do not like to give negative feedback is not surprising. They know that the recipient is likely to be defensive or hurt. However, many people avoid even patting others on the back for good performance. Some managers seem to feel embarrassed or threatened about giving favorable feedback that a subordinate or coworker deserves. Employees sometimes request feedback, but they usually do not do so when the results are likely to be negative and they cannot avoid accepting blame.

Unfortunately, many managers do not know how to give feedback, to say nothing of coaching and developing subordinates. Some do not even see giving feedback as part of their jobs. Indeed, they may view performance discussions as a distraction from day-to-day operations. They decry the expense of individual development that may result from feedback discussions, and they fear loosing an employee's loyalty and friendship from negative feedback. Managers' reluctance to give feedback is especially problematic in organizations faced with tight resources and employee cutbacks. Standards of performance are increasing in these firms, and more and higher quality work is expected of everyone who remains. Marginal performance cannot be tolerated for long.

ELEMENTS OF FEEDBACK

Performance information may be objective, resulting from clearly visible performance output. Moreover, the amount and type of information may be under the control of the employees, who can select the information they want about how well they are doing. On the other hand, performance information may be subjective, arising from formal and informal evaluations made by others. Employees may seek such information on their own. More likely, their supervisor or coworkers deliver the information, whether employees want it or not. Employees may be receptive or defensive depending on factors such as the favorability of the feedback, the source's intention to be constructive, and the employee's self-confidence. The source's willingness to give feedback depends on factors such as the source's ability to communicate, the source's comfort with giving a performance evaluation face-to-face or in writing, and the source's ability and desire to coach the employee in using the information to improve performance. Giving feedback may also depend on whether the organization expects performance feedback to be delivered as part of the management process.

Unfortunately, feedback has its dark side. For instance, managers may avoid giving feedback or may deliberately give destructive feedback. I cover the psychological, social, and situational antecedents of these all too common occurrences. I show how people give and seek feedback in ways that manage others' impressions of them. I relate destructive feedback to harassment and other forms of treatment abuse and discrimination on the job. I show how to encourage constructive feedback, develop functional feedback and growth-oriented interpersonal relationships, and discourage destructive feedback and dysfunctional interpersonal relationships.

HUMAN RESOURCE PROGRAMS

Mindful of human resource practice, I present examples of feedback methods integrated with different appraisal techniques. I also offer guidelines for improving the value of feedback and its use by recipients. This should help managers who struggle with the difficulty of discussing an individual's performance face-to-face with that individual. I show how improved feedback processes can be integrated into more effective and comprehensive human performance systems. Psychological and organizational barriers that intervene in the giving of effective feedback are discussed. I show how to design feedback systems for collecting reliable and telling information about performance from multiple sources and viewpoints, and I present ideas for program development that can be used in managerial assessment and training.

The volume is intended to be valuable for designing employee development programs, training supervisors in performance management, establishing more challenging jobs, building an integrated human performance system, and creating environments that enhance employees' career motivation. I cover ways to provide interdependent group members with information that increases their coordination and cooperation. I also demonstrate how to hold managers accountable for giving and using feedback.

A Word About Legal Issues

Managers must be aware of the legal implications of feedback. The performance review process must be conducted in a professional and fair manner, focused on behaviors and outcomes (not personalities) and free of discrimination unrelated to job performance. Any performance appraisal system used to make an employment decision about a member of a protected class (e.g., based on age, race, religion, gender, or national origin) must be a valid system (i.e., an accurate measure of performance associated with job requirements), or it may be challenged in the courts (based, for instance, on Title VII of the 1964 Civil Rights Act, the Civil Rights Act of 1991, and the Age Discrimination in Employment Act of 1975). The use of rating systems that depend on subjective criteria and personality trait evaluations rather than evaluations of behavior may very well be worse than using none at all. Appraisals are subject to raters' subjective biases and prejudices (see chapter 5). Appraisal systems linked to goal setting must involve an ongoing procedure, such as the review process recommended in this volume (chapter 10). If only an annual or semiannual review meeting occurs that covers only the most recent performance information, it may not be a valid system, or may not provide acceptable justification for personnel decisions.

In addition to frequent performance discussions, ongoing documentation in behavioral terms is recommended. However, it must be remembered that this material is discoverable in a court suit, so it must be accurate and factual. The supervisor should be clear with the subordinate at the outset of the performance period about how the appraisal will be used. Also, managers should review their appraisals of subordinates with the next level of supervision as a way of holding the manager accountable for a thorough and fair evaluation.

A related legal and social issue is sexual harassment. Harassment can easily masquerade as feedback. Sexual harassment involves sexual favors or the creation of an environment that tolerates unwelcome sexual advances or language. The organization should have a clear policy prohibiting such behavior. Moreover, the performance review guidelines and associated training should include reference to this policy and should indicate that care should be taken to guard against creating a hostile environment in the review process. This includes any sexual advances, innuendos, or vulgar statements that an employee could consider hostile or objectionable.

OVERVIEW

This volume is divided into four sections. The first section covers perceptual processes that influence how people perceive themselves and use feedback, and how they perceive others as they prepare to give feedback. The second section describes means of collecting feedback data (appraisals, multisource feedback surveys, and assessment centers). The third section outlines ways to support people in using feedback (performance review and coaching) and hold them accountable for performance improvement. The final section examines current organizational and technological trends that influence feedback, ultimately leading to a feedback-oriented, continuous learning corporate culture.

The first section on person perception includes four chapters. Chapter 2 covers how and why feedback works. It examines why some people are so uncomfortable giving and receiving feedback. I enumerate the many potential benefits of feedback, distinguish between constructive and destructive feedback, and describe conditions that enhance feedback effectiveness.

Chapter 3 shows how people evaluate themselves. I review the literature on variables that determine the gap between self-ratings and ratings from others. This feedback gap is supposed to signal the need for development. However, some people may not see the need for change when they evaluate themselves more highly than others evaluate them. I look at variables that determine the extent to which people evaluate themselves accurately, revise their self-perceptions, establish goals for performance improvement, and make learning an ongoing process.

Chapter 4 continues the discussion about person perception by turning to interpersonal dynamics associated with giving and receiving feedback. It covers reactions to formal and informal feedback, self-regulatory mechanisms, feedback seeking, and impression management.

Chapter 5 focuses on how people process information about others as sources of feedback. The chapter covers research on the accuracy of interpersonal perceptions. It describes cognitive processes people use to encode, store, and decode information before giving feedback. The chapter discusses the effects on rater motivation, observation skills, and information-distorting biases.

The second section of the book describes methods for collecting feedback data. Chapter 6 describes traditional performance appraisal methods including a variety of commonly used rating methods. The chapter even covers "ratingless" appraisals as a way to avoid labeling people with a numeric rating.

Chapter 7 begins a discussion of multisource feedback surveys. These popular surveys collect ratings from a variety of sources: supervisors, subordinates, peers, and customers. The chapter explains why multisource feedback is used by so many companies as input for development. It outlines the pros and cons of using multisource feedback for development alone or for both development and administrative decisions. Guidelines for developing and implementing multisource feedback methods are offered.

Chapter 8 considers how employees react to multisource feedback and the extent to which it relates to behavior change and performance improvement. The chapter offers recommendations for evaluating multisource feedback programs. Chapter 9 describes assessment centers, computerized assessment, and business simulations as other sources of feedback.

The third section of the book indicates ways to support the use of feedback. Chapter 10 examines the manager's role as a provider of feedback. It describes how people come to realize that they really do need to change. Goal setting is examined as a key factor in making feedback useful. Feedback is likely to have little value if people do not use feedback to set goals for improvement and then achieve their goals. The chapter also emphasizes the manager's role in performance management, recommending ways for supervisors to conduct constructive performance reviews with their subordinates.

Chapter 11 expands the discussion of performance management beyond the review to encompass an ongoing process of feedback monitoring and development. The chapter describes ways for supervisors to support their subordinates' performance management by providing resources for their development and by serving as a coach. The chapter covers the role of external executive coach and shows how senior managers can learn to be effective coaches, cascading coaching down through their organizations.

Chapter 12 considers ways to hold managers accountable for giving and using feedback. Forces and mechanisms that contribute to feelings of accountability are described as means of increasing attention for careful ratings and serious deliberations about the meaning of feedback.

The final section of the volume, Future Directions, reflects how changes in organizations are influencing the importance and use of feedback. Chapter 13 discusses feedback in teams and cross-cultural organizations. Teams have become an increasingly common method for getting complex, cross-functional work done in organizations because of the need for input from people with different skills. Also, organizations have become more global, expanding operations and forming partnerships around the world. The chapter looks at how teams (including virtual teams with geographically dispersed members) form shared expectations and use feedback about the performance of individual team members and the team as a whole to meet the organization's performance goals. The chapter also reports research on cultural effects of performance ratings in multinational organizations.

Chapter 14 concludes the book by describing the effects of changing technologies and jobs on feedback and development. It shows how computer-based technologies offer ways to collect and deliver feedback, set goals, receive coaching, and learn new skills. I define a feedback oriented corporate culture, ways to increase employees' feedback orientation, and methods to support continuous learning.

In summary, this volume shows the value of meaningful feedback. Feedback is important for communicating changing job requirements and providing a basis for setting goals to guide performance improvement and career development. Feedback is essential for managing in times of increasing organizational complexity. It is important for strong self-esteem and accurate attributions of positive and negative outcomes. Also, feedback is vital for effective performance management: directing behavior, coaching, overcoming marginal performance, and reinforcing excellent performance.

I

PERSON PERCEPTION

2

How and Why Feedback Works

Feedback is the information people receive about their performance. It conveys an evaluation about the quality of their performance behaviors. Giving feedback is "the activity of providing information to staff members about their performance on job expectations" (Hillman, Schwandt, & Bartz, 1990, p. 20). Feedback is an important part of the education process. Test grades let students know what they have achieved and what they must learn to do better next time. People at work give feedback to reinforce others' good behavior and correct their poor behavior. The recipient of feedback judges its value and determines whether to accept and act on the feedback, reject it, or ignore it. Feedback has different purposes at different career stages. It helps newcomers learn the ropes, midcareer employees to improve performance and consider opportunities for development, and late career employees to maintain their productivity. Managers are an important source of feedback because they establish performance objectives and provide rewards for attaining those objectives. Other sources of feedback are coworkers, subordinates, and customers.

This chapter, based in part on London, 1995c, describes why people feel uncomfortable about feedback. I consider the benefits of feedback and provide some initial suggestions for ensuring that feedback is worthwhile. I draw on the scientific literature to learn about the characteristics of feedback, feedback providers, and feedback recipients that may determine whether feedback is effective. Finally, I distinguish between constructive and destructive feedback purposes, styles, and behavior.

FEELINGS ABOUT FEEDBACK

Consider how you respond to feedback. Do you like being told how well you are doing on a project? Although you think you have done a good job, do you feel more confident hearing commendation from others? When you think you could have done a better job, do you still feel good when others think you did a good job? Is it important for you to know what people think about your work? (Fedor, Rensvold, and Adams, 1992, used questions on these topics to measure employees' reactions to feedback.)

Do you perceive receiving feedback as risky? Do you believe your boss would think worse of you if you asked him or her for feedback? Would you be nervous about asking your boss or coworkers how they evaluate your behavior? Do you feel it is not a good idea to ask your coworkers for feedback because they might think you are incompetent? Are you embarrassed to ask your coworkers for their impression of how you are doing at work? Would your coworkers think worse of you if you asked them for feedback? Do you believe it is better to try figuring out how you are doing on your own instead of asking your coworkers for feedback? (These questions are based on Ashford's [1986] willingness to seek feedback scale.)

Even someone who shies away from seeking feedback directly may still crave it. Do you find yourself eavesdropping on other supervisors to get different points of view about your performance? Do you pay close attention to how your supervisor acts toward you to figure out where you stand? Do you keep your ears open in case your supervisor has any more information about your performance? Do you pay close attention to the feedback your supervisor gives to your coworkers? (These questions are based on Ashford and Tsui's [1991] scale for assessing employees' feedback-seeking behavior.)

Feedback is a touchy issue in organizations. Of course people like being told when they are doing well, but they probably do not take the risk to request feedback unless they are pretty sure the information will be positive. Indeed, they may ask for feedback in a way that ensures that they only get favorable information. In general, people are apprehensive about being evaluated. They fear failure, and they would just as soon not know what others think of their performance rather than receive painful information even if it could help them. Learning from feedback often requires overcoming a mental block—the tendency to rationalize, ignore, or avoid feedback.

Many people feel the same way about giving feedback as they do about receiving it. Some managers see little practical value in the performance feedback discussion. They foresee primarily aversive consequences from giving negative feedback (Napier & Latham, 1986). Managers generally view the feedback discussion as an unpleasant situation to be avoided, postponed, and handled hurriedly (Kopelman, 1986; Meyer, 1991). Therefore, unless they want deliberately to abuse someone, they shy away from giving negative feedback. They know it puts the receiver on the defensive and leads to an uncomfortable situation at best. Being tactful and clear at the same time is difficult. Managers also may feel embarrassed about giving positive feedback. Feeling that they are laying bare inner feelings, they worry that they will be perceived as ingratiating. They may believe that saying something positive now makes it harder to say something negative later, or they may fear that the receiver will expect a reward they cannot provide.

Consider a few examples. Some of these are examples of feedback in action; some represent failures in feedback giving; some represent desire for feedback; and some represent problems of not giving feedback. A sales manager who recently lost his job in the latest company downsizing asked his boss, "Why me?" The boss gave him several examples of customers who had complained. The manager wondered why his boss had not mentioned these problems earlier.

Here is another example. A supervisor wanted to let a subordinate know he had done a great job on a project, but she did not want the subordinate to expect a raise the supervisor could not provide. She therefore did not say anything at all about the subordinate's performance.

Next, consider a graphics designer who liked working with a particular client because the client was clear about what she liked and did not like. The client usually was satisfied, and told him so. Other clients would accept a job with little comment. Some of them, however, would not return with new business, and the designer was never sure why.

Think about a company that started a new rating program that asked subordinates and coworkers to rate every manager each year. Managers in the company tended to ignore the feedback reports. They did not have a chance to rate top management, and they saw no reason why they should pay attention to the way their subordinates evaluated them.

A young manager with only 2 years of experience after college felt she should have clearer career direction. She wished she had a plan that would move her ahead in the business. She did not know what kind of future she had with the company. She envied a colleague in another department who had frequent discussions with her manager about career opportunities. Her friend had a good idea what she would have to do to be promoted, and she even had a career plan that indicated the types of assignments she should have during the next 5 years.

One of the first lessons learned by newly appointed members to a quality improvement team was that total quality management requires data on customer satisfaction. The team developed indexes of performance quality and a tracking mechanism to collect and analyze the information.

Self-managing work teams in an automobile parts plant reviewed their production data at the end of each day. They tracked results weekly to evaluate fluctuations in performance and test the effectiveness of improvement methods.

As a final example, negotiation team members in a labor dispute met after each bargaining session to discuss the opposing team's reactions to offers and counteroffers presented during the session.

These examples show that performance feedback comes in many forms. Moreover, feedback is important to individual and group performance. Now we consider why it works.

THE BENEFITS OF FEEDBACK

Research on feedback indicates a number of reasons why it is so important to enhance work outcomes. Feedback has a number of positive effects. Consider the following effects based on literature reviews by Ilgen, Fisher, and Taylor (1979), Larson (1984), London (1988), and Nadler (1979): Feedback directs behavior (i.e., it keeps goal-directed behavior on course). Feedback influences future performance goals, essentially creating objectives for achieving higher levels of performance in the future. Employees know what they can do well, and how much better than can do if they try harder. Positive feedback itself is reinforcing. Even if it does not lead to some material outcome, such as more money, people appreciate knowing when they have done will. Such feedback heightens their sense of achievement and internal motivation. Feedback increases employees' abilities to detect errors on their own. They know what performance elements are important and what levels of performance are expected. As such, feedback sets standards of performance, and employees learn to evaluate themselves against these standards. In addition, feedback enhances individual learning. Employees realize what they need to know and what they must do to improve. Seeking self-knowledge is a prerequisite for and motivator of growth and improvement.

Feedback has other benefits as well. It increases motivation by demonstrating what behaviors contribute to successful performance. It helps people clarify their beliefs about the effects of their behavior. They learn the extent to which their good behavior contributes to rewards and their poor behavior contributes to their being deprived of these rewards or being punished in some way. They also learn what aspects of the situation beyond their control influences these outcomes. Feedback increases the salience of the information and the importance of the feedback process.

People used to receiving feedback learn to seek it out. Also, they know how to ask for feedback they can use. In a group setting, feedback focuses group members' attention on the same performance elements and provides all of them with a common perspective. This is helpful when group members depend on each other to complete the task, when they have different roles, and when they want their teammates to like them.

Feedback increases in the amount of power and control employees feel. This applies to both the source of feedback and the recipient. Providers of feedback understand how information can improve others' performance. Recipients of feedback recognize how information helps them take control of their own performance. Regular feedback helps them feel they can cope with performance problems by being able to make incremental changes in their behavior and see the effects. Feedback increases employees' feeling of involvement in the task. They recognize how they contribute to the task, and they feel a sense of task ownership and importance. Feedback about individual performance coupled with information about environmental conditions and opportunities helps employees form a career identity that is challenging and potentially rewarding. In negotiations, feedback is a mechanism for evaluating offers. In decision making, feedback about the results of the decision helps groups and individuals to recognize cognitive biases (e.g., the tendency to overly weight information that is worded negatively) and avoid these biases in the future.

In summary, feedback has value because it directs and motivates behavior. It has reward value in and of itself. It provides paths for career development. It contributes to increased self-awareness and willingness to engage in self-assessment. It enhances supervisor–subordinate relationships, fosters group development, and improves service quality and customer responsiveness. However, the benefits of feedback depend a great deal on how the feedback is delivered.

THE SOURCE'S REACTIONS

Feedback is a dynamic process between source and recipient, and giving feedback affects the source as well as the recipient (Larson, 1984). For instance, supervisors say that they like subordinates to whom they give positive feedback and dislike subordinates to whom they give negative feedback. Also, giving feedback may increase the ease with which supervisors recall specifics about subordinates' behavior. In addition, giving feedback may increase supervisors' feelings of control over subordinates, especially if subordinates actually improve their performance. However, supervisors may perceive that they have less control over subordinates if the feedback is followed by declines in performance.

Subordinates realize when their supervisors prefer to avoid giving negative feedback. Employees who believe they are performing poorly use feedback-seeking strategies that minimize negative performance feedback as a way of maintaining their positive self-esteem (Larson, 1988). As a consequence, they receive less negative feedback than may be warranted. This makes worse an already poor relationship between the supervisor and subordinate. As the performance problem persists, the supervisor is likely to see it as more severe, becoming increasingly angry and resentful toward the subordinate (Baron, 1988). When the feedback is public, supervisors try to be consistent, making it harder to correct the situation by giving accurate feedback.

CONSTRUCTIVE FEEDBACK

Feedback is constructive when it offers concrete information that can be used. The intent is to help (i.e., to maintain, correct, or improve behavior). It is provided in such a way that it is used by the recipient. It is clear and easily understood. Moreover, it is interpreted similarly by the source and recipient.

Constructive feedback is not necessarily positive, although it may begin with positive feedback to capture the recipient's attention and involvement. The focus is on the recipient's behavior. It does not blame the recipient or threaten the recipient's self-concept. It takes into account the recipient's ability to comprehend and absorb the information. Too much information or data that are too complex may be distorted, ignored, or misunderstood. In addition, constructive feedback is frequent. Giving feedback should be a common practice, not an unusual occurrence that seems to have momentous implications. Moreover, it should be timely so that the recipient knows just what behaviors and performance outcomes are in question. Feedback should occur immediately or soon after the behavior or performance it is intended to critique.

Feedback should be relevant to elements of performance that contribute to task success and that are under the recipient's control. In addition, feedback should come from a credible source, one taken seriously and believed to be accurate. Recipients will have a difficult time denying or ignoring such information. Feedback should be accompanied by explanation so the recipient understands how it can be applied to improve task performance. The source of the feedback should not take it for granted that the recipient will know what to do with the feedback. Also, support mechanisms should be available to help the recipient profit from the feedback. These may include training or special job assignments that allow the recipient to practice and improve.

Understandably, supervisors are hesitant to give negative performance feedback to subordinates they like. Poorly performing subordinates receive less feedback than highly performing subordinates (Larson, 1986). However, when managers give poor performance feedback, they tend to be more specific than when they give positive performance feedback in order to be as helpful as possible to the poor performer. Managers delay evaluating and giving feedback to moderately low performers, and they evaluate them with more positive distortion than they evaluate moderately high performers (Benedict & Levine, 1988). Positive distortion includes selective transmission of bad news in which only neutral messages are provided and unpleasant portions are avoided. Inflating the ratings decreases the possibility that feedback will be received negatively. Moreover, distortion increases when the raters feel they will be publicly accountable for the feedback (i.e., subordinates know who is giving the negative feedback).

In general, people are more willing to give feedback and guide its effective use when the recipient can control the results, the results are positive, the source and recipient get along well, and the source and recipient agree (Larson, 1984). Also, people are more willing to give feedback when the information is salient (perceived to be important by the recipient and source), the feedback is tied to organizational rewards such as a pay raise, the source of feedback is dependent on the recipient in some way (e.g., for excellent performance), the source is responsible for providing the data (it is in the source's job description), and there are positive norms in the organization for giving feedback (e.g., other managers do it and it is widely accepted as part of the management role).

Contrasting Constructive and Destructive Feedback

Constructive feedback is specific and considerate (Baron, 1988). It may recognize that some portion of the cause for poor performance results from factors beyond the subordinate's control. Also, constructive feedback attributes good performance to internal causes, such as the subordinate's effort and ability. This assumes, of course, that these attributions are appropriate. The feedback does not blame people for negative outcomes, and it recognizes people for their accomplishments. When a problem or weakness is evident, suggestions are made for improvement. Sample statements from the feedback source include the following: "I think there's a lot of room for improvement"; "You did the best you could under the circumstances"; "You should give more attention to . . . ." Destructive feedback is the obverse, including general comments about performance, an inconsiderate tone, attribution of poor performance to internal factors, and possibly threats. The feedback source might say, "You didn't even try." "You can't seem to do anything right"; or "If you don't improve, I'll get someone else to do it."

Not surprisingly, people react more positively to positive feedback. Managers who receive more favorable feedback are more likely to accept the results as accurate, less likely to be defensive, and more likely to use the feedback for development (Brett & Atwater, 2001). One study found that this was especially the case for feedback from subordinates, more so than for feedback from peers (Facteau, Facteau, Schoel, Russell, & Poteet, 1998). Managers who feel accountable for using feedback are indeed more likely to use it to guide their development (Leonard & Williams, 2001).

In several laboratory studies, Robert Baron (1988) reported that undergraduates receiving destructive feedback expressed lower self-efficacy on subsequent tasks than those receiving constructive feedback. Destructive feedback led subordinates to feel more anger and tension, and to report that they would handle future disagreements with the source of feedback through resistance and avoidance instead of collaboration and compromise. Furthermore, Baron (1988) found that employees believed that poor use of criticism was a more important cause of conflict than some other factors, such as competition over resources or disputes over jurisdiction. Later research found that trainees who received feedback attributing their performance to factors within their control had higher task efficacy and improved learning (Martocchio & Dulebohn, 1994).

Destructive Behavior

We can learn about the nature and effects of destructive feedback from studies of abusive behavior (Bassman, 1992). Although abuse in the workplace may not be as blatant as in other settings, it still occurs, and can be destructive to employees' careers and self-esteem. Moreover, it may take the form of illegal behavior (e.g., sexual harassment or treatment discrimination). Profiles of domestic abusers include feelings of weakness and powerlessness (Fleming, 1979). Abusers are unable to tolerate frustration, have a low level of impulse control, frequently are overly dependent emotionally on their victim, and exhibit excessive jealousy. They have two sides to their personality, presenting a nice person to the outside world (the pillar of the community) while exercising a form of domestic terrorism at home. Couples who deal ineffectively with conflict use aversive control strategies (e.g., criticism) as ineffectual ways to alter each other's behavior. Abusive, destructive behavior is learned, and abusers often come from families with a history of similar behavior.

This pattern also may hold for abusers in the workplace, including supervisors who give abusive feedback. The supervisor's power may lead him or her to manipulate the subordinate, losing sight of the subordinate's feelings and abilities. The hierarchical power of the organization means that supervisors who harass subordinates control a variety of resources. This makes abused employees similar to other victims of abuse (Bassman, 1992). The victim's oppositional or succumbing reactions reinforce the abuser, creating a gradually escalating series of punishing behaviors. Such a cycle may apply to supervisors who are insecure about their own power. Powerless authority figures use coercive methods to provoke resistance and aggression. This prompts them to become even more coercive, controlling, and restrictive (Kanter, 1977). Such aversive control strategies tend to multiply over time and tend to be reciprocated, resulting in long-term costs and dysfunctional relationships (Jacobson & Margolin, 1979).

Examples of Constructive and Destructive Feedback

Behaviors associated with constructive and destructive feedback depend on the nature of the relationship between supervisor and subordinate. Consider three types of relationships: those characterized primarily by control, reward, or affiliation. In control-dominated relationships, the supervisor's motivation is to control or be in a position of power over the subordinate. In reward-dominated relationships, the supervisor uses available rewards to affect the subordinate's behavior. In affiliation-dominated relationships, the supervisor wants to maintain a friendly relationship with the subordinate. Each of these dominant role relationships helps us to understand different types of constructive and destructive feedback. It should be kept in mind that negative feedback can be constructive or destructive depending on how it is presented. Positive feedback may be destructive under some circumstances, for instance, if the value of the positive behavior is minimized or undervalued by the source.

Characteristics of control include power, negotiation, demeanor, tone, and values. The supervisor's intention in constructive, control-dominated relationships is to empower the subordinate and concentrate on ways they can both win. The supervisor is respectful and patient and adheres to the Golden Rule: "Do unto others as you would have them do unto you." The supervisor's intention in destructive, control-dominated relationships is to be domineering. The supervisor behaves as if this were as zero sum game in which only the supervisor or subordinate can win and one of them must lose. The supervisor is curt and expects the subordinate to "do as I say, not as I do."

Characteristics of reward-dominated relationships are behavior continuity, confidence building, evaluation and reward, attribution, timing, and focus. The supervisor's intention in constructive, reward-dominated relationships is to encourage and reinforce a can-do attitude. The supervisor praises the subordinate, attributing favorable outcomes to the subordinate's behavior and ability and negative outcomes to environmental factors beyond the subordinate's control. Feedback is given soon after the behavior occurs, and the focus is the task itself. The supervisor's intention in destructive, reward-dominated relationships is to discourage the subordinate. The subordinate's confidence is diminished if not destroyed through belittling, disparagement, ridicule, and demeaning words and actions (e.g., labeling or name calling). Positive reinforcement is withheld and negative reinforcement is given. Favorable outcomes are attributed to external causes, whereas negative outcomes are attributed to the subordinate's behavior or ability. Feedback is delayed, and the focus is on the subordinate as a person rather than the task.

Characteristics of affiliation-dominated relationships are expression of feelings and, more generally, communication. The supervisor's intention in constructive, support-dominated relationships is a controlled expression of his or her feelings. Communication is open, two-way, clear, frequent, and face-to-face. The supervisor reveals information about him- or herself as a way to gain confidence and trust and provide a level playing field for honest discussion of the subordinate's strengths and weaknesses. The supervisor strives to be fair and treat subordinates equally. The supervisor provides the subordinate with considerable attention and may deliberately or unwittingly increase or foster learning (a positive Pygmalian effect; Eden, 1992). The supervisor's intention in destructive, support-dominated relationships is to vent, personally benefiting from emotional catharsis regardless of its effects on the subordinate. Communication is closed and one-way. Messages are oblique and confusing. In general, communication is infrequent and indirect. Feedback is given indirectly by talking behind the subordinate's back. The supervisor is self-protective and secretive about his or her own characteristics, not wanting to reveal information that may suggest weaknesses and lack of dependability. The supervisor discriminates unfairly in evaluating and providing information to subordinates, demonstrating personal biases unrelated to the needs of the task or organization. The supervisor provides the subordinate with little attention and may deliberately or unwittingly prevent learning (a negative Pygmalian effect; Oz & Eden, 1994).

Characteristics of all types of relationships (whether based on control, reward, or affiliation) are focus, behavior, and rationality. Constructive relationships are typified by the supervisor's focus of the feedback on the subordinate. The supervisor's behavior is tolerant and supportive. Also, the supervisor's rationality is "20-20," meaning that the supervisor has a reasonably accurate and complete picture of his or her feedback intentions and the subordinate's likely reactions. Destructive relationships are typified by the supervisor's focus on him or herself. The supervisor's behavior is intolerant and, in the extreme, abusive. Moreover, the supervisor's rationality is myopic, that is, generally shortsighted and careless as to the short- and long-term effects on the subordinate. The supervisor is likely to attribute the feedback to the welfare of the subordinate ("I'm doing this to challenge the individual, to get him or her moving"). "Corrective lenses" are needed at least to stop the destructive behavior and hopefully move to a more constructive mode. Such interventions, described later, may include training, a behavioral reinforcement schedule, methods to increase self-awareness, or removal from the situation.

WHEN FEEDBACK IS NOT AVAILABLE, SELF-REGULATION TAKES OVER

Brink (2002) investigated the effect of perceived performance discrepancy on changes in self-efficacy and goals. The perception of goal attainment was the discrepancy between a previous goal and self-generated feedback. Formal feedback increases performance by explicitly informing people of exactly how they performed. This helps people to compare their performance with their goals. They then are able to evaluate their past performance and the goal-performance differential to determine whether future goals need to be altered. However, people often do not have formal feedback in their daily activities, and they need to rely on their own perceptions. They gain implicit feedback by performing the task while actively and continuously noting to themselves how well they are doing. This internal feedback is a substitute for external feedback, and can be as effective when it is reasonably accurate. However, people with high learning goals (Dweck & Leggett, 1988) are less concerned with monitoring their performance and less bothered by failure. They continue to learn and achieve regardless how well they are doing.

Brink (2002) studied undergraduate students' classroom goals and self-efficacy. Their goal-perceived performance discrepancy (subtraction of their self-set goal for a grade on an examination from their expected/estimated exam grade) was related to change in self-efficacy before and after the test. The greater the goal-perceived performance discrepancy, the more their expected or estimated grade exceeded the goal, and the better they felt about their ability to succeed. Students with a learning goal orientation were less likely to adjust their self-efficacy based on their goal attainment on the examination, whereas those with a high performance goal orientation (students who learned for the grade) were more likely to adjust their self-efficacy in relation to their perceived goal accomplishment. As the students' self-efficacy increased, their goals for future test performance increased.

The results showed that even without external feedback, people consider the relation between their prior goals and their self-observed performance, whether they perceive their performance accurately or not. These results are consistent with Bandura's (1986) theory that self-monitoring is important to self-regulation. People observe their own performance, diagnose how well they are doing, determine how much further they have to go, and then adjust their thoughts about their own ability and goals for the future. Although feedback is critical for goal setting and self-regulation, people derive their own feedback when necessary. However, failure may have a differential effect depending on goal orientation. Those who are "in it" for the reward (e.g., grade) are more responsive (in terms of their sense of self-efficacy and future goals) to perceived performance than those who are continuously striving to learn and do better regardless of how they happen to be doing at the moment. (See chapter 4 for a more extensive discussion of self-regulation, self-monitoring, and feedback seeking.)

CONCLUSION

This chapter recognizes that employees do not like to give or receive feedback. Yet feedback has many benefits in terms of directing, motivating, and rewarding job behaviors that are important to high performance. In particular, feedback is critical to the goal-setting process as a way for employees to track their progress and set new goals for further achievement. I describe characteristics of effective feedback and ways to avoid destructive feedback. Finally, I note that when feedback is not available, which often is the case, people evaluate their own performance.

This chapter raises the following points:

1. People generally do not react positively to feedback. They are naturally apprehensive about being evaluated. Also, people worry about how others will react to feedback.
2. Feedback directs, motivates, and rewards behavior. It is the basis for development and career planning. Moreover, it contributes to the building of effective interpersonal relationships.

3. Effective feedback is clear, specific, frequent, and relevant to important job behaviors.
4. Feedback is a dynamic process between source and recipient. Also, giving feedback affects both the source and the recipient.
5. Constructive feedback attributes poor performance to external causes, such as situational factors beyond the subordinate's control, when the external attribution is warranted. That is, it does not blame people for negative outcomes that are not their fault. Also, constructive feedback attributes good performance to internal causes, such as the subordinate's effort and ability. That is, it recognizes when an individual should be praised for positive outcomes.
6. Destructive feedback is abusive. Although the word "abusive" may seem extreme as a descripion of workplace behavior, it occurs, and can be destructive to employees' careers and self-esteem.
7. The nature of the boss–subordinate relationship determines how feedback is manifested. Constructive feedback in control-dominated relationships empowers the recipient and concentrates on ways that the recipient and source can both win. It increases the recipient's sense of independence and self-control. In reward-dominated relationships, it encourages and reinforces a can-do attitude. It increases goal clarity and challenges the recipient to do better or overcome disabilities or barriers on his or her own. In affiliation, support-dominated relationships, it allows a controlled expression of feelings. It leads to increased mutual trust and confidence.
8. When external feedback is not available, people create their own internal feedback.

The next chapter provides the foundation for a better understanding of feedback. It examines factors that influence how people process information about themselves.

3

How People Evaluate Themselves

This chapter examines how people use feedback to form and revise their self-concept. The gap between self-ratings and feedback from others (e.g., subordinates, peers, superiors, or customers) should help people determine the need to behave differently. People are most likely to recognize the need for change when the ratings of both self and others (e.g., subordinates) tend to be unfavorable. However, they may not see the need to change when feedback from others is unfavorable and self-perceptions are favorable. This is when change may be needed most, but it also is when defense mechanisms, such as denial, come into play.

There is a conflict between the psychodynamics of defensiveness and growth. A key question highlights this conflict: Under what conditions does one reaction to feedback dominate over another? Managers who experience failure tend to inflate their self-ratings as a way to salvage their self-concept (McCall & Lombardo, 1983). Managers who experience success (e.g., receive a promotion) tend to agree with their coworkers' assessments of them (McCauley & Lombardo, 1990). That is, they are likely to see their strengths and weaknesses in the same way that others see them. However, people who judge themselves more favorably than others do are likely to be poor performers. This happens because they do not get along with those who are rating them, or they do not understand the expectations others have for their behavior. People who evaluate themselves more unfavorably than others do often have inconsistent levels of performance. They are concerned about improving their performance, but they are not likely to attempt hard tasks or set difficult goals (Bandura, 1982).

People who consistently evaluate themselves higher or lower than others rate them have little insight into their strengths and weaknesses. They are unlikely to use performance feedback to alter their self-image and behave differently (Ashford, 1989). Nevertheless, feedback can improve the accuracy of their self-image over time. Eventually, unfavorable feedback will decrease the extent to which one overrates one's self-image (Atwater, Rousch, & Fischthal, 1992). Until that point is reached, overraters set goals that are too high for their capabilities, thereby increasing their chances of failure. They do not see the need for training until it is too late. Underraters—those who evaluate themselves less favorably than others see them—set goals that are too low for their capabilities. They will not get a chance to test their abilities and improve their self-concept.

Self-awareness is having an accurate understanding of one's strengths and weaknesses, usually measured by agreement between ratings of oneself and ratings made by others. Self-concept is the view one has of oneself that results from self-awareness. In this chapter, I examine the extent to which people evaluate themselves accurately, looking in particular at the agreement between self and other ratings, and between self-ratings and the way people think others rate them. I cover the meaning and emergence of self-ratings by exploring research on how feedback is related to self-awareness and self-concept. Next, I consider personality characteristics related to the way people react to feedback. Learning goal orientation is an important characteristic that influences how a person is likely to use feedback—for development or for accomplishing a performance goal. Finally, I argue the reasons why self-assessment can be valuable.

DO PEOPLE EVALUATE THEMSELVES ACCURATELY?

People have a natural tendency to overestimate the quality of their own performance or the importance of their effort and contribution. Nevertheless, the way people evaluate themselves is important to them and their employer. Self-assessments help people understand their work environments and the demands placed on them. Still, they generally rate themselves in a way that at least maintains their self-image.

Consider the possible combinations of agreement between self-ratings and ratings from coworkers, and between self-ratings and objective performance indicators. The evaluations of coworkers and self-evaluations might be the same, but both may not agree with objective measures. This could happen when ratings by others are affected by employees' attempts to manage others' impressions of them. In another case, self-ratings may agree with objective performance indexes but not with the ratings of others. This would occur because employees know themselves better than raters know them (Ashford & Northcraft, 1992; London, 1995a).

Susan Ashford (1989) identified three types of agreement: (a) agreement between individuals' self-ratings and their beliefs about how others perceive their behavior, (b) agreement between self-ratings and other's ratings, and (c) agreement between perceptions of others' assessments and others' actual assessments. The elements of the first type of agreement, individuals' perceptions of themselves and the way they assume others see them, tend to be highly correlated. There is less agreement between actual ratings by others and self-ratings—the second type of agreement. The way people believe others see them and the way people actually do see them, the third type of agreement, tend to be modestly related. In general, people overestimate the similarity between their self-perceptions and the way they think others see them (Mabe & West, 1982). That is, self-appraisals and the ratings of others generally are not equivalent. As a result, we would not want to use self-appraisals as a substitute for the ratings of others. Still, as we see later, self-ratings may be valuable for comparison purposes and as a way to diffuse defensive reactions to feedback.

Self–Other Agreement

People are generally lenient when evaluating themselves (Harris & Schaubroeck, 1988). Therefore, self-ratings are not likely to be accurate predictors of performance ratings made by others. People who evaluate themselves higher than others do (so-called overestimators) are likely to be low performers (Atwater, Rousch, & Fischthal, 1995). Individuals who evaluate themselves lower than others rate them (underestimators) tend to be mixed in their performance (Yammarino & Atwater, 1997). However, self-ratings are a reflection of self-concept, and thus may be related to some measures, such as leadership and managerial behavior, that in turn affect performance (Atwater, Ostroff, Yammarino, & Fleenor, 1998). That is, although lenient (overly positive), self-ratings can be discriminating in indicating the frequency of different behavior types and how well these behaviors are accomplished.

Halverson, Tonidandel, Barlow, and Dipboye (2002) pointed out several problems with research on this topic. The measures of performance associated with agreement all are derived from ratings, and thus may be influenced by the same subjective biases (e.g., common rating errors). Self–other agreement indexes need to be correlated with objective measures of performance to determine their relevance. Also, the predictability of the agreement measures will depend on the raters' knowledge of the performance dimensions rated. For this reason, self–subordinate agreement should be more highly related to measures of leadership than self–peer and self–subordinate ratings.

Halverson et al. (2002) corrected these problems in a study of the relation between self–other agreement and rate of promotion for a sample of Air Force personnel. Rate of promotion reflects leadership effectiveness across several positions with several supervisors. As predicted, they found that agreement between self-ratings and ratings by subordinates was positively related to promotion rate, whereas self–peer and self–supervisor agreement were not. Those who were in high self–subordinate agreement had the highest rate of promotion. Promotion rate decreased as the favorability of ratings decreased. Lower promotion rates occurred for extreme underestimators. Extreme overestimators had the lowest promotion rates.

The agreement measures predicted promotion rate above and beyond the components, suggesting the value of self–subordinate agreement as an indication of self-awareness. Note that this study examined the relation between self–other agreement and prior promotion record. Research is needed to study whether self–other agreement predicts future promotion and performance measures.

In summary, people who evaluate themselves higher than others do are likely to be poor performers. Agreement between self-ratings and ratings by subordinates may be a good predictor of promotion rate.

How We Think Others See Us

People tend to think others see them in the same way they see themselves (Shrauger & Shoeneman, 1979). However, there is less agreement between self-ratings and the ratings of others. People form judgments about how others evaluate them by both the feedback they receive and how they see themselves (Kenny & DePaulo, 1993). They filter feedback through their self-concept. This is the reason why people overestimate the agreement between their self-evaluations and how they think others see them. Not surprisingly, people who are more egocentric tend to think that others see them in the same way they see themselves (Fenigstein & Abrams, 1993). However, if they believe that those rating them (e.g., supervisors) control valued rewards, such as pay raises, they are more accurate in judging how others see them (Kenny & DePaulo, 1993). Thus, people seem less likely to have exaggerated thoughts about how others view them when there is going to be a concrete outcome from the ratings of others.

The very strong self-perceptions of some people are carried over to a belief that others perceive them quite clearly and have good insight into their personalities. When asked to guess how others see them, these individuals think about how they see themselves. They evaluate their own performance and suppose that others will evaluate them similarly. Over the course of many interactions, an individual's self-perceptions actually may influence how others see him or her. This is especially likely for people with high self-confidence who convey to others what they think of themselves in a clear and convincing way. As an example, take John, a vice president (VP) for marketing. He tends to have a favorable, if not inflated, view of his performance. He thinks others see him in the same way. How could they not? As a gregarious individual, he is not above talking about his accomplishments.

When some people are asked to evaluate themselves, they think about how others react to them. Rather than look inward, they look outward. These individuals are likely to develop self-evaluations that agree with others' ratings of them. If they receive signals that they are highly regarded, they are likely to see themselves the same way. However, if they see signs that they are not highly regarded (e.g., they feel they are being ignored or they hear rumors that others think their work is lacking), they may come to doubt their abilities. For example, consider Mary, the director of the office of finance for a municipal government agency. She is constantly concerned about the opinions of the various managers her office serves. She is delighted when she receives feedback that a report was well-received. However, when there are problems, for instance, a report was unclear and led to many questions or a report was not completed on time, she tends to blame herself. Although her profession demands close attention to detail, her colleagues feel that she is highly self-critical.

Thus, there is likely to be a dynamic interaction between self-perceptions and the ratings of others. Self-views can rub off on others just as others' evaluations can affect how people see themselves. Agreement between self-rating and the ratings of others may therefore start out low but increase over time.

When it comes to rating other people, raters tend to agree. People are able to perceive differences among others. That is, they can agree among themselves about the behaviors of others. They observe the same behavior, consider the same available information, and come to the same conclusions (Fenigstein & Abrams, 1993). However, people are less adept at recognizing how others see them. After all, they have a vested interest in their self-concept and in hoping that people evaluate them favorably. When they get feedback, they initially explain it in a way that agrees with their self-image. If the feedback persists in diverging from that self-image, the self-image may bend in the direction of the feedback or provoke more intense defensiveness. This happens more rapidly if the person giving the feedback is also making decisions about valued outcomes.

Feedback that is misleading, incomplete, or inaccurate will have dysfunctional consequences. For example, lenient (noncritical) feedback to people who overestimate their performance will reinforce their positive self-image and maintain their low performance. Ambiguous or incomplete feedback to individuals with a low self-image will not improve the view they have of themselves.

Summary

People tend to evaluate themselves leniently to affirm or enhance their self-image (Harris & Schaubroeck, 1988). People interpret feedback through their self-concept. Still, self-assessments can help people to interpret feedback. One study found that managers whose self-ratings corresponded to their subordinates' ratings of them had been promoted faster, suggesting that seeing oneself in the same way that subordinates do is associated with successful leadership. People tend to think that others see them the way they see themselves. However, people really are not very adept at recognizing how others see them.

EMERGENCE OF SELF-AWARENESS

Self-awareness refers to having an accurate view of one's strengths and weaknesses, which is important in understanding how people react to feedback. Presumably, feedback increases self-awareness. However, self-awareness and the resulting self-concept do not stem from receiving feedback from others about one's performance. Rather, they emerge from an individual's exploration of his or her own perceptions and experiences. Building on Carl Rogers' (1980) idea that positive change results primarily from reducing the gap between how people see themselves and the way they experience the world, Goodstone and Diamante (1998) stated that feedback will help individuals if they process the information in a deliberate, conscientious way, and if the changes suggested by the feedback are consistent with organizational goals and needs. This sense-making and change process resulting from feedback needs to be supported by empathetic understanding, positive regard, and genuineness from one's boss, coworkers, mentor, external coach, or family and friends. Feedback is the starting point. Support from others helps individuals to overcome resistance to feedback (instead of feeling threatened), helps them to focus on behavior changes consistent with organizational objectives, and reinforces their efforts to change.

Relation Between Feedback and Self-Awareness

Cohen, Bianco, Cairo, and Geczy (2002) studied the extent to which performance outcomes are related to self-awareness (as measured by 360-degree feedback, a survey technique that collects performance ratings from peers, subordinates, supervisors, and sometimes customers; see chapter 7). Data were collected at Avon Corporation, a leading seller of beauty and related products with $6 billion of annual revenue operating in 143 countries with 3.5 million independent sales representatives. Their 360-degree feedback instrument is based on six roles Avon's leaders are expected to play: learner, global partner, developer, strategist, achiever, and change agent. The instrument is based on 19 sets of behaviors (competencies) and 75 specific practices linked to the 6 leadership roles.

Avon's 360-degree feedback instrument is meant to enhance leaders' self-awareness about their fit with Avon's leadership model. The instrument is not used for promotion or compensation decisions. Raters complete it online anonymously. Studying data from a sample of 460 top leaders in Avon, Cohen et al. (2002) found that leaders' self-awareness was not high (i.e., their self-ratings did not agree with others' ratings of them). This is a typical finding in the literature on 360-degree feedback. In particular, most leaders rated themselves lower than their bosses rated them. However, the leaders rated themselves higher than their peers rated them. The implication is that the leaders tended to think less of themselves as leaders than their bosses, but more of themselves as leaders than their colleagues. The study also showed that separate performance ratings associated with the company's leadership development were positively related to supervisor ratings on the 360-degree feedback instrument. Leaders who disagreed with their colleagues' ratings were likely to be rated below expectations on leadership development.

Examining reasons for these findings, the authors surmised that colleague's ratings were surprising because the culture in the company generally is affirming. However, raters apparently tended to be honest, not lenient, perhaps because the ratings were anonymous. Also, the tendency in the company is for leaders not to share their feedback with those who rated them. The authors concluded that feedback must be built into development plans, and that the leaders need to be held accountable for carrying out these plans.

Personal Qualities That Influence Self-Assessment

Individual characteristics may affect how people rate themselves. For instance, intelligence, internal locus of control, and achievement orientation are related positively to the accuracy of self-evaluations (Mabe & West, 1982). People are less subject to biases in self-ratings when they are higher in intelligence, believe that they can take actions to produce positive outcomes, and desire to achieve. Biases in self-ratings include the tendency to be lenient, the attribution of poor outcomes to external conditions, and the need to impress others. Introversion and interpersonal sensitivity are positively related to accuracy of leadership self-perceptions (Rousch & Atwater, 1992). Also, leadership success tends to be related positively to realistic and less lenient self-evaluations of leadership (Bass & Yammarino, 1991). In a study of 204 managers in a financial services organization, Goffin and Anderson (2002) reported that managers who inflated their self-ratings relative to their supervisors' ratings of them were higher in achievement motivation, higher in the tendency to describe self in desirable terms (not surprisingly), lower in anxiety, and higher in social confidence (self-esteem).

The way people evaluate others also is associated with their personal characteristics. Similarity between the rater and ratee in terms of education, race, gender, and other elements of background are related to rating others more accurately. Not surprisingly, raters who know the ratee better are more accurate. As a result, subordinates may be able to rate their manager's supervisory behavior better than the manager's boss. In addition, there is a higher relation between self-ratings and ratings by others in organizations that encourage supportive interpersonal relationships (e.g., evaluate managers on their teambuilding and communication skills) than in organizations that pay little or no attention to interpersonal relationships and that may even promote poor work group dynamics (e.g., through poor communication and inadequate explanation of role relationships) (Yammarino & Dubinsky, 1992).

Summary

Self-awareness emerges from an exploration of personal experiences and perceptions. Feedback is a part of this experience. Research has found that performance outcomes are related to self-awareness, as measured by self–other agreement. Personal qualities, such as personality characteristics, are related to the way people evaluate themselves and others. Next, we consider how personality affects the way people are likely to react to feedback.

PERSONALITY AND REACTIONS TO FEEDBACK

Personality is likely to reflect the extent to which a person accepts, values, and uses feedback. Smither, London, and Richmond (2002) reviewed the literature on personality performance generally as it relates to personality and reactions to performance feedback. Personality refers to controlled temperament or dispositions that influence the pace and mood of a person's actions (Hogan, Hogan, & Roberts, 1996). Personality is likely to be evident in the distinctive ways that people deal with others who reoccur in a variety of situations. In other words, people with certain personality characteristics tend to behave in the same, identifiable way almost regardless of the particular situation. Personality therefore is likely to affect how people react to feedback and their use of the feedback for development. Moreover, personality is likely to be related to job performance because it affects the difficulty of the goals people set and their motivation for achieving them (Buss, 1991). Traits such as emotional stability and believing in one's own efficacy and internal control are likely to foster higher job performance (Judge & Bono, 2001; Schmit, Kihm, & Robie, 2000). Personality measures have been found to add significantly to the prediction of performance beyond predictions based on measures of ability and experience from interviews, biodata, and assessment centers (Cortina, Goldstein, Payne, Davison, & Gilliland, 2000; McManus & Kelly, 1999). For instance, one consistent finding is that people high in such variables as conscientiousness, agreeableness, and emotional stability tend to be rated by others as high in job performance in a wide variety of jobs (Barrick, Stewart, & Piotrowski, 2002; Brooks, 1998; Dalton & Wilson, 2000). These personality variables are especially important in jobs that involve interpersonal interactions and require interpersonal sensitivity (Mount, Barrick, & Stewart, 1998; Witt, Burke, Barrick, & Mount, 2002).

Before feedback is used, it needs to be accepted and internalized (Ashford, 1986).Recipients higher in flexibility and wanting to make a good impression are likely to have a positive reaction to feedback, as compared with recipients lower in general well-being (Ryan, Brutus, Greguras, & Hakel, 2000). Self-enhancement theory predicts that people are more likely to be open to positive feedback than negative feedback because they naturally want to create and confirm a positive image of themselves. The theory also suggests that people are likely to be threatened by and likely to reject negative feedback (Kluger & DeNisi, 1996). However, they may not reject negative feedback if they believe that the long-term benefits outweigh the immediate negative feelings (Korsgaard, Meglino, & Lester, 1997). This view is supported by goal theory and control theory, which suggest that people who encounter negative feedback are likely to set goals for improvement, whereas people who encounter positive feedback are less likely to set development goals because they are not motivated to change (Carver & Scheier, 1982; Locke & Latham, 1990; Lord & Hanges, 1987). People are more motivated to use feedback for development when they are conscientious, low in anxiety, high in self-efficacy (believing they can make positive things happen), and high in internal control (believing they bring about things that happen to them as opposed to believing they are at the mercy of others' actions) (Colquitt, LePine, & Noe, 2000).

Smither, London, and Richmond (2002) studied the extent to which personality predicts multisource ratings of leadership effectiveness, reactions to feedback, and use of feedback for development. Specifically, they followed 116 male officers in an elite unit of the U.S. military. The subjects completed various personality instruments before being rated on a 360-degree feedback measure. The psychologists who delivered the feedback to the subjects evaluated their reactions immediately after the feedback was discussed. Also, the officers rated their own use of the feedback 6 months after receiving it. The study found that officers high in agreeableness were rated more highly. Officers low in neuroticism were more likely to be rated by a psychologist as motivated to use the feedback. Officers high in responsibility rated themselves as feeling obligated (accountable) to use the feedback results. Officers high in extraversion were more likely to indicate that they sought additional feedback. Officers high in responsibility were more likely than others to state that they were participating in developmental activities. Those high in conscientiousness were more likely to report that they improved as a result of the feedback.

Consider the practical implications of the general finding that personality is related to reactions to feedback and its use. Coaches who deliver the feedback and help managers interpret and apply it need to customize how they deliver 360-degree feedback to managers on the basis of the managers' characteristics. (Atwater, Waldman, & Brett, 2002). Smither, London, and Richmond (2002) suggested that feedback providers must be prepared to deal with recipients' defensive reactions to unfavorable feedback. They should be alert to the tendency many people have to rate themselves positively, the reason why self-ratings are not highly related to ratings by others (Conway & Huffcutt, 1997). An nderstanding of managers' personality profiles may help their bosses and coaches recognize who is most likely to be receptive to feedback. Managers low in conscientiousness, emotional stability, openness to experience, agreeableness, or extraversion may need more time, attention, and help in their use feedback than managers high in these personality variables. Those low in these characteristics are likely to be defensive. Their supervisors and coaches can talk to them about the benefits of using feedback to set development goals and seek additional feedback on whether they have changed their behavior and improved their performance. Coaches can benefit from training in psychology that allows them to understanding the relevance of personality and assess personality characteristics. Without experienced and knowledgeable coaches, feedback may be misinterpreted or fall on deaf ears.

Learning Goal Orientation

Learning goal orientation, an aspect of personality or personal disposition, refers to what the recipient of feedback hopes to gain or learn from the feedback. As a result, it is important as a predictor of reactions to feedback. Goal orientation has been defined as a three-factor construct involving (a) mastery (the desire to acquire new skills and knowledge and to improve one's competence), (b) prove (the desire to demonstrate one's competence and to be perceived favorably by others), and (c) avoid (the motivation to prevent others from forming unfavorable impressions about one's ability and competence (Dweck & Leggett, 1988; Elliot & Harackiewicz, 1996; VandeWalle, 1997; VandeWalle, Brown, Cron, & Slocum, 1999). A mastery goal orientation, which also can be called a learning goal orientation, tends to be related positively to feedback seeking, whereas a prove or avoid goal orientation tends to be related negatively to feedback seeking (VandeWalle & Cummings, 1997). That is, people with a goal to learn and improve continuously for the sake of skill and knowledge development are likely to be disposed favorably to feedback and, indeed, seek it out. However, those who want to avoid negative impressions or to demonstrate their competence are likely to feel less sanguine about feedback.

Botwood (2002) found that goal orientation was related to reactions to self-perceptions of performance (self-feedback) and to feedback from others. An example of self-feedback would be whether one feels competent performing a task. Positive self-feedback would be acknowledging that one did something well (e.g., took the initiative to meet with a client to discuss pending issues), whereas negative self-feedback would be acknowledging that one did something poorly (e.g., missed an important deadline). In a survey of 115 employees reading a vignette about a work experience, Botwood (2002) found that employees high in mastery goal orientation felt more positive emotions after positive self-feedback and less positive emotions after negative self-feedback. Not surprisingly, employee high in prove goal orientation reported feeling more positive emotions after receiving positive feedback from others and less positive emotions after receiving negative feedback from others. High avoid goal employees felt less positive emotions after receiving negative feedback. Although this study was not based on actual feedback experiences, it suggests that goal orientation affects how people are likely to feel about and react to feedback.

Summary

Personality is likely to affect how people react to feedback. For instance, conscientious, high self-efficacy people are more motivated to use feedback. This will be useful information for coaches and supervisors who help people use feedback (see discussion on the coaching process in chapter 11). One important characteristic influencing the use of feedback is the learning goal. People with a mastery goal welcome feedback to help guide their continuous development, whereas people with a prove drive want to be perceived favorably by others, and people with an avoid drive do not want to call others' attention to their weaknesses for fear they will form unfavorable impressions.

WHY SHOULD EMPLOYEES BE ASKED TO EVALUATE THEMSELVES?

Given the problems with self-assessments, why should people be asked to evaluate themselves? Self-assessment is valuable for several reasons noted by Ashford (1989, p. 135). It recognizes the self as a source of feedback. It can be helpful for self-regulation and for tracking goal achievement. It is important in increasingly turbulent organization environments that require employees to sort out supervisory and peer preferences as well as evaluative criteria. In addition, self-assessment helps to reduce ambiguity in the environment (e.g., about performance expectations and one's capability to meet these expectations). People form perceptions of themselves based on direct or indirect feedback from others, objective performance standards or explicit performance expectations, and observations of how the behavior of others is evaluated (Wofford, 1994). Thus, feedback provides comparative information for calibrating one's own behavior and feelings. Self-assessment questions are both measurements and cues. The self-assessment items tell the rater what elements of behavior are important to the organization.

Enhancing Self-Assessment Accuracy

Self-assessments are more likely to be accurate when they are based on objective, easily measured performance dimensions (e.g., number of units produced or one's ability to communication) than on subjective and ambiguous dimensions (e.g., one's organization sensitivity). Also, self-ratings are likely to be higher than ratings by others; overestimation is more common than underestimation.

There are a number of good reasons for encouraging accurate self-perceptions (Ashford, 1989). Accurate self-assessment can increase the match between self-assessment and the assessments of others, making it easier for employees to understand and use feedback. Accurate self-assessments allow employees to tell the extent to which they are meeting their supervisor's expectations or the performance standards for the job. Accurate assessments can help to set a realistic level of aspiration for future achievements. Employees can develop accurate beliefs about their ability to achieve more difficult goals, which in turn can increase their motivation, their desire to devote energy to the task, and their willingness to persist in goal accomplishment. However, these outcomes will not occur if employees fail to assess their progress on relevant behaviors or if they focus on irrelevant behaviors.

These possible outcomes suggest several challenges to accurate self-assessment (Ashford, 1989). Employees must gather information while dealing with randomness, conflicting cues, and ambiguity. They must obtain information while protecting their self-image as an autonomous and self-assured person.

Importance of Information Quality.   People easily distort feedback. They tend to overestimate their abilities and performance (Ashford, 1989). Also, they are quick to recognize any flaws in the reliability or validity of information about their performance, particularly if the information is unfavorable. However, feedback is hard to deny or ignore when it is objective and easily measured and understood. An employee will think less of a supervisor's personal judgments of his or her sensitivity to organizational politics than of the supervisor's written descriptions of specific behavioral incidents.

Anticipated Reactions to Feedback.   People decide whether to seek feedback, and they may have a choice of sources, including the possibility of asking several people. Their feelings about their own likely reactions to feedback may guide these decisions. For instance, they may anticipate that unfavorable feedback will make them feel bad, so they hesitate to seek the feedback unless they are relatively certain it will not be negative (Ashford, 1986). Jeff Casey, Subimal Chatterjee, and I examined how people think they will react to consistent and inconsistent feedback from two sources (Casey, London, & Chatterjee, 1995). The student subjects thought that managers would be happier with equal feedback as long as it was the same as or higher than their self-assessment. However, they thought managers receiving inconsistent feedback would increase their postfeedback self-assessment. When feedback is inconsistent, people's fear of negative information may outweigh their satisfaction with the positive information. However, when reevaluating their self-assessment, the ambiguity in the inconsistent feedback provides justification for self-enhancement. Therefore, to avoid biases that may affect reactions to the feedback and later revision of self-image, it is important that people receive consistent information, or at least information that suggests agreement among raters.

Dependence of Reactions on Favorability of Feedback and Agreement. People protect their egos by selectively attending to or interpreting information in a way that allows them to maintain a positive self-image. The extent to which self-protection is necessary depends on the agreement between self-evaluations and the evaluations of and others. Consider several possibilities identified by Ashford (1989). One possibility is that the evaluations of both self and others are positive. This leads to favorable feelings and self-affirmation. Another possibility is that the assessments of both self and others are negative. Although self-affirming, this may lead to discouragement, procrastination, or lack of action. A third possibility is that self-assessment is positive and the assessment of others is negative. This is not unusual (Harris & Schaubroeck, 1988). Maintaining a favorable self-assessment in this case constitutes self-delusion unless the person receiving the feedback has a good justification for denying the data or attributing the unfavorable feedback to a cause other than him- or herself. If the unfavorable evaluation is justified and ignored, the dysfunctional behavior is likely to continue, to the individual's detriment. Yet another possibility is that self-assessment is negative and the assessment of others is positive. This is less common, of course, but when it does occur, it can be highly dysfunctional. Individuals in this situation are likely to set lower standards for themselves than they are capable of achieving, with the result that they do not try as hard as they should.

Ways to Improve Self–Other Agreement.   Changing an individual's self-image is not easy, particularly if the individual has been conditioned to think of him- or herself in negative terms. An effort should be made to ensure that formal evaluations occurring annually or semiannually should be used as a basis for making important personnel decisions (e.g., pay raises and job assignments). This puts teeth into the performance feedback, making the evaluations salient and meaningful to the raters and recipients. However, feedback givers should consider that increased salience may increase the recipient's defensiveness and will not lead automatically to more accuracy in self-ratings. Annual or semiannual performance reviews are not a substitute for frequent, specific, and behaviorally oriented feedback throughout the year. This feedback, coupled with feedback from the formal reviews, will help to increase accuracy in self-ratings.

Summary

Not surprisingly, self-assessments are more likely to be accurate when they are based on easily measurable, objective criteria. When self-ratings agree with ratings from others, employees are more likely to accept the feedback. However, they may not learn from the feedback and change their behavior as a result. That is, when self–other ratings agree and they both are positive, no change in behavior is needed. When they agree and both are negative, the recipient's self-perceptions are affirmed. That does not mean that the individual will take action even though the feedback calls for it. People who underestimate their performance in the eyes of others may adjust their self-perceptions upward but not change their behavior. People who overestimate their performance in the eyes of others (the most frequent case) may have trouble facing facts, and may look for ways to deny or rationalize the negative or lower than expected feedback. Specific and frequent feedback is likely to increase self–other rating agreement and increase the likelihood that the feedback recipient will take action to improve his or her performance. However, in actuality, feedback often is subjective and infrequent.

CONCLUSION

In conclusion, our self-concept stems from our perceptions and interpretations of our experience. Self-concept may change through experiences that challenge the self-concept and increase self-awareness. Self–other agreement on performance measures are part of that experience and influence self-awareness. Understanding self–other agreement and its contribution to self-awareness is likely to influence reactions to feedback. Personality factors, such as conscientiousness and learning goals also may influence reactions to feedback. The literature reviewed in this chapter suggests the following conclusions:

1. People are lenient when it comes to evaluating themselves. However, self-ratings are a reflection of self-concept, and may be related to leadership and managerial behavior, which in turn is likely to affect performance.
2. Agreement between our self-perceptions and others' perceptions of us is important because we are more likely to change our behavior when we accept others' evaluations of our weaknesses. Our self-perceptions tend to agree substantially with the way we believe others see us. However, agreement between our self-perceptions and the way we actually are viewed by others is much lower. Nevertheless, self-perceptions can change with direct feedback.
3. Our personality affects how we react to feedback. People are more motivated to use feedback for development when they are conscientious, low in anxiety, high in self-efficacy, and high in internal control.
4. Self-enhancement theory predicts that people are more likely to be open to positive feedback than to negative feedback because they naturally want to create and confirm a positive image of themselves. Conversely, people are likely to be threatened by and likely to reject negative feedback unless they believe they can benefit from it.

5. Managers low in conscientiousness, emotional stability, openness to experience, agreeableness, or extraversion may need more time, attention, and help in their use feedback than managers who are high in these personality variables. Those who are low in these characteristics are likely to be defensive.

6. Supervisors and coaches can vary how they deliver 360-degree feedback to managers depending on their likely reactions. For instance, they should know who is likely to be defensive and be prepared to deal with it. They should be alert to the tendency many people have to rate themselves positively.

7. A learning goal orientation references the desire to acquire new skills and knowledge and to improve ones competence.

8. The more that self-ratings agree with the ratings of others, the more individuals are likely to see feedback as valid.

9. Self–other agreement may be enhanced simply by providing feedback more frequently and basing feedback on objective, measurable criteria.

This chapter examines the evolution and potential value of self-perceptions. The next chapter examines factors that influence how people evaluate others.

4

Feedback Dynamics

There are many sources of feedback. A source can be anything from an impersonal monthly sales report picked off an in-house computer system to a salary bonus. Here, I refer to interpersonal sources of feedback. These may include one's boss, subordinates, peers, other employees, customers, or suppliers. Some feedback comes without asking. It might come in the form of the annual performance appraisal review or a multisource feedback survey report. At other times, feedback must be sought. Yet people often may shy away from seeking feedback. When they do ask how they are doing, they may have an ulterior motive—for instance, to get someone to say something nice about them. They may wonder how asking for feedback will affect what the source will think and say. They may wonder whether their asking will highlight behaviors that may otherwise have gone unnoticed. They may ask in a way that they hope will make a favorable impression on the source. This chapter considers the nature of informal feedback, self-regulatory mechanisms that influence feedback reactions, the extent to which people seek feedback on their own, and how feedback seekers try to manage the impressions other people have of them.

INFORMAL FEEDBACK

Informal feedback about a person's job performance comes from numerous sources: supervisors, peers, subordinates, customers, and suppliers. Indeed, feedback is just about continuous in that we observe and react to others as they interact with us. This assumes that one is in a work environment involving people with whom one can discuss performance issues, or at least observe reactions to one's performance. Hence, people who spend considerable time working alone (e.g., telecommuters) may need to make special efforts to seek meaningful feedback. Similarly, their supervisors may need to make special efforts to keep open lines of communication about performance.

One-on-One Feedback

In one-on-one situations, people convey information about each other to each other. In the process, they express and fulfill their needs and expectations (London, 1995a, chapter 9). We learn from others when they make direct statements (e.g., "I don't understand what you mean" or "You need to work on that"), ask questions (e.g., "Why were you so rough on him?" or "Why didn't you let her get a word in edgewise?"), and react to you (e.g., look puzzled, surprised, or confused). Such feedback occurs spontaneously in any interaction. We pay attention to how others act toward us and the casual, unsolicited feedback remarks they make (Ashford & Tsui, 1991). Other cues are more indirect. For instance, we observe how quickly others return our phone calls, how often they come to us for advice, and how long we are kept waiting when we have an appointment. The danger is that we may misunderstand or draw erroneous conclusions. This depends on our insight into interpersonal relationships in general, and the closeness of the specific relationship.

Insight into interpersonal relationships requires an understanding of the expectations we have for each other. People expect to hear about task achievement and competence from their coworkers, whereas they expect to hear about personal feelings and social relationships from their friends, some of whom may also be work associates (Gabarro, 1990). As a relationship develops over time, people disclose more about themselves to others, and they feel more comfortable giving others feedback. This probably is more likely to happen with peers than with supervisors or subordinates. The relationship becomes closer and more direct as people deal with problems and dilemmas (Altman & Taylor, 1973). Self-disclosure, exploration, testing, and negotiation deepen over time. A well-developed relationship is characterized by spontaneity of exchange, efficient communication, and mutual investment.

Mutual exchange relationships occur when both parties give and receive something of value. According to social exchange theory, the development of interpersonal relationships depends on the expectation that continued interaction and commitment will be more rewarding than weakening or discontinuing the relationship (Organ, 1988). At work, relationships between two people evolve as they develop expectations about what the task is, what the outcomes of the joint endeavor should be, and how they should work with each other. Social exchange is based on implicit obligations and trust. The value of the exchange may depend on the identities and status of the two parties relative to each other. Such a social exchange occurs between a supervisor and a subordinate, as when a supervisor provides a subordinate with choice assignments or opportunities for career development.

Development of the social exchange relationship requires knowing something about the other party—what the other party needs and values as well as the social processes the party can benefit from and enjoy. For instance, individuals may value information, influence, favors, or just friendship. Each party has expectations about how he or she can benefit and what must be rendered in return. However, these expectations and the timing of their delivery are not specified. Neither party knows the extent of the other's expectations and whether they have been fulfilled.

Norms of reciprocity guide the social exchange by imposing implicit standards about when and how the receiver of benefits must repay the donor. People want to reciprocate with those who benefit them (Bateman & Organ, 1983). Those who feel they are benefiting from a relationship will try to provide something in return, and this fosters the relationship (Greenberg, 1990). The fairness of the exchange can affect its continuation and growth.

Interpersonal feedback can be an important part of mutual exchange and development of a close relationship. Close acquaintances and friends establish ways of providing each other feedback that conveys clear information accepted as constructive. However, relationships are fragile. Those that are not fully developed can easily unravel when explicit destructive feedback catches the recipient off guard, causes embarrassment, or suggests mistrust. Even in close relationships, a tactless comment can be insulting and undermine the relationship. Situational norms also influence appropriate comments. People who have worked together for years may feel comfortable discussing performance issues, but not personal behaviors, such as personal appearance.

In summary, informal feedback entails a host of interpersonal dynamics that influence reactions to feedback. People develop expectations of each other and norms of reciprocity. These expectations and norms influence how honest and direct they are with each other and how much they are likely to learn about themselves as they exchange information. Social dynamics influence what people say and how they say it. As a result, that reactions of people to feedback can be controlled or self-regulated. Next, I describe the self-regulatory mechanisms that influence feedback interactions.

MECHANISMS FOR SELF-REGULATION

Consider how people regulate their activities in relation to their perceptions of the world. Some people are more sensitive to the behavior and feelings of others. Some are internally focused, trying to elicit reactions that confirm their self-opinion. Others try to protect themselves against unfavorable information about themselves even at the expense of never learning about their strengths. Still others try to create situations that verify a negative self-image and prevent them from being successful.

Conscientiousness

People who are conscientious are likely to seek feedback to regulate their behavior. Conscientious people are organized, efficient, goal-oriented, and persistent. Also, they are likely to be better performers than those who are low in conscientiousness (Barrick & Mount, 1991). People high in conscientiousness are likely to take on difficult, unattractive, but necessary tasks (Steward, Carson, & Cardy, 1996). Moreover, they are highly motivated and think constructively about what they can accomplish.

Self-Monitoring

Some people are more sensitive to feedback and more willing to respond constructively to it than others. These people are known as *self-monitors*. (For more information on self-monitoring, see Anderson, 1990; Snyder, 1987; Snyder & Gangestad, 1986.) Self-monitors are attuned to what the external environment requires and expects of them. They vary their behavior to meet the needs of the situation. Low self-monitors are influenced primarily by their attitudes, values, and related personality traits. They do not modify their behavior to adapt to changing situations or circumstances (Reilly, Warech, & Reilly, 1993). High self-monitors are responsive to group norms, roles, and other features of the social situation, and as such, they display a variety of behaviors depending on the situation. They constantly compare and adjust their behavior to an external standard (the expectations or reactions of other people) or internal standard (their own concerns and values). As such, high self-monitors are alert to feedback, attuned to the source's motivation and expertise in providing the feedback, and ready to change their behavior when the feedback is valid. High self-monitors tend to agree with the following items from the self-monitoring scale developed by Snyder (1974):

- I can make impromptu speeches even on topics about which I have almost no information.
- I guess I put on a show to impress or entertain others.
- In different situations and with different people, I often act like very different persons.
- I may deceive people by being friendly when I really dislike them.

Low self-monitors respond negatively to the preceding items, but respond positively to the following:

- I find it hard to imitate the behavior of other people.
- In a group of people, I am rarely the center of attention.
- I am particularly good at making other people like me.

Self-Esteem

Another individual characteristic, separate from self-monitoring, is *self-esteem*—how positive one feels about oneself. High self-esteem enhances a person's adaptability and resilience in the face of barriers. Low self-esteem makes an individual vulnerable, that is, emotionally reactive, sensitive, and intolerant of barriers.

People high in self-esteem respond positively to the following statements from Fedor, Rensvold, & Adams (1992):

- I feel that I'm a person of worth, at least on an equal basis with others.
- I feel that I have a number of good qualities.
- I am able to do things as well as most other people.
- I take a positive attitude toward myself.
- On the whole, I am satisfied with myself.

People low in self-esteem respond positively to the following:

- All in all, I am inclined to feel that I am a failure.
- I feel I do not have much to be proud of.
- I wish I could have more respect for myself.
- I certainly feel useless at times.
- At times I think I am no good at all.

High self-esteem should moderate the reactions of high self-monitors to feedback. That is, high self-monitors who are high in self-esteem likely will respond to feedback most constructively. Positive feedback bolsters their self-esteem, and critical feedback motivates them to change their behavior to match expectations (or at least try to do so). On the other hand, high self-monitors with low self-esteem are likely to be threatened by critical feedback and hence engage in self-protective, defensive mechanisms that limit their likelihood of obtaining such feedback in the future (e.g., they do not seek feedback). Also, they tend to discount or ignore positive feedback. They are therefore unlikely to benefit from feedback and may suffer from fear of it. Low self-monitors, regardless of selfesteem, are likely to be impervious to feedback, whether negative or positive, constructive or destructive.

Self-Affirmation

People seek self-affirming information as a way to maintain their image of themselves (Steele, Spencer, & Lynch, 1993). This may be initiated by an event that threatens the image in some way, for instance, receiving negative feedback in an area the individual believed was a strong point. Self-affirmation is a rationalization and self-justification process that happens through continuous interpretation of one's experiences until the self-image is restored. People with high self-esteem have more ways to maintain or restore their self-image than people with low self-esteem.

Self-Protection Mechanisms

Self-protection mechanisms are ways that people affirm their self-image (Wohlers & London, 1989). For instance, they may implicitly ask for distorted information, as when they request praise ("Did I do okay?"), or compel others to say good things about them. People who use self-protection mechanisms receive less accurate information about themselves, and as a result, have less understanding of their abilities. Arthur Wohlers and I defined four types of self-protection mechanisms: denial, giving up, self-promotion, and fear of failure. Table 4.1 describes how these mechanisms are manifest in behavior.

TABLE 4.1
Self-Protection Mechanisms

Denial
  Reacts negatively to feedback
  Blames others for failure
  Never admits mistakes
  Inhibits others' performance
  Accurately perceives one's own performance [inverse]
  Frequently asks for feedback [inverse]
  Gives credit where it is due [inverse]
  Accurately perceives others' performance [inverse]
  Accurately describes events [inverse]

Giving up
  Abandons difficult tasks
  Avoids being compared with better performers
  Tunes out others who perform better
  Would leave a job because coworkers perform better
  Allows negative feedback to lower performance
  Dislikes better performers
  Tries hard on difficult tasks [inverse]
  Sticks to tasks until he or she succeeds [inverse]

Self-promotion
  Makes sure others know about successes
  Asks for praise
  Feels concern about status symbols
  Talks about own good performance
  Makes others feel compelled to say good things about his or her performance
  Does not admit one's own contribution to a group's success [inverse]

Fear of failure
  Points out own strengths when criticized
  Entertains fear of failure
  Gets upset by own poor performance
  Tries to prevent others from doing well
  Tries to convince others they are wrong
  Tries to raise others' opinions of self
  Downplays own weaknesses
  Feels concern about making the "right" career moves

Adapted from Wohlers & London, 1989.

Self-Handicapping

Self-handicapping strategies are another way that people protect their self-image. People rationalize events in a way that is flattering to them. This allows them to increase their pride when they succeed and avoid shame when they fail. Self-handicapping is a way to ensure that they will be able to interpret the outcome of their behavior in the most flattering way (Jones & Berglas, 1978). For instance, they avoid information about their own abilities. They prefer not to know how they did, so they avoid feedback or situations that will make it clear to themselves and others that they were responsible for a particular outcome. People who have low self-esteem are most likely to engage in self-handicapping (Tice & Baumeister, 1990). These individuals are unsure of themselves and prefer not to know the truth about their abilities. This is especially likely then they doubt their ability to do something well or believe the evaluator is likely to be highly critical of their behavior.

Summary

Self-regulatory mechanisms influence our openness to feedback and the extent to which we shield ourselves from feedback. Some people are highly sensitive to the way others react to them. Others have a strong self-esteem, rendering them open to new ideas about their strengths and weaknesses. Others are highly protective of their self-image. They seek self-affirmation and guard against negative feedback. Although self-regulation helps us protect our self-mage, it prevents us from realizing our full potential. An accurate self-assessment is likely to help us recognize what we can do well and what we cannot do well, and therefore helps us direct our goals and behavior in ways we can be successful. However, as I pointed out in the preceding chapter, self-appraisals tend to be lenient. Moreover, some people describe themselves differently depending on the impression they want to create in a given situation (Schmit & Ryan, 1993). Also, supervisors may be lenient just because they think their subordinates will have a somewhat exaggerated view of themselves (London, 1995a, chapter 3). This reciprocity coupled with self-protection may limit the value of feedback. In the next section, I consider the extent to which people actually seek feedback.

ASKING FOR FEEDBACK

As I suggested earlier, the extent to which we seek feedback and the way we seek it depends on our self-image and the mechanisms we use to maintain our self-image (Ashford & Tsui, 1991). It also depends on our purpose. Feedback seeking can be a way to gather accurate information about ourselves. It also can be used as an impression management technique (i.e., to shape and influence what others think of us). In addition, feedback seeking can be used to protect our ego (Morrison & Bies, 1991). We consider the costs and benefits of asking for feedback. We consider the source's expertise, and accessibility and one quality of the relationship we have with the source (Morrison & Vancouver, 1993). People with a high need for achievement and self-esteem choose sources high in expertise and relationship quality. Those with high performance expectations choose sources high in reward power. Also, those who need to improve their performance the most are least likely to seek feedback (Karl & Kopf, 1993).

Motivation to Seek Feedback

The motivation to seek feedback is not entirely straightforward. Feedback may be useful for correcting errors and reducing uncertainty, but it may be dysfunctional if it threatens self-esteem. Also, low performers who need feedback most may be the most reluctant to seek it.

There are a number of reasons why people seek feedback (as I reviewed chapter 2). These stem from the potential value of feedback for reducing uncertainty (by determining whether one's behavior is accurate and how it is evaluated), signaling the relative importance of various goals, creating the feeling of competence and control, allowing calibration of self-evaluations, and giving the employee a chance to defend his or her ego.

Many people actively seek feedback (Ashford & Cummings, 1983). The feedback may be obtained by monitoring the environment or by active inquiry. However, people worry about the effects of asking for feedback. Consider how you would respond to the following statements about the cost of requesting feedback (adapted from Fedor et al., 1992):

- If I asked my supervisor to evaluate my performance, he or she would become more critical of me.
- I would look incompetent if I asked my supervisor for additional information about my performance.
- I get embarrassed asking my supervisor for performance information.
- It takes too much effort to get my supervisor to talk to me about my performance.
- My coworkers do not tell each other how they are doing, although they may talk about others' performance behind their backs.

Consider how often you directly ask others, "How am I doing?" How often do you talk to your supervisor about your performance or ask for more performance information than you are given. People worry about the costs of asking for feedback in terms of the effort required, the possibility of losing face, and the amount and type of inferences required.

Acceptance of Feedback

When employees receive feedback, they evaluate its accuracy. They make an attribution about whether the feedback applies to them or whether it is the result of other factors (e.g., the source's motivation to hurt or praise the recipient, or situational conditions beyond the recipient's control). When people accept feedback and attribute the cause to themselves, they are likely to set meaningful, realistic goals that have the potential to improve their performance (Taylor, Fisher, & Ilgen, 1984).

Several personality variables influence employees' feedback seeking and reactions to feedback. People low in self-confidence are likely to be apprehensive of being evaluated. These individuals engage in ego protection mechanisms, as discussed earlier in this chapter. They tend to deny or avoid negative feedback, and in general try to control the feedback they receive. Employees high in self-confidence are likely to welcome feedback. These individuals tend to engage in self-assessment and self-regulation. People high in self-esteem rate themselves high, especially when the appraisal is based on ambiguous performance dimensions (Harris & Schaubroeck, 1988). Those with a self-serving bias take credit for success and attribute blame to external causes (Levy, 1991). People high in internal control make more accurate attributions about their role in causing events and are willing to attribute negative events to themselves and positive events to others when appropriate. Those low in internal control are more likely to rate themselves leniently and protect themselves from criticism (Levy, 1991). (People high in internal control recognize that they can affect positive outcomes, whereas those high in external control believe that they have little control over outcomes.) Overall, people with enough courage to seek unfavorable feedback are able to increase the accuracy of their self-understanding. They are likely to recognize accurately how others view their work (Ashford & Tsui, 1991).

Brown, Ganesan, and Challagalla (2001) investigated the processes by which information seeking through monitoring (observing) and inquiry (asking) are related to role clarity and performance. They found that both methods of seeking information were necessary to enhance role clarity. Furthermore, employees with high self-efficacy were able to use the combination of inquiry and monitoring most effectively to increase role clarity, whereas employees with low self-efficacy were not.

Self-efficacy differs from self-esteem (Brown et al., 2001). Self-efficacy is individuals' beliefs that they have the ability and resources to succeed at a particular task (Bandura, 1997; Stajkovic & Luthans, 1998). Those who have these beliefs are likely to have higher motivation and task focus, exert more effort, have lower anxiety, and experience less self-defeating negative thinking (Bandura, 1997). Self-efficacy reflects individuals' evaluations of their own personal capability, whereas self-esteem reflects evaluations of self-worth. Brown et al. (2001) argued that because individuals high in self-efficacy are relatively free from cognitive distractions, biases, and distortions, they should be better able to clarify role expectations by seeking information. Also, by seeking greater amounts of information, they should achieve greater role clarity and reach higher levels of performance. In contrast, individuals low in self-efficacy are likely to be distracted by intrusive negative thoughts and subject to negative cognitive biases and uncertainties about their abilities. As a result, they will not seek, and may even avoid, information that could clarify their roles and help them improve their performance.

Furthermore, Brown et al. (2001) argued that both inquiry and monitoring are necessary for information seeking to clarify roles. The benefits of inquiry and monitoring are synergistic and greater than the sum of their separate effects. The meaning and significance of information obtained by observing can be clarified by asking about details or ambiguities. Information obtained by asking can add context, framework, or schema that helps interpretation of more ambiguous information obtained by observation (Thomas, Clark, & Gioia, 1993; Weick, 1995). Inquiry without monitoring can lead to incomplete information and responses biased by socially desirability or impression management (e.g., information the others think you want to hear). In contrast, monitoring without inquiry may lead to ambiguous information or inferential errors.

In a survey of 279 salespeople from two Fortune 500 firms, Brown et al. (2001) found that neither inquiry nor monitoring alone is sufficient to improve role clarity, even for employees with high self-efficacy. Indeed, monitoring was negatively related to role clarity when inquiry was low, indicating that faulty inferences about the meaning and significance of information obtained by observation are likely when not accompanied by asking. Similarly, inquiry and role clarity were not significantly related when monitoring was low, indicating that information acquired by asking alone is insufficient to enhance role clarity. Employees high in self-efficacy use information more effectively than those with low self-efficacy, who seem to be less capable of integrating information and using it effectively to improve role clarity.

Brown et al. (2001) concluded that employees who already are likely to perform well (those with high self-efficacy) increase their advantage over time by integrating and interpreting information to clarify their role and improve their performance. They self-regulate goal-directed behavior by seeking feedback proactively. This is likely to generate a continuous increase in performance and provide a continuous advantage, thereby further enhancing self-efficacy. Employees low in self-efficacy do not seek information effectively by both asking and observing.

Summary

People can learn a great deal about themselves by asking for feedback. However, this takes courage. As we discussed in the preceding section, people's self-protection tendencies often prevent them from asking for feedback, and when they receive it, from reacting to it positively. People with high self-efficacy are likely to be more open to feedback and willing to seek it on their own. Organizations benefit from managers and employees who are self-directed and whose self-efficacy and information seeking are supported by their leaders. An information-rich environment is important. Moreover, individuals need to be encouraged to seek clarifying information by both observing and asking for information. Also, they need to be alert to personal tendencies that influence their feedback seeking. Feedback interactions are influenced by how we want others to think of us. This is the topic of the next section.

IMPRESSION MANAGEMENT

Impression management refers to ways people try to influence others' perceptions of them. Consider the extent to which you use the following job-focused tactics (adapted from Ferris, Judge, Rowland, & Fitzgibbons, 1994): play up the value of a positive event for which you have taken credit; try to make a positive event for which you are responsible appear greater than it actually is; try to take responsibility for positive events, even when you are not solely responsible; try to let your supervisor think you are responsible for positive events in your work group; or arrive at work early to look good in front of your supervisor.

Now, consider the extent to which you use the following supervisor-focused tactics: take an interest in your immediate supervisor's personal life; praise your immediate supervisor on his or her accomplishments; do personal favors for your supervisor; volunteer to help your immediate supervisor on a task.; compliment your immediate supervisor on his or her dress or appearance; or agree with your supervisor's major ideas.

People try to influence others' impressions of them in a variety of ways. They may try to do it directly through such assertive behaviors as ingratiation, intimidation, or self-promotion, or they may act defensively through such behaviors as apologies, restitution, and disclaimers (Kumar & Beyerlein, 1991). Another way to manage the impressions of others, or at least try, is to associate or disassociate oneself in relation to an event (e.g., "boasting" in a way that links you to a favorable event or disclaiming a link to an unfavorable event) (Gardner, 1992).

When people seek feedback, they often are concerned about how asking for feedback affects what the source of the information thinks of them. Seeking unfavorable feedback can enhance the source's opinions of the employee's performance. However, seeking favorable feedback can decrease the source's opinions (Morrison & Bies, 1991). Recognizing that seeking feedback affects others' impressions of them, people may ask for feedback in a way that will enhance what others think of them (Ashford & Northcraft, 1992). They consider whether it is better to ask for feedback sooner after a favorable event after than an unfavorable event, and when the source is in a good mood. They consider whom to ask. Good performers ask sources who have high reward power, and poor performers ask sources who have low reward power. They also consider how to ask. They may try to ask for feedback in a way that calls attention to favorable aspects of the performance. People are especially attuned to what others think of them when these others control rewards, when the feedback is given publicly (e.g., during a staff meeting), and when a formal performance evaluation is imminent.

People tend to avoid seeking feedback when others are watching (Gardner, 1992). Having an audience increases anxiety and nervousness from being evaluated, especially for people who are "publicly conscious" (i.e., sensitive to how others react to them). They are hesitant because they perceive impression management costs from asking how they are doing. They fear that seeking feedback will be perceived as a sign of insecurity, uncertainty, lack of self-confidence, or incompetence. Obviously, employees are concerned about what their bosses think of them because their bosses control pay, promotions, job assignments, and other valued job outcomes. They try therefore to create a favorable impression by, for example, setting higher public goals and providing excuses and apologies for poor performance. If the organization's norms make feedback a frequent occurrence and it is okay to request it, then employees will be more likely to seek feedback.

Learning About Impression Management

Gardner (1992) offered the following recommendations for using impression management in reacting to feedback. He emphasized the importance of being aware of your impression management behavior and the image you project. Size up your audience and the situation (how the people with whom you interact may influence your performance). Recognize the dangers of the strategy you have chosen. Also, realize that impression management is not a substitute for high performance. Indeed, demonstrating excellence is the surest way to make a good impression. Just be yourself. Do not try to be something you are not because people will see through the facade.

Furthermore, Gardner offered recommendations for those on the receiving end of impression management (i.e., the supervisor, coworker, or customer) in observing others. Be aware of your personal characteristics and the situational features that make certain types of impression management strategies more likely (e.g., status differences). Minimize personal, situational, and organizational features that foster undesirable performance (e.g., situations in which resources or people are scarce or performance requirements or standards are ambiguous). Look for ulterior motives and avoid being overly influenced by dramatic behavior.

Consider the difference between the ability to manage impressions and the motivation to manage impressions. This distinction can be understood by two 8-item scales listed in Table 4.2. (These scales, developed by Reilly et al.,

TABLE 4.2
Items Reflecting Motivation and Ability to Manage Impressions

Motivation to manage impressions
   1. I am highly motivated to control how others see me.
   2. I feel there are many good reasons to control how others see me.
   3. Controlling others' impressions of me is not important to me. [inverse]
   4. In social situations, one of my goals is to get others to form a certain kind of impression of me.
   5. I never try to lead others to form particular impressions of me. [inverse]
   6. I do not try to control the impression others have of me when I first meet them. [inverse]
   7. I try to affect others' impressions of me most of the time.
   8. At parties and social gatherings, I do not attempt to say or do things that others will like. [inverse]

Ability to manage impressions
   1. When I feel that the image I am portraying is not working, I can readily change it to something that does.
   2. Even when it might be to my advantage, I have difficulty putting up a good front. [inverse]
   3. I am not particularly good at making other people like me. [inverse]
   4. In social situations, I have the ability to alter my behavior if I feel that something else is called for.
   5. I feel a bit awkward in company and do not show up quite as well as I should. [inverse]
   6. I have trouble changing my behavior to suit different people and different situations. [inverse]
   7. Once I know what the situation calls for, it is easy for me to regulate my actions accordingly.
   8. I have found that I can adjust my behavior to meet the requirements of any situation in which I find myself.

From Reilly, R. R., Warech, M. A., & Reilly, S. (1993). Reprinted with permission.

1993, were based on a factor analysis of a larger set of items from Leary [1983] and Gangestad & Snyder [1985].) They suggest ways that people manage others' impressions.

Summary

The extent to which people ask for feedback is influenced by their desire for others to think highly of them. We all want to be liked and respected, and as employees, we want others, especially our supervisors, to evaluate our performance highly. We do not want to call attention to negative aspects of our performance, even when we think we can benefit from learning how others see us. When we ask for feedback, we are concerned about how merely asking and thereby causing others to think about our performance may influence the impression they have of us. The self-esteem of many people is too fragile for them to take the risk. They care too much about what others think, sometimes for good reason (e.g., in the case of the supervisor who controls important outcomes such as their salary increases and promotional opportunities, not to mention their very jobs).

Research suggests that seeking positive feedback can backfire, causing others to think we are courting favor. However, it turns out that seeking unfavorable feedback can enhance others' opinions of us.

CONCLUSION

People's reactions to feedback may depend on the nature of the feedback (constructive or destructive) and the relationship they have with the feedback source. People seek feedback from a variety of informal sources during their everyday interactions at work. Mechanisms for self-regulation, such as the desire to enhance and protect one's self-image, affect a person's receptivity to feedback. In this chapter, I discuss variables that affect motivation to seek feedback and the likelihood that feedback will be accepted and used (e.g., a person's self-monitoring tendency). I also make the point that people should understand how they use feedback seeking as an impression management tool. The chapter suggests the following conclusions:

1. Informal feedback comes from numerous sources as we interact with others. We can view feedback within the context of one-on-one relationships, group dynamics, and negotiations.
2. Norms guide the social exchange by imposing implicit standards about when and how the receiver of information must repay the source. Interpersonal feedback can be an important part of the mutual exchange and the development of a close relationship.
3. People regulate their activities in relation to their perceptions. They vary in their sensitivity to others' behavior and feelings, their desire to confirm their self-opinion, their need to protect themselves against unfavorable information, and their tendency to create situations that verify a negative self-image and prevent them from being successful.
4. The way and the extent to which people seek feedback depend on their self-image and the mechanisms they use to maintain that self-image. Feedback seeking can be used to gather accurate information about oneself or as a technique to control what others think of oneself.
5. Impression management techniques include assertive behaviors such as ingratiation, intimidation, or self-promotion and defensive behaviors such as apologies, restitution, and disclaimers. In general, people should be alert to their impression management behavior and the image they project.

Now that we have examined the value of feedback (chapter 2) and how people evaluate themselves (chapter 3) and react to feedback (chapter 4), we turn to how people evaluate others.

5

Processing Information About Others

Now that I have covered how people evaluate themselves as they receive feedback, I consider how people process information about others as the source of feedback. I draw on research in psychology that explains the accuracy of interpersonal perceptions. (For an in-depth review of this literature, see London, [1995a], chapters 3, 4, and 6, and London, [2001], chapters 1 and 2.) I consider the cognitive processes people use to encode, store, and decode information before giving feedback. Also, I show how rater motivation, observation skills, information distorting biases, and empathy for others influence rater accuracy. I begin by turning to the basic psychological and cognitive processes that underlie evaluations—a field called "person perception."

PERSON PERCEPTION THEORY AND RESEARCH

The social psychological processes of person perception explain how managers form impressions of others and use this to provide them with feedback about their job performance. *Person perception* refers to the processes by which we form impressions and make inferences about other people in response to the behaviors, words, and interactions we observe between ourselves and others and between other people (Klimoski & Donahue, 2001). This occurs over time and culminates when one person (e.g., a manager) is asked to evaluate another (e.g., a subordinate or peer). The evaluation is likely to be subject to a number of factors that affect the accuracy and usefulness of the judgment for the purpose at hand. Klimoski and Donahue (2001) argued that person perception incorporates various levels of analysis, including the perceiver, the person(s) perceived, the relationships between them, and the situation. The perceiver's goals, motivation, and cognitive skills and processes need to be considered. Also, the perceiver is an active participant in the process, interacting with the individual evaluated, thereby inducing behaviors that then are incorporated into the perception and the favorability of the resulting judgment.

The way we perceive others may be influenced by expected patterns of behaviors, called *scripts* or *schemas*. These are well-learned behavioral sequences that define typical reactions to environmental conditions (Abelson, 1976). The schemas we hold about the way people should behave under certain conditions tell us what information and events to monitor. The initial information we get about a person and the situation suggests a relevant schema. This causes us to arrive at conclusions that influence our later perceptions. Cues that distinguish one person from another are especially likely to gain our attention and prompt a schema.

We are primed to use some schemas. For instance, if we view ourselves as high achievers, we categorize others on the basis of competence, labeling them as "competent" or "incompetent." We may use schemas that fit how we feel at the moment. Mood may affect the type of schemas used, their intensity, and the strictness with which they are applied. When we are in a good mood, we are likely to be favorably disposed toward others and to rate them positively. Conversely, when we are in a bad mood, we are likely to rate others more harshly.

Cognitions about others are shaped by the previously formed schemas we have about traits, roles, situations, and events. For instance, the initial beliefs we have about a person may be shaped by whether the individual is tall and thin as opposed to short and fat, African American as compared with Asian, or the like. An event schema forms our expectations about people within that context, for instance, a job interview. We "know" how people are supposed to dress and act in an interview. Deviations from expectation draw our attention, whereas we may not fully internalize perceptions of behaviors and responses to questions that are expected. Schemas are stereotypes that function in our minds as first impressions. They form our expectations and color how we interpret or selectively perceive forthcoming information about the individual. On the one hand, schemas have a valuable function in helping us to sort through information and make judgments quickly. On the other hand, they may cause us to ignore valuable information that disconfirms initial impressions.

Schemas, combined with perceptions, lead us to attribute reasons for a person's behavior. We observe and interpret a behavior through the schema. Moreover, in the absence of specific observations, we infer knowledge, traits, dispositions (typical behavioral tendencies), intentions, and membership in one or more social categories, such as "outstanding performer" (Nickerson, 1999). Our first response in being asked to judge another person or event may be to take obvious features and categorize them according to our schemas. We do this automatically (i.e., without much thought).

Our motives and goals influence how much control we exert over the inference process (Klimoski & Donahue, 2001). If we see little cost to being inaccurate (e.g., we will not be held accountable for our judgment), we use schemas as shortcuts to make rapid evaluations. If we are motivated and have the resources to be more precise in our judgments, then we may take more time and go beyond these shortcuts to collect information thoroughly and make judgments we can defend. There are times and conditions that motivate us to seek full information and process it carefully (e.g., when others tell us to take care, or when we realize the importance of the judgments). At other times we are motivated to confirm our initial expectations or stereotypes, perhaps because we see no value in working harder to make a better judgment, or because we want to confirm our expectations and support our stereotypes. After all, confirming our prior beliefs is reinforcing, and disconfirming them may be upsetting. Also, personal desires may enter into our judgments (e.g., not wanting to recognize that others are better at their jobs than we are). Our mood and emotions may influence our perceptions (Forgas, 1995). For instance, we may be more positively disposed to others when we feel good about ourselves. Klimoski and Donahue (2001) concluded that "while we may sometimes be dispassionate in our observations and assessments of others, it is far more likely that we will be ego-involved as there are personal consequences that follow as our social judgments translate to decisions or actions" (p. 36).

The idea that person perception is embedded in a larger social context means that judgments go beyond the eye of the beholder to include the beholder's interactions with and influence on the person evaluated. The perceiver may wittingly or unwittingly affect the target's behaviors by asking certain questions, making certain statements, or nonverbally provoking reactions that demonstrate what the perceiver wants to see. Game playing and positioning may play a role as the target tries to manage the perceiver's impressions (Kozlowski, Chao, & Morrison, 1998). This may be complicated further when people are asked to evaluate each other and set up implicit situations (e.g., tit-for-tat or "you scratch my back and I'll scratch yours), suggesting that evaluations may be influenced by what people want and expect from each other, not what they observe.

A word must be about said stereotypes. *Stereotypes* are exaggerated beliefs about a group (Operario & Fiske, 2001). We may apply stereotypes as we identify a person as a member of the group. The mind typically activates stereotypes automatically. They are elusive in that they are sometimes hard to identify and even more difficult to influence or change. Also, they seem to pervade organizations and society. Usually, the stereotype deals with likability or competence, but rarely both (Fiske, Glick, Cuddy, & Xu, 1999). Unfortunately, stereotypes can be used to explain or justify inequalities in organizations. People can hold ambivalent stereotypes in that they include both negative and positive beliefs (e.g., likable but incompetent or the reverse). This allows people to deny being uniformly bigoted against a particular group while continuing to justify status inequalities. Because stereotypes can affect the actions of both the perceiver who holds them 1 and the target about whom the stereotype applies, the stereotype can have the appearance of truth and become a self-fulfilling prophesy. For instance, if a member of a certain group is believed to be incompetent and treated as such, that person is less likely to have opportunities to learn and demonstrate competence.

Fortunately, we do not have to put up with stereotypes. Controlling stereotypes is both an individual and organizational responsibility (Operario & Fiske, 2001). Personal motivation to avoid stereotyping and organizational interventions can help to alleviate their effects. Personal standards can override societal beliefs, and social norms and standards of fairness can undermine stereotypes. Organizations can help to overcome stereotypes in performance appraisals, job assignments, and other job-related decisions in several ways. Managers can be held accountable for their judgments and decisions. People will be more deliberate in their evaluations if they know they may be required to justify their decision and if valued outcomes are at stake. Emphasizing the mutual interdependence between supervisor and subordinate can remind the supervisor that cooperation and fairness are important, thus lessening the possibility that a stereotype will influence the supervisor's evaluations of the subordinate. Another way to reduce stereotypes is to inform people about how they can stereotype others without even knowing it. Training in the unconscious mechanisms by which stereotypes operate can help people to control their thinking and judgments.

Besides trying to affect the thought processes and decisions of individuals, organizations can examine managers' evaluations and decisions about subordinates and their daily treatment of subordinates to determine whether some groups are disadvantaged relative to others (Operario & Fiske, 2001). Employee attitude surveys and supervisor ratings by subordinates can be a source of data to ensure fairness. Consultants can be hired as objective third parties to interview employees about their treatment. Performance ratings and promotion decisions can be examined to ensure fair treatment. Also, managers should be reminded frequently that they are responsible for egalitarianism no matter how much pressure they are under to meet goals. The organization should demonstrate that differences between people are valued, and managers who have good records for hiring and promoting people of diverse backgrounds should be rewarded.

Perhaps people would have an easier time justifying their evaluations if they had a good understanding of how they form opinions about others. In general, people do not have a good idea about how they form impressions of others (Reilly & Doherty, 1989; Slovic & Lichenstein, 1971). For instance, research shows a low relationship between the attributes raters consider important in evaluating people and those derived from statistical analyses (Nisbett & Wilson, 1977).

As an example, say Margaret, a department supervisor, is asked to rate each of her nine subordinates on five dimensions of performance and then to give each person an overall performance rating. Suppose she must do this twice a year and has done it now for 3 years. That gives us quite a lot of data to analyze. Assume that the subordinates' jobs have remained fairly static over this period and nothing has happened to change Margaret's mind about what dimensions of performance are most important to overall performance. When asked which dimensions she feels have most important (i.e., have more weight) influence on her overall rating, Margaret will be happy to tell us. However, if we then analyze her ratings across the years, statistically predicting the overall rating based on the set of performance dimensions, the dimensions that have higher weights in the prediction equation are not likely to match those she says are important.

When raters such as Margaret are given these statistically derived weights, they develop a better understanding of how they evaluate others, and they are able to learn how to form more accurate judgments (Summers, Taliaferro, & Fletcher, 1970; Surber, 1985). Moreover, they are more insightful about the importance they place on specific performance dimensions after they have had time to practice in similar situations with clear feedback about the quality of their judgments (Reilly & Doherty, 1989, 1992). Over time, as raters are given information about their cognitive processes, they can become fairly good at accurately identifying the weights they use and how they make decisions about others.

In summary, the way we perceive others is heavily influenced by schemas—our prior conceptions and viewpoints that help us interpret our observations. This is a give and take process as we interact with other people and try to influence their impressions as they try to influence ours. Stereotypes derived from societal beliefs can be overcome or avoided by holding people accountable for their judgments. Organizations should hold managers accountable for their perceptions and evaluations of their employees, including documentation to support their evaluations. This would be easier, perhaps, if people had a better understanding of how they form their judgments. Next, I consider how person perception processes affect performance ratings on surveys and performance appraisal forms.

COGNITIVE MODELS OF PERFORMANCE APPRAISAL

Principles from social cognition and cognitive psychology have been used by researchers and theorists to explain raters' cognitive processes in performance appraisal. Unfortunately, research has had little impact on ways to design better performance appraisal systems (Murphy & Cleveland, 1995). We still need research in three areas originally identified by Ilgen, Barnes-Farrell, and McKellin (1993): "(a) the investigation of the content of cognitive variables, (b) the identification of work group and organizational factors that influence these variables, and (c) the design of appraisal systems that incorporate cognitive principles(p. 362)." As an example, the nature of the rating environment may influence ratings. When raters feel confident that they can be open and honest without jeopardizing themselves, ratings are less likely to be lenient (Padgett & Ilgen, 1989). Such rater confidence may improve when raters are encouraged to document their observations over time before the rating.

Automatic Versus Careful Cognitive Processing

When raters observe behavior, they usually compare it with preconceived impressions (images or schemata) (Beach, 1990). If the performance they observe conforms to their expectations, their observations are automatically categorized and not considered further. This state of mindlessness is characterized by an overreliance on categories and distinctions from the past. As a result, raters are oblivious to novel or alternative aspects of the situation (Langer, 1992). Their observations fit into an existing cognitive category, and no additional thought is needed to interpret them. However, if their expectations were not met, then they need more careful (deliberate or controlled) cognitive processing to understand the observation (Sanders, 1993). The raters then ask themselves a series of questions: Is there a need for more information? Might the observed outcomes be caused by the situation rather than the individual being evaluated? If the answer is yes, could the individual being evaluated have changed the situational conditions to alter the outcomes? The answers will determine whether the raters attribute the outcome to the situation or to the individual being rated. If the performance discrepancy is attributed to the individual, then the favorability of the observation will affect the favorability of the evaluation. If the observation is attributed to the situation, then the favorability of the observation will not influence the favorability of the evaluation.

People given the task of evaluating others are likely to start with the assumption that the behavior they observe is intentional. That is, they are biased against situational explanations (Mitchell & Wood, 1980). This occurs because the rating situation focuses attention on the ratee. If the ratee is experienced, the raters assume that performance outcomes resulted from the ratee's actions, not particularities of the situation. However, experienced raters tend to recognize and take into account situational constraints that may influence performance. They also take into account the reasons the ratee gives for the performance outcome. Regardless of the reason, however, the more serious the performance outcome, the more raters are likely to attribute the outcome to the ratee rather than the situation (Murphy & Cleveland, 1991).

Raters' evaluations are influenced by social and situational factors (Judge & Ferris, 1993). For example, a supervisor's ratings of a subordinate are likely to be more favorable when the supervisor has more opportunity to observe the subordinate. Close observation by the supervisor will motivate the subordinate to work harder. This may occur when the supervisor has fewer subordinates and thus more opportunity to know and work with the subordinate. Supervisors may be inclined to give more favorable ratings if they believe that unfavorable ratings are not worth the trouble because they make subordinates angry and defensive. Supervisors may rate subordinates more favorably when the subordinates convey a positive image of themselves and seem to pressure their supervisors to provide equally favorable judgments or suffer their ire. Another reason for favorably biased ratings is liking. Supervisors may be inclined to favorably evaluate subordinates they like because not to do so would be incongruent, not to mention the possibility of interference with the friendship.

Effects of Rater Motivation on Rating Accuracy

Raters who want to provide more accurate ratings (perhaps because they want to be able to back up their judgments in case of confrontation with an employee) and have been trained in doing so are likely to pay more careful attention to how they observe, encode, recall, and integrate information about the ratee. In one study, giving raters a monetary reward for being more accurate increased accuracy (Salvemini, Reilly, & Smither, 1993). In this experiment, one third of the college student raters were offered the incentive before observing the performance of ratees on a videotape. Another third were offered the incentive after viewing the tape, but before making the ratings. One third of the raters received no incentive offer. Those who had the incentive before making their observations increased their accuracy in rank ordering ratees. The incentive was given early enough in the evaluation process to affect the full range of cognitive precesses: attending to, encoding, and recalling behaviors. Learning about the incentive after the observations could influence only the recall and integration processes. As a result, the raters who learned about the incentive later were likely to process information automatically during the attention and encoding stages. Consequently, they were not as able to recall the specifics of this information later when they were motivated to make accurate evaluations.

Encouraging Recall

A number of factors may decrease rater accuracy such as rater biases, motivation (or lack thereof), and insufficient information. Controlling these factors may improve accuracy. For instance, if we know that rater biases and motivation affect ratings, we can at least make raters aware of these factors and encourage them to seek more detailed and concrete information. Performance appraisal researchers usually assume that ratings are a function of the rater's memory of specific observed behaviors, and that memory and rating accuracy are positively related (Feldman, 1981). However, ratings may be based on previously formed impressions rather than memory of recent observations. Therefore, the effects of preconceived impressions may be lessened if raters are requested to recall recently observed behaviors before making their ratings (Woehr & Feldman, 1993).

Effects of Rater Expertise

Expert raters are those who have been trained to avoid biases and have experience making accurate ratings. Hence, expert raters are likely to agree with each other and with objective performance indicators (Funder, 1987; Zalesny & Highhouse, 1992). However, experts may disagree among themselves if situational characteristics are perceived differently. For instance, one rater may believe that situational conditions were a major determiner of performance, whereas another rater may arrive at a different conclusion. Also, the way the expert rater recalls information may depend on the rater's similarity to the ratee. Thus, experts may be subject to biases and differentially influenced by situational conditions. Even trained raters may make the mistake of jumping to a conclusion with little investigation (Kelley, 1972).

Attribution Biases

A common bias is attributing favorable events to ourselves and unfavorable events to factors beyond our control (Herriot, 1989). Another is believing that other people have the same expectations, beliefs, and attitudes that we do. We tend to blame our poor actions on the environment. However, when other people behave the same way, we tend to attribute the behavior to their dispositions. Generally, we underestimate the effects of situational conditions on others and overestimate dispositional factors. A reason may be that we pay attention to our environment when thinking about ourselves, but pay attention to others and ignore the environment when evaluating others (Storms, 1973). Additional attributional errors include assuming mistakenly that we behave the same way regardless of the situation, believing that others face the same situational conditions that we do, and thinking that we have enough information to form an accurate evaluation.

Impression Management

People are concerned about managing the impressions others have of them. They do this by using such strategies as ingratiation, intimidation, exemplification (i.e., being a model of exemplary behavior and dedication), supplication (i.e., trying to have others pity them and help them with their troubles), and face saving (Copeland, 1993; Gardner, 1991). Trying to affect the impressions others have of us is not unreasonable. It is natural to put our best foot forward. After all, we want social approval. Also, impression management tactics can be effective. Subordinates who try to manage supervisor's impressions of them receive higher ratings from the supervisors (Wayne & Kacmar, 1991). In addition, supervisors are less critical of subordinates who use impression management (Dobbins & Russell, 1986). People who are good at ingratiating themselves to others tend to be better liked and receive more pay raises and favorable performance appraisals than their coworkers (Gardner, 1991). Unfortunately, being overly ingratiating is likely to make a negative impression on others.

Nonverbal cues are important to the way we learn about others. Such cues include eye contact, facial expression, distance, and gestures (Gifford, 1994). Some cues are inherent in a person's being, such as race and gender, whereas other cues are transitory and under the individual's control (e.g., gestures, eye contact, and interpersonal distance). People use these cues to manage the impressions others have of them. Also, impression management includes saying things that flatter others or oneself or conform to others' opinions.

People are more likely to engage in impression management when they think it will be beneficial. Therefore, managing a supervisor's impressions is likely to be viewed as important because supervisors control valued outcomes. However, managing impressions of subordinates is likely to be viewed as less important. This may change when subordinates are asked to provide upward ratings of the supervisor. However, if these ratings are solely for developmental purposes (i.e., they can be use to identify areas for improvement, but have no direct consequences), then managers may not try to influence their subordinates' impressions of them. Of course, the managers may feel different if upward feedback is incorporated into the evaluation process and used to make salary or promotion decisions about the managers.

To summarize, this section considers a number of factors that influence how managers and other employees translate their perceptions and judgments into performance ratings of their coworkers (subordinates, peers, and supervisors). Ratings are affected by social and situation factors, such as the opportunity to observe and the image of themselves that people try to convey. Raters' motivation to pay attention, recall behaviors observed, and base their judgments on fact will influence the accuracy of their ratings. Having an incentive (e.g., a monetary reward) for accuracy and being asked to recall observed behaviors are ways to enhance accuracy. Even experienced raters and experts in their fields may be subject to biases. Also, ratings may be affected by the impressions others try to create. The next section considers further how raters' characteristics influence their evaluations.

INDIVIDUAL CHARACTERISTICS AFFECTING EVALUATIONS

Our skills and personality tendencies influence how we perceive other people. This section discusses observation skills, self-monitoring tendencies (our sensitivity to the environment), and empathy as individual difference variables influencing person perception.

Observation Skills

Observation skills include gathering and recording data about job performance without judgment or bias. Skilled observers understand the effects of individual characteristics and situational conditions on people's behavior. Some people are better observers than others because they are able to monitor and recall cues in various situations. Good observers generally are experienced observers similar to the people they are observing, high in self-awareness, high in cognitive complexity, and socially intelligent (Boice, 1983). Moreover, they are able to make swift and accurate judgments of other people. Admittedly, this is not the same as acquiring an in-depth understanding of those observed, but it is enough to predict future behaviors.

Self-Monitoring

As discussed in the preceding chapter, high self-monitors are those who are sensitive to others' reactions to them. They have an understanding of others' behaviors. For example, high self-monitors are more accurate than low self-monitors in making judgments about others' emotions (Snyder, 1974). Being high in self-monitoring helps employees in job situations that call for interpersonal sensitivity, such as a gender-nontraditional jobs (e.g., men in the nursing field) (Anderson, 1990; Anderson & Thacker, 1985). These employees must not only perform well, but also show that they belong in the role. They benefit greatly from the adaptive self-presentation skills of high self-monitoring.

Empathy

Empathy is the ability to understand others' feelings and emotions. People high in empathy can take the perspective of others and understand the situations in which they find themselves while remaining at a social distance from those observed (Stinson & Ickes, 1992). Such individuals are able to distinguish between factors in the environment that influence a person's behavior and aspects of the person's past that influence his or her behavior. Empathy is not just a matter of intelligence. People are likely to be empathetic in understanding the emotions of those they know well. One study found that well-acquainted partners were more understanding of each other's emotions than strangers (Stinson & Ickes, 1992). This may occur because friends exchange information and disclose their feelings to each other. In addition, of course, friends have a more detailed understanding of each other's lives. They are also likely to share knowledge structures. As a result, friends are more accurate than strangers in reading another person's thoughts and feelings about imagined events in another place or time.

CONCLUSION

This chapter began by examining person perception theory and research and exploring what people know about how they evaluate others. In general, they do not know much. I describe some cognitive models to help understanding of the performance appraisal process in light of possible situational constraints and motivational dynamics that influence rater accuracy. I consider how impression management influences evaluation and self-perception processes. I also consider how individual characteristics such as observation skills and empathy influence judgments of others.

The major learning points from the chapter can be summarized as follows:

1. The way we perceive others is influenced by our goals, motivation, and cognitive skills. It also is influenced by how we interact with others, eliciting responses and making judgments about those responses, possibly causing situations that confirm our initial beliefs.
2. Cognitive schemas (preconceived beliefs or stereotypes) affect how we interpret information about others. Schemas help us sort through information and make judgments quickly, but they may bias our perceptions, causing us to ignore valuable information.
3. We can control our own and others' stereotypes. We can be aware of them and how they influence our judgments. Also, organizations can train managers to avoid rating errors and hold them accountable for their judgments.
4. We are not good judges of our own evaluation processes.
5. Cognitive processes of person perception indicate that when we observe another's performance, we compare it with our expectations. If our expectations are met, we automatically process and categorize the information, and the observation is not considered further. If our expectations are violated, we initiate more controlled and thoughtful processing that may lead to a change in our perspective and evaluation of the individual.
6. Our evaluations of others will be more accurate and probably more favorable when we have had more time to observe them.
7. Our skills and personality tendencies may influence how we perceive other individuals. However, whereas appraisals tend to be biased, they can be made more accurate with the right support.
8. In asking for feedback and giving it, we intentionally or unintentionally manage the others' impressions of us.
9. Our observation skills, self-monitoring tendencies (sensitivity to the environment), and empathy affect how we evaluate others. Observation skills can be learned and improved.

Now that I have set the stage by examining how people form impressions of themselves and others, the next section begins a review evaluating sources of feedback. These are ways that organizations provide feedback formally and informally, and ways that individuals should consider in their search for constructive feedback.

II

PERFORMANCE EVALUATION METHODS

6

Performance Appraisals

Feedback can come from any number sources. It can be visible in the tasks we do as we see the pace and quality of our work. It can come from reports, such as monthly sales figures. It also can come from other people: supervisors, subordinates, peers, and customers. This chapter concentrates on the traditional supervisor performance appraisal rating. I describe rating methods and also "ratingless" appraisals as a source of feedback. Also, I present self-assessment as a way to highlight the employee's responsibility for performance tracking and for using the feedback for development and improvement. I begin by considering what is measured: contextual, adaptive, and task performance.

DIMENSIONS OF PERFORMANCE

Johnson (2001) compared the contribution of contextual performance (sometimes referred to as organizational citizenship performance) and task performance to judgments of overall performance. *Contextual performance* comprises behaviors that show (a) job dedication (job-task conscientiousness) such as volunteering for a task or activities that are not formally part of the job, showing extra effort, suggesting improvements, demonstrating initiative, taking extra responsibility, and demonstrating functional participation; (b) organization dedication (organizational citizenship performance) such as following organizational procedures and rules, and supporting organizational objectives, complying with organizational values and policies, staying with the organization during hard times, favorably representing the organization to outsiders, demonstrating loyalty and obedience, sportsmanship, civic virtue, and conscientiousness; and (c) interpersonal facilitation (interpersonal citizenship performance) such as helping and cooperating with others, assisting or helping coworkers, and exhibiting social participation, interpersonal facilitation, altruism, and courtesy. Contextual behaviors are less job specific and more likely to be more strongly related to personality than to task performance.

Task performance consists of activities that directly transform raw materials into the goods and services produced by the organization or maintain the technical core of the enterprise by replenishing supplies, distributing products, and providing planning, coordination, supervision, and staff functions that allow for efficient functioning.

Adaptive performance, or learning, a third element of performance, can be construed as separate from task and contextual performance. It is the proficiency with which employees change their behavior to meet changing situational demands. Adaptive performance consists of activities that handle emergencies or crisis situations; demonstrate physically orientated adaptability; solve problems creatively; learn work tasks, technologies, and procedures; demonstrate interpersonal adaptability; display cultural adaptability; handle stress; or deal effectively with unpredictable or changing work situations. These actions have elements of task performance in that they encompass behaviors geared toward completing a task. They also have elements of interpersonal citizenship. Handling stress is contextual (i.e., it supports the social, organizational, and psychological context of work), but overlaps interpersonal and organizational citizenship and task performance. It includes such behaviors as remaining composed when faced with difficult circumstances or a demanding workload (perhaps an element of job-task conscientiousness), not overreacting to unexpected news or situations, managing frustration by directing effort to constructive solutions instead of blaming others (perhaps an element of interpersonal citizenship), demonstrating resilience and professionalism in stressful circumstances, and acting as a calming influence to which others look for guidance.

Johnson (2001) used a method to derive a set of weights reflecting the relative contribution of each predictor to overall performance when considered by itself and in the context of the other predictors. In an analysis of ratings from 842 supervisors of 2,308 employees representing eight job families in a large organization, dimensions of contextual performance made a unique and relatively important contribution to overall performance. The study also found that adaptive performance for handing work stress and job–task conscientiousness were related to task and contextual performance measures. Handling stress was more highly related to contextual performance than task performance. Also, it was a compound dimension involving different elements of contextual performance: interpersonal citizenship (e.g., acting as a calming influence that others look to for guidance), organizational citizenship performance (e.g., demonstrating resilience and professionalism in stressful circumstances), and job-task conscientiousness (e.g., remaining composed in the face of difficult circumstances or a highly demanding workload).

Elements of contextual performance varied in their importance to overall performance depending on the job family (Johnson, 2001). For example, the highest relative weight for organizational citizenship performance occurred for the customer service and sales job family, in which employees had the most personal contact with people outside the organization. Hence, supervisors placed more importance on representing the organization in a favorable way in this job family than in others. In support job families, wherein the main function was to help other people get their work done, supervisors placed more weight on interpersonal citizenship performance. Moreover, contextual performance was more important in positions for which task requirements were less demanding.

In summary, performance appraisals may require supervisors to evaluate an employee's performance in terms of contextual, task, and adaptive elements of performance. Jobs vary in the extent to which each of these categories of performance are relevant. Supervisors should understand the relative importance of these different job elements to the particular job they are evaluating. This also implies that supervisors should vary the type of support they provide for employees to help them perform well. In other words, task structure may be needed on jobs for which task dimensions are predominant, whereas social support may be needed on jobs for which contextual or adaptive dimensions are predominant. It also implies that supervisors need to collect appropriate information about the relevant job elements. Task performance information may be easier to observe and interpret than contextual performance information. The former may be available from objective data about the quantity and quality of service delivered or the widgets produced by the employee or the employee's department. The latter may be available by talking to people and observing interpersonal interactions. Once the supervisor understands the nature of the job and the sources of information, the information needs to be collected in a systematic way, provided as feedback, and integrated into the organization's performance management process for use in making compensation, job placement, and training decisions and assignments.

RATING DYNAMICS

The supervisor is the traditional source of performance appraisal and feedback. Most organizations require at least annual appraisals and a feedback discussion. During the discussion, the supervisor explains the appraisal to the subordinate and asks for a signature to attest that the appraisal was explained to the subordinate (not that the subordinate necessarily agreed with the appraisal). Some appraisal forms may provide space for the subordinate to write his or her own opinion. The annual performance appraisal often leads to some change in compensation, although feedback about performance and implications for improvement and career development should be separate from discussions about pay to avoid or reduce rater and ratee defensiveness and to focus attention on performance issues (Lawler, 1999). Some organizations suggest or require more frequent appraisals and feedback discussions that do not have implications for pay. This section examines alternative

rating formats and an alternative to ratings, the "ratingless" narrative appraisal. Self-appraisals and the cost–benefit of appraisals also are discussed.

Rating Formats

The traditional rating form has a series of items, each of which is rated on a
numeric scale, with scale points described by adjectives such as "very good"
or "exceeds expectations." Considerable research attention has been given
to rating formats in an effort to find procedures that yield the most accurate
ratings (Murphy & Cleveland, 1995). Consider the difficulty of the performance appraisal task: "Raters are faced with observing, storing, recalling,
integrating, and judging the effectiveness of behaviors for a number of ratees. Finally, they must translate this judgment onto a rating scale" (Steiner,
Rain, & Smalley, 1993, p. 438). Compound this with rater biases, lack of
enthusiasm, and the period covered by the review. Rater inaccuracies and
disagreement among raters evaluating the same individual are not surprising
under these circumstances.

The fewest rating errors occur when scale formats include concrete, behavioral descriptions that are understandable, observable, and important to
the job. Items that are general, focused on personal characteristics, unclear,
judgmental, or not critical to the job are likely to result in the most rating
errors. Rating scales based on job analyses with input from people doing the
job are likely to be the clearest and most acceptable to the raters and the
recipients of the feedback. The items may be phrased as behavioral expectations (i.e., what the employee could be expected to do), or they could be
behavioral observations, examples of actual employee behaviors observed
by the supervisor. Figure 6.1 provides some examples of rating scales. (For
more details about performance appraisal scales, see a good text in human
resource management, such as that by Cascio, 1986).

The process of evaluating others entails cognitive processes and measurement models applied in a rating format that supposedly is a mechanism
for "helping raters to search for ratee behavior in an efficient and organized
way and to translate this behavior into evidence relevant for making accurate evaluate judgments about a ratee's performance" (Borman et al., 2001,
p. 966). Another consideration is how the type of format affects the quality
of feedback. Do formats vary in how understandable they are to both the
rater and ratee? Consider some common rating formats:

- Graphic rating scales (GRS): presents a rating scale for each performance dimension, with each scale (having three, four, or five, more
  scale points) anchored usually with general statements, such as "low,"
  "middle," "high." This is easily understood by raters and ratees. Ratings are clear and easy to present in feedback discussions. However,
  because the scales are not very descriptive, the ratings are likely to
  require detailed explanation and justification.

Simple Graphic Rating Scale

Circle one response for each performance category:

Quantity of performance: Ourstanding   Above   Average   Below   Unacceptable
                                         Average   Average

Quality of performance: Ourstanding   Above   Average   Below   Unacceptable
                                         Average   Average

Comments:

_____

Behaviorally Anchored Rating Scale for a General Manager

Gives Feedback to Subordinates

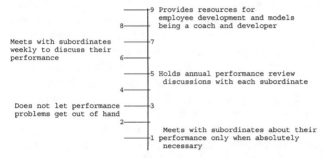

Note: Each item is scaled by an independent group of managers in the firm to fall at these
points. The items provide examples of the type of behavior typical of each point on the
performance scale. The rater is instructed to indicate the one number that best applies to the
ratee. Other scales are constructed for other performance dimensions. A variation is the
Behavioral Expectations Scale which words representative items in terms of what the ratee could
be expected to do. That way, the rater does not have to have actually observed the behavior
during the performance period.

_____

Ranking System
    Sometimes used in conjunction with ratings, this system asks the manager to rank order
subordinates from highest to lowest. Managers in the same department at the same organizational
level may meet to rank all immediate subordinates on one list. They discuss each subordinate and
then attempt to agree on a rank order.

FIG. 6.1. Examples of rating scales.

- Behaviorally anchored ratings scales (BARS): places behavioral statements reflecting critical incidents at different places on the rating scale
  according to their effectiveness level. When feedback is given, the behaviors on the scale exemplify the types of behaviors the rater means,
  and as a result, may make feedback clearer, enabling the supervisor to
  give the subordinate more specific behavioral examples.
- Mixed standard scales (MSS): provides an effective, midlevel, and ineffective behavioral example representing each performance dimension,
  and the rater indicates whether the ratee's effectiveness was more than,

less than, or the same as that described in each behavioral statement. The increased specificity is likely to be useful during feedback.

- Performance distribution assessment method: generates a modal performance-level score, a variance-in-performance score, and a negative range avoidance score (showing how well the ratee avoids ineffective performance). Supervisors (raters) may have trouble making these judgments. A question for feedback discussion is whether the subordinate (ratee) can absorb this information. Supervisors should provide subordinates with the scales before the feedback discussion and possibly start the discussion with an explanation of the method. The method may need to be used several times before subordinates become familiar with receiving the feedback.

- Computerized adaptive rating scales (CARS): presents raters with successive pairs of statements. Each statement has been prerated on a scale to indicate its level of performance. Raters do not see these scale values, but rather select from each pair of statements the one that more closely reflects the person evaluated. In the second pair of statements, one statement will have a scale effectiveness value somewhat above the effectiveness value of the statement chosen first as the more descriptive. The other statement will have a scaled effectiveness level somewhat below the effectiveness value of the initially chosen statement. The second choice would revise the initial estimated ratee effectiveness level, and two more statements would be chosen for the next pair, and so forth until there is no change in the description of the ratee, with the level of rating on the performance dimension being the scale value of the most descriptive item. This method provides more precision in the rating. The end result may be more difficult to explain during feedback. A feedback discussion strategy may involve working through the scale with the subordinate, using it as a basis for discussing aspects of performance and the subordinate's behavioral tendencies.

The CARS format was developed by Borman et al. (2001) in an experiment that compared different rating methods. These authors considered CARS to be more in line with raters' cognitive processes, helping them to calibrate their perceptions so that their performance judgments about the behaviors they observed are more precise. The method is based on Thurstone's (1927) law of comparative judgment, which holds that people's reactions to stimuli are subjective, vary from one instance to another, and are normally distributed. Stimuli can be placed on an interval scale based on ratings from a number of experts. Pairs of statements then are presented to a rater evaluating another person (e.g., supervisor evaluating a subordinate). For each pair, the rater chooses the statement that is more descriptive of the ratee. The scale value of the more descriptive item would be a more precise a rating derived from a more linear numeric scale, which provides only ordinal-level measurement. Borman et al. (2001) applied the adaptive testing orientation of item response theory (IRT) to the method such that each successive pair of items provides a more precise estimate of the ratee's performance.

Borman et al. (2001) used a laboratory study involving videotaped vignettes of six office workers depicting prescribed levels of contextual performance. The vignettes were rated by 112 subjects: 33 employees and 79 university students with prior work experience. Examples of behavioral statements were as follows: "refuses to take the time to help others when they ask for assistance with work-related problems" (reflecting very ineffective performance on the dimension of Personal Support), "expresses own personal satisfaction in being a member of the organization when asked by outsiders" (reflecting effective performance on the dimension of Organizational Support), and "consistently completes work on time or ahead of time, even when deadlines seem impossibly short" (reflecting very effective performance on the dimension of Conscientious Initiative).

The study found more reliable ratings and substantially greater validity and accuracy for CARS than for GRS or BARS. Although this was a laboratory study, prior laboratory studies using similar methods on techniques other than CARS had found few differences between rating formats (Borman, 1979). The authors concluded that there are two reasons why CARS produced more favorable results than GRS and BARS: (a) The behavioral statements in the CARS format are more and more targeted directly toward the ratee, and (b) the method of iterative paired-comparison judgment provide a more precise assignment of a numerical rating than the judgment tasks used by other rating formats.

A "Ratingless" Narrative Appraisal

Some authorities recommend eliminating grading altogether. For instance, Herbert Meyer (1991), a former human resource executive at General Electric and later a professor of psychology at the University of South Florida, believes that attaching a numeric score or overall adjectival grade (e.g., satisfactory) to the review is demeaning and unnecessary. Any administrative actions, such as a salary increase or a promotion, communicate an overall appraisal better than a grade. Meyer (1991) recommended that supervisors write narratives (general descriptions with behavioral examples), but not provide numeric ratings. To show that this is not far fetched, Table 6.1 includes some commonly asked questions and expert answers about the ratingless appraisal.

Self-Appraisals

Meyer (1991) also considered the value of incorporating self-appraisals into the performance appraisal discussion. With this approach, the subordinate

TABLE 6.1
Questions and Answers About the Ratingless Appraisal

Ratingless appraisals are narrative descriptions with examples of behaviors that reflect performance. Supervisors write a few short paragraphs or perhaps several pages, but they do not attach one or more numeric values to reflect their judgments. The following questions and answers should be considered to determine the feasibility of this method.

Is poor performance likely to be identified and addressed?

The narrative appraisal should be part of a larger system of performance excellence that ties together objective setting, development planning, and periodic performance review and feedback. Marginal performance will have to be identified and dealt with by addressing issues of capability and motivation, giving direct and constructive feedback, setting realistic goals and consequences, and tracking performance. The intention of the performance review is to encourage communication about performance between managers and subordinates, provide documentation, and not let performance problems slide.

Do we eliminate both ratings and rankings?

Yes, both should be eliminated. The goal of the new process is to move away from evaluating and categorizing people toward providing more detailed, descriptive summaries of performance linked to specific objectives. The ratings, even without forced choice, are subjective, likely to be inconsistent across groups (e.g., "exceeding objectives" may mean different things to different managers), and not necessarily backed by solid and well-documented performance information. Encouraging the meaningful review without the rating will focus attention on performance rather than distract attention to an artificial category.

How do we handle compensation under this type of system? How do we differentiate and support the compensation?

Compensation decisions should still be made by the supervisor or peer groups of managers on the basis of subordinates' accomplishments.

How do we communicate performance about a subordinate to other departments (e.g., when the subordinate is being evaluated for transfer or promotion), especially if other departments use numeric appraisal ratings?

Given differences in standards and the subjective way that rating categories are commonly used, traditional performance appraisal ratings are not always helpful for staffing purposes. Narrative appraisals should provide far more in-depth information for making staffing decisions about people. Employees' strengths and weaknesses should be more apparent in the narratives than could be conveyed by a single rating and the brief documentation that usually accompanies the rating. The more extensive information about employees should give a selecting manager more confidence in making decisions about them.

What about dotted-line relationships where there is dual reporting and different compensation systems, as might occur in multiple teams or matrix management environments?

Such organizational structures require planning and coordination. Dual reporting relationships suggest that the employee's managers need to agree on how time will be split. If the work is independent (e.g., involving totally different projects for each manager), then separate appraisal processes and commensurate merit treatment can be carried out independently by each manager. If the work is interdependent, then the managers can agree on how they will work with the employee to set goals, give feedback, and write the final appraisal. The managers may meet together with the employee, or one manager can take the lead, getting input from the other manager all along the way.

How do we make sure that motivation is not negatively influenced? How do we ensure that this system will drive performance in a positive way and move the organization forward?

A process that encourages frequent communication about objectives, development, and performance should enhance motivation and clarify linkages to company and department

TABLE 6.1 (cont.)

goals. The process can highlight any major departmental goals (e.g., customer responsiveness, quality, awareness of corporate objectives, and creativity) to ensure that these are reflected in the objectives.

How do you include customer input? How much should customer input be included?

Customer input is important and should be gathered by the manager before he or she writes periodic performance reviews and the final appraisal. In general, input is important from multiple sources, and managers should be encouraged to contact the employee's subordinates, peers, and other departmental supervisors, as well as paying customers, to obtain information. The employee can be asked to nominate several people who are familiar with the employees.

Can we provide the forms in electronic process?

Yes. For instance, such a form could have several columns, allowing the manager to type goals or objectives in the left-hand column and related performance review and methods of accomplishment in the middle and right-hand columns.

How are performance appraisals done and used with project work, for instance, when a major project has been completed?

Frequent feedback should be encouraged, and feedback during and at the completion of the project certainly is desirable. The performance excellence process should require a review and feedback several times during the year at designated, regular intervals (e.g., once every 3 or 4 months). The issue of what constitutes a project might best be stated in terms of what constitutes an objective. An objective may be general (e.g., deliver high-quality products on time). Objectives can be project based, but should also include a set of performance standards reflecting how the project will be carried out. For instance, therefore, a project involve completing a media package for a particular department, and doing so on time in a manner that demonstrates knowledge of the client's needs.

How do we ensure there there will be no surprises at the end of the year? How often should appraisals and feedback sessions be conducted?

Periodic feedback should ensure that there will not be surprises. Reviews should occur quarterly or every 4 months.

What is the linkage to ongoing feedback and ongoing development? How do we ensure that managers are held accountable for the development of subordinates? How do we measure the development? How much input should come from the subordinates?

As evident from my responses to earlier questions, I envision a complete process that ties together objectives, development, and ongoing feedback. One of the objectives for a manager's job should be developing subordinates. As such, managers should be evaluated on how well they carry out the goal-setting and performance review process and how much attention they give to their subordinates' professional growth and development (to do better on their current jobs, to prepare for anticipated changes in job requirements, and to prepare for other jobs in line with their career interests and corporate needs).

How do we communicate the rollout of this program to employees?

Rollout should have several components: an announcement from the senior vice president in the form of a memo or video message; a memo or brochure describing the process; and half-day orientation meetings (i.e., training workshop) to discuss the principles of the programs, policies and procedures, expectations, and examples of constructive meaningful narrative appraisals and poor narratives. The orientation can be delivered by departmental managers (a good developmental experience for managers who are part of a fast-track advancement program), and a video of the training can be made for new entrants to the department.

Adapted from London, 1995b.

takes the lead in the appraisal process. The supervisor's role is to give the employee recognition and suggest changes in behaviors or activities. He wrote:

> The appraisal feedback interview is a very authoritarian procedure—a parent–child type of exchange. Most modern organizations are moving away from authoritarian management toward an involvement-oriented working environment. A performance review discussion based on the subordinate's self-review fits an involvement-oriented climate much better than the traditional top-down performance review discussion. It also has the advantage of forcing the manager into a counseling mode, rather than serving as a judge. Research has shown that performance review discussions based on self-review prove to be more productive and satisfying than traditional manager-initiated appraisal discussions. (p. 68)

Supervisors are likely to need training in how to be a "counselor" and react to problems, such as how to deal with who subordinates who have an inflated self-evaluation or, conversely, an unnecessarily self-deprecating view.

Meyer (1991) suggested that the conventional, one-way approach to feedback is sometimes appropriate when the subordinate is dependent on the supervisor, as is the case of new employees, trainees, or people in highly structured jobs. As subordinates become more experienced and the relationship grows between the supervisor and subordinate, self-appraisals are likely to be more valuable. They increase the subordinate's dignity and self-respect; place the supervisor in the role of counselor, not judge; enhance the subordinate's commitment to goals and development plans that emerge from the discussion; and avoid defensive reaction on the part of the subordinate.

However, several problems with self-review should not be ignored (Blakely, 1993). It violates traditional mores about the proper relationship between boss and subordinate. Its value may be limited by a self-serving bias that inflates self-appraisals, especially if the appraisal is to be used for administrative purposes and not solely for development. Because people tend to rate themselves leniently, by completing the self-rating, they are essentially preparing in advance for the feedback discussion. The self-appraisal may crystallize their position, and this could increase the potential for an adversarial discussion. Also, supervisors may be lenient because they are sensitive to subordinates' self-judgments and prefer to avoid confrontation.

The Cost–Benefit of Appraisals

In many organizations, performance appraisals and feedback discussions are done poorly, and because managers shy away from giving feedback, appraisals may not be done at all. Clearly, documentation of performance is needed to support personnel decisions, such as those regarding compensation and promotion. Documentation is needed especially when the decisions are negative and the organization needs supporting material to justify a decision that may be protested by the people affected. Also, performance appraisals can be central to stimulating feedback. However, the formal process, and especially the process of ranking employees, can engender defensiveness and hard feelings. Clearly, this reaction will not contribute to a feedback-oriented, continuous learning environment. Other processes such as 360-degree feedback (see the next chapter) or continuous quality improvement processes (see chapter 13 on "teams") may reduce the need for formal appraisals.

The primary issue in these discussions is not how to identify and plan for future skill development, but rather how to negotiate agreement with the employee that the rating is correct and acceptable enough to justify a decision, such as the merit pay outcome. If the employee cannot accept the decision and believes it is less than what it should be, the employee is likely to withdraw in some way. This issue is more than one of dealing with defensive behaviors. Disagreement may occur if there has been little prior communication or feedback with the employee.

Perhaps a contingent approach should be taken to the conduct of performance appraisal discussions. For example, some subordinates are less defensive when their supervisor begins a performance review discussion by asking for their self-evaluation. In other cases, delegating feedback may be better (e.g., having a coach or human resource manager deliver the news). In other cases, however, the supervisor should consider ways to convince the manager such as positioning the positive, flattering feedback first and providing the flattery. In general, more research is needed on conducting constructive performance appraisal discussions.

Summary

A number of different rating formats exist. The most common method, a simple graphic rating scale, may not yield as precise and accurate ratings as other methods, such as computerized adaptive rating scales, which are more difficult to prepare and require computer technology. Appraisals do not even have to include ratings, especially if the prime purpose is feedback for performance improvement. Self-appraisals can be very useful as a way to reduce the feedback recipient's defensiveness. Whereas self-ratings tend to be inflated, as discussed in chapter 3, self-assessment engages people in the process of their own performance review. Some people view themselves more critically than others view them when it comes to discussing their performance for purposes of guiding their development rather than giving them a salary increase. In general, feedback needs to be provided in ways that are palatable, that put forth recognized and accepted justification for decisions and offer clear directions for development. This may mean positioning the feedback in a way that the recipient can digest it. As such, the particular rating format may be less important than what is done with the information, including how supervisors deliver the feedback and what the recipients do with the information to guide their performance improvement and career development. Still, ratings serve a purpose in demonstrating that administrative decisions are performance based.

Whereas performance appraisal and feedback are related but distinguishable processes, the quality of the appraisal and the context in which it is made likely will affect its value for feedback and for improving performance. The next section indicates ways to reduce rater errors and generally improve the quality of performance appraisals, which in turn should improve their value for feedback.

TOWARD MORE VALUABLE APPRAISALS

Barnes-Farrell (2001) outlined the constraints that make performance appraisal difficult for managers. Time constraints make it hard to record relevant behaviors as they are observed. Memory constraints make it hard for managers to recollect all the relevant information when completing a performance appraisal form. Managers who have a number of subordinates are likely to spend more time with some of them than others. As such, managers are not able to engage in systematic observation of relevant information for all of them. For some subordinates, managers have an overload of information and may have trouble sorting through it all and focusing on critical areas of performance. For other subordinates, managers have too little information, or uneven information in that their attention may be centered on a highly negative or positive situation. Subordinates may draw their manager's attention to certain information, for instance, sharing positive events and making light of negative events. Subordinates help managers make sense of situations and can, in the process, affect their managers' perceptions of the reasons for the events. Subordinates can attribute negative outcomes to factors beyond their control and positive outcomes to their own actions. Unless managers gather more data on their own, they are likely to trust their subordinates' explanations. Conflicting information may lead managers to draw erroneous conclusions. For instance, having some positive and negative information about a subordinate may lead to the conclusion that the subordinate is an underachiever with high potential but low motivation, or that inconsistent negative outcomes must be the result of external causes.

The performance appraisal process takes place within the context of the social interaction among the manager, each subordinate, and the team of subordinates. The manager needs to maintain and enhance these relationships while evaluating each individual's accomplishments. The social dynamics are likely to influence the evaluation judgments. In addition, performance appraisal is complicated by multiple goals: to distinguish between subordinates for better payment of the best performers, and to identifying strengths and weaknesses for development. The pay decision requires making overall judgments about each subordinate's accomplishments and then comparing subordinates. The development evaluation requires a comprehensive review of each subordinate separately that involves looking at skills, knowledge, and behaviors that contribute to performance outcomes.

Also, as I discussed in the chapter 5, the manager's motivation may affect the evaluation process. Some managers are willing to invest more time, emotional energy, and cognitive effort in the appraisal task than others. The less information the manager has and the more pressing the demand for a judgment, the more likely it is that the manager's appraisal will be affected by the stereotypes, leniency, halo, or other rater errors.

Barnes-Farrell (2001) also noted how changing organizational conditions are likely to influence the quality of appraisals. Flatter organizational structures mean that managers have more subordinates reporting to them and less time to work with each. An emphasis on teamwork deemphasizes individual differences in performance and emphasizes team relationships and work quality of the team as a whole. With this approach, individual performance appraisal may be viewed as hurting teamwork. New work arrangements such as geographically dispersed and telecommuting work arrangements make collecting performance information difficult. Fortunately, new information technologies allow high-quality data to be collected and recorded from multiple sources and records to be maintained over time (see the discussion in the nest chapter and chapter 14 on collecting performance ratings from multiple sources using Internet technology).

The most significant barrier to enhancing the accuracy of performance ratings is inability to identify factors that predict raters' ability or motivation to provide accurate ratings (Murphy & Cleveland, 1995). Jawahar (2001) examined the effects of raters' attitudes about performance appraisal accuracy and their self-monitoring on leniency (elevation accuracy) of ratings and personnel decisions. Positive attitudes about the appraisal process and the organization in general should be related to trying harder to evaluate performance accurately. Self-monitoring, a stable dispositional characteristic, is the tendency to act according to one's attitudes (Snyder, 1979). Self-monitors are predisposed to be lenient because they want to maximize the approval of others and minimize their disapproval (Jawahar & Stone, 1997; White & Gerstein, 1987).

In Jawahar's (2001) study, 210 university managers who were also part-time graduate students completed measures of self-monitoring and attitudes toward accurate appraisal. Six weeks later, they were asked to read descriptions of two employees. Each employee was described by 25 critical incidents. One employee was rated. The other served as a standard of comparison. This other employee was clearly more favorable, thereby avoiding the ceiling effect of evaluating the one employee and allowing room for participants to inflate their ratings. Expert ratings were used to assess participants' accuracy. In addition to the ratings, participants made pay increase recommendations for the employee rated (e.g., using a 9-point scale ranging from "strongly oppose a pay increase" to "strongly support a pay increase").

Results showed that attitudes were not related to ratings or decisions. Self-monitoring was negatively related to accuracy of ratings and decisions, and not related to attitudes about appraisal. Attitudes were more strongly related to accuracy of ratings and decisions for those who were low in self-monitoring. The findings showed that high self-monitors are likely to behave in accordance with current situational influences and anticipation of consequences. For instance, they are likely to manipulate information to justify their decisions, particularly if they are held accountable for their decisions (Fandt & Ferris, 1990). Therefore, their behaviors are not as likely as those of low self-monitors to be consistent with their previous attitudes. In contrast, the behaviors of low self-monitors reflect their feelings and attitudes without regard to situational or interpersonal consequences.

Jawahar (2001) considered what practitioners can do to keep high self-monitors from evaluating others leniently. One possibility is to make them feel more secure so that they do not feel that they need to avoid the disapproval of others. All raters could be required to meet with their subordinates and review their performance informally several times a year. High self-monitors would thereby feel more comfortable with the rating process and be less concerned about incurring others' (e.g., the ratee's) disapproval at the time of the formal appraisal, and so would be more accurate in their evaluations. Another possibility is a training program in skills for observing and evaluating subordinates, providing feedback, and coping with subordinates' emotional responses.

The preceding discussion suggests that raters' motivation and sensitivity to the probable reaction of others to them are likely to influence their ratings. In addition, raters tend to make a number of errors common to raters. These should be recognized, and steps should be taken to reduce or eliminate them through training.

Common Rating Errors

Managers' judgments of others' performance may be affected by a variety of perceptual errors. These common biases often are evident in performance ratings, although they may pervade narrative descriptions of performance even when ratings are not made. They include the following:

- *Leniency*: the tendency to give overly favorable ratings on all performance dimensions regardless of actual performance
- *Severity*: the tendency to give overly negative ratings on all performance dimensions regardless of actual performance
- *Halo*: the tendency to allow perceptions of one performance dimension to influence ratings of other, unrelated performance dimensions

- *Similarity*: the tendency to give overly favorable ratings to ratees who are similar to the rater in characteristics unrelated to performance (e.g., age, race, or gender)
- *Central tendency*: the tendency to give midrange ratings of all performance dimensions regardless of actual performance (e.g., ratings of 3 on 1 to 5 scales)
- *First impression*: the tendency to allow one's first impression of the ratee to influence ratings. (This is especially relevant to employment interviews, but applies also to ratings of subordinates in which a manager develops an immediate impression of a new subordinate, then allows this impression to color subsequent judgments of the subordinate's performance.)
- *Recency effect*: the tendency to allow a recent incident to influence judgments of performance dimensions for the entire performance period.

Such errors suggest the need for training to reduce managers' errors of judgment and increase their rating accuracy.

Rater Training

One approach to performance appraisal training is to alert managers to common errors of judgment so they can spot them in the way they evaluate others and guard against them. Other approaches change the evaluation method rather than the rater. Appraisal methods that have clear performance dimensions expressed in behavioral terms are likely to reduce rating errors. In general, the more ambiguous the performance dimensions and the less likely their relation to observable job behavior, the more raters' biases affect the ratings. Other approaches try to make managers better observers of performance, assuming that if they have a clear recollection of job behaviors and a clear understanding of performance standards, their judgments will be relatively bias free.

Observation Skills Training. Observation skills can be improved by (a) giving observers prior experience in judging the topic and object of interest, (b) using good actors as models, (c) making the discriminations as discrete and defined with familiar terminology as possible, (d) allowing judges to see the context that may have provoked the observed actions, and (e) allowing observers sufficient time to observe (Boice, 1983).

Rater Error Training. Training methods to increase insight may include training people to observe cues, ask for additional information, and search for disconfirming evidence. People can learn to ignore biases, such as confirmation bias (leaning toward one perspective and seeking support for one's initial view and avoiding disconfirming evidence) and hindsight bias (believing that the world is more predictable than it really is because what happened often seems more likely afterward than it did before hand) (Russo & Schoe-maker, 1992). Also, people can learn how to conceptualize and process perceptions so they can learn to think about what they perceive and the judgments they make (Perkins, 1981).

Frame of Reference Training. Another training approach entails giving raters a frame of reference for evaluating the accuracy of their ratings as part of the training in addition to lecture and discussion concerning job be-haviors and rating dimensions. One study compared frame-of-reference and rater-error training with a control condition called "structure of training" that presented examples of typical job behaviors and rating dimensions, practice ratings, and discussions about ratings (Stamoulis & Hauenstein, 1993). This control condition produced results similar to those of the frame-of-reference training. Raters still may improve dimensional accuracy from training lim-ited to lecture and discussion of job behaviors and rating dimensions coupled with rating practice. These authors also suggested that frame-of-reference and rater-error training should be used together (a) to increase the corre-spondence between the variability in observed ratings and the variability in actual ratee performance and (b) to provide practice in differentiating among ratees (instead of focusing on rating errors). This may be accomplished by lecture and discussion of job behaviors and rating dimensions coupled with general performance examples, rating practice, and general rating feedback.

CONCLUSION

This chapter reviews traditional approaches to performance appraisal, par-ticularly supervisor ratings. I describe rating formats. However, I suggest the use of ratingless narrative appraisals to avoid threatening "grades." This is especially valuable after an organizational downsizing. The survivors may benefit from detailed, constructive feedback rather than ratings that label people, perhaps with unnecessary harshness. Also, I also recommend incor-porating a self-appraisal into the performance review process. The major points from the chapter can be summarized as follows:

1. The supervisor is the traditional source of performance appraisal and feedback, and the appraisal process usually involves a feedback dis-cussion with the subordinate, thereby mandating explicit feedback if conducted properly.
2. Some organizational policies and cultures support serious attention to feedback and development by making them an important (expected and rewarded) part of the way organizations operate.
3. Rating formats can be designed to accentuate a focus on behaviors (rather than general opinions of personality, for instance). Such rating scales enhance rater accuracy and generate constructive information.

4. Ratingless appraisals can avoid the defensiveness that often accompanies grading and focus the recipient's attention on behaviors and directions for development and performance improvement.

5. Self-appraisals should be incorporated into the performance review process. Beginning a performance review with a self-appraisal increases the recipient's involvement in and commitment to the process and diffuses the recipient's defensiveness.

6. Raters' motivation to provide ratings they can defend, situational conditions that allow time to observe behavior, and raters' self-monitoring tendency (sensitivity to how others react to them) affect ratings.

7. Managers should be alert to common errors in evaluating the performance of others such as leniency, halo, central tendency, similarity, and recency. They should be alert to these common rating errors to guard against them.

8. Appraisal methods that have clear performance dimensions expressed in behavioral terms are likely to reduce rating errors.

The next chapter turns to another source of feedback: multisource ratings. These so-called 360-degree feedback processes collect ratings from peers, subordinates, customers, supervisors, and self. This can be a useful supplement to supervisory ratings, and a valuable tool in helping the employee to plan development activities.

Ranking System

Sometimes used in conjunction with ratings, this system asks the manager to rank order subordinates from highest to lowest. Managers in the same department at the same organizational level may meet to rank all immediate subordinates on one list. They discuss each subordinate and then attempt to agree on a rank order.

7

Multisource Feedback Methods

Multisource feedback refers to ratings that can come from subordinates, peers, supervisors, internal customers, external customers, or others. When feedback comes from all the locations around a person (boss, subordinates, suppliers, customers) it is also called "360-degree" feedback. Usually, multisource feedback is collected for managers or supervisors, but it could be collected for any employee, with the raters depending on the employee's role in the organization. Multisource ratings are not always collected from all possible sources. For instance, sometimes only upward ratings are collected (i.e., subordinates are asked to rate their supervisor). Multisource ratings are collected through surveys using computer, telephone, in-person interviews, or paper-and-pencil questionnaires . The survey may be administered annually or more often. For example, a division of Motorola collects ratings quarterly by computer for automatic averaging of scores and providing of feedback reports to managers.

Multisource feedback is growing in popularity and importance as a method for evaluating employees and providing them with input for development. A 1995 report indicated that all Fortune 500 companies used or were planning to use multisource feedback (London & Smither, 1995). A 1996 paper reported that 25% of companies use some form of upward or multisource feedback survey process (Antonioni, 1996). Four years later, another report indicated that as many as 12% to 29% of all U.S. organizations were using this method (Church, 2000). Clearly, the use of multisource feedback has not diminished, and in all likihood has increased.

There are several reasons why multisource feedback is such a popular method for evaluating performance. The feedback contributes to individual development by providing information on worthwhile directions for learning and growth. It builds self-awareness, which in turn increases self-reflection and perhaps a greater understanding of others and how they react to you. This, in turn, could prompt managers to think more about the potential consequences of their actions toward others. Managers may feel accountable to respond to others' ratings of them. When administered over time, the survey results provide a way for managers to track changes in their own performance as they try to react to previous feedback and change their behavior.

From an organizational perspective, multisource feedback promotes organizational development by specifying dimensions of managerial behavior that are important to the organization's management. In this way, it clarifies management's performance expectations. It recognizes the complexity of managerial performance, realizing that performance is viewed differently by different constituencies, and that managers need input from these different sources for a comprehensive view of their performance (Latham & Wexley, 1981; Tsui & Ohlott, 1988). The supervisor does not have sufficient information or perspective to be the sole reviewer. Supervisors often are reluctant to evaluate subordinates honestly. They want to avoid having to confront the subordinate with negative information (Fried, Tiegs, & Bellamy, 1992). Also, managers may need to behave differently with subordinates, peers, supervisors, and customers. Managers confronting organizational change recognize the importance of being attuned to the changing expectations of multiple constituencies, and they realize that this requires continuous learning.

This chapter and the next presents the growing body of knowledge about multisource feedback. I describe how multisource feedback is used for development and to make decisions about people. I review multisource feedback methods including guidelines for item generation, report format, and ways of feedback delivery that make the feedback more valuable to the recipient. In the following chapter, I review how employees react to multisource feedback and the extent to which it relates to behavior change and improvement in performance.

MULTISOURCE FEEDBACK AS A PROCESS

Multisource feedback should be viewed as part of an ongoing performance management and development process, not as a discrete, stand-alone event (London & Tornow, 1998). Even if the multisource survey results are not used for a formal evaluation of managers, it still is part of the performance monitoring and improvement process. This includes setting performance goals, finding areas for improvement, taking action to learn and practice new skills and behaviors, and tracking different elements of performance from different perspectives including those of subordinates, peers, supervisors, customers.

Multisource feedback is best used as a support mechanism for gaining input about your performance. You could regularly ask your boss, peers, and subordinates for input, but this takes time, and you may not get honest feedback when you put people on the spot. Also, you may not ask the right questions or receive the answers in an objective way. With a 360-degree survey, all managers are evaluated in the same way on the same set of per-formance for the same purpose. You can compare your results with average scores obtained from others and from scores you received in the past. Of course, you need to interpret your results and judge their value. Did raters within a group (e.g., all subordinates) disagree and by how much? What does this disagreement say about the value of the average rating? Has the agreement among raters increased over time, perhaps because you are more consistent in your management style as a result of the multisource feedback? Is being more consistent important? Maybe you need to vary your behavior because your subordinates have different needs. Perhaps you have attended a management style course that provides a context for evaluating your sub-ordinates' needs and managing in relation to their individual differences in capability and motivation. Ongoing feedback will help you determine how your behavior is perceived and whether your personal goals for development are paying off. Multisource feedback becomes a calibrating vehicle within this overall performance–management/development process.

USING MULTISOURCE FEEDBACK FOR DEVELOPMENT AND ADMINISTRATIVE DECISIONS

Multisource feedback may be used solely to guide the recipient's develop-ment. Alternatively, it may be used by upper management to make decisions about the person rated as well as to help the person identify areas for per-formance improvement and career development. Incidentally, multisource feedback also can be used to evaluate organization change and development by averaging results across managers in a department or the organization as a whole and examining levels of performance and changes in performance over time (Timmreck & Bracken, 1997). As a tool for organization develop-ment, multisource feedback can be used in team-building discussions about the overall quality of management in the organization. Following changes over time across the organization can demonstrate the overall benefit of feedback to the organization as it promotes a feedback-rich climate. Most companies use multisource feedback solely for development. Increasingly, however, companies also are using the results to make administrative deci-sions about managers (Timmreck & Bracken, 1997).

Use for Development

When multisource feedback is used for development alone, the managers who were rated generally are the only ones receiving their results, unless they choose to share the results with others (Cialdini, 1989; Van Velsor & Leslie, 1991). This highlights the importance of managers using the information for their own development. The organization takes responsibility for a rating process that protects rater confidentiality, for a computer-generated report of the results, for help in interpreting the reports, and for training and development opportunities (Kaplan, 1993). Recipients of the feedback must take responsibility for interpreting their results and using the information to guide their development and performance improvement.

Use for Administrative Decisions

Increasingly, organizations use multisource feedback for administrative purposes, such as decisions about merit pay and advancement (London & Smither, 1995). This makes the feedback all the more salient to the individuals receiving it. But the process is likely to feel threatening to managers, especially to those who are worried about the quality of the interpersonal relationships they have with their colleagues. Such managers will say that they do not trust the process. Efforts are needed taken to demonstrate the reliability and validity of the ratings in providing meaningful information that cannot easily be undermined by raters who want to get even with or impress ratees.

The Pros and Cons of Using 360-Degree Feedback for Administration and Development or for Development Alone

There are several reasons why multisource feedback should be used for development and not for administrative decisions (London, 2001). Because ratings are provided anonymously, raters are less likely to be lenient when they know their ratings will not be used for making decisions about the managers they are rating. Keeping the results confidential promotes the psychological safety, which in turn encourages managers receiving the feedback to be less defensive. When managers are asked to rate themselves, which usually is the case, they are able to compare their self-concepts with the way others see them and to explore the reasons for any differences. Executives may believe that having to base decisions on the results detracts from their own judgment and accountability, essentially reducing their discretion over key personnel decisions.

Executives may not be prepared to discuss the feedback results with their subordinate managers (see chapter 12 on how executives and managers can learn to coach their subordinates). Also, managers may feel uncomfortable talking to their supervisor about how others view their performance, finding the situation threatening and stressful (Dalessio, 1998). It may take time for the organization to develop a culture that supports feedback. Using 360-degree data for decisions may prompt defensiveness and decrease the chances for using the data constructively. It may be a cause dysfunctional relationships, as might happen if managers avoid feedback discussions or construct rationalizations to save face. This is more likely to happen if the data are used to make decisions about managers who have to explain their results to their boss. The credibility of multisource feedback results may be in question if raters have a vested interest in the results, as they would if their manager's annual bonus depends in part on the ratings of subordinates who want their manager to be treated well in hopes that they, in turn, will also be treated well. Managers may try to influence how their subordinates rate them by implying rewards for positive results. Also, if subordinates or others (peers or customers) are chosen by the managers, they may not select impartial people.

There are, however, some good reasons for using multisource feedback to make administrative decisions (London, 2001). Important personnel decisions, such as those involving termination, promotion, and compensation, should be informed by information from different perspectives. This is especially important when supervisors do not have daily contact with the managers who report to them (e.g., in flat organizational structures whose executives have many managers reporting to them), and when performance cannot be easily quantified by the use of objective measures. Another reason is simply that if good information is available, it should be used to help in making better personnel decisions that benefit the organization. Knowing that ratings will be used in this way may encourage people to be more exact in their judgments, particularly if they might be called to task to explain them (to a lesser degree if they are not). Executives are likely to gather information about managers from different sources before making decisions about them anyway. Multisource feedback formalizes and standardizes this process for all managers, not just for those executives would like information for a special reason. Therefore, raters may be less biased than they might be if an executive approached them about a certain manager, in which case they may tell the executive what they think the executive wants to hear. Overall, using the data to make decisions increases the likelihood that managers will take their results seriously and use them to change their behavior and improve their performance.

Overall, the use of 360-degree feedback depends on the organization. Probably, the most productive way to introduce the process is to use it first for development alone. Then, after employees become used to the technique and the resulting data, and receiving feedback becomes routine, the organization can begin to incorporate it into administrative decision making. This may take several years. In any case, as emphasized in the next section, all raters and those rated should be clear about the purpose of the process.

WAYS TO INCREASE THE VALUE OF MULTISOURCE RATINGS

There are a number of ways to limit rater distortion and increase the value of multisource feedback results for development and administrative decisions (London, 2001). Survey results can be examined to determine the average ratings and the variation in ratings across raters. Systematic biases, such as leniency, can then be identified. Giving raters feedback about distortion in data from prior ratings, or at least alerting them to possible rater errors, can encourage them to avoid these errors in the future. Raters can be given other performance data (e.g., objective measures such as sales) for comparison with their ratings to help them understand how well their judgments relate to these other measures.

In general, it is important to clarify for the raters and the managers receiving the results how the data will be used, whether for development, administration, or both. This should be clear before the ratings are collected. Bracken (1996) proposed that different sets of multisource ratings be collected for development and administration. Ratings that focus on managerial behaviors can be collected, say, every 6 months for purposes of development. Ratings that focus on managerial outcomes tied to organizational and departmental goals can be collected once a year for purposes of administrative decisions.

In general, when implementing a multisource feedback survey process for the first time, organizations would be wise to use the results for development only during the first several years. In that way, defensiveness and impression management game playing are less likely to enter the equation, and participants will feel less threatened by the process. Use for development will create a continuous performance improvement mindset that recognizes the value of feedback. Over time, as employees, managers, and executives become more comfortable with the process and discussions about the feedback results, the organization can change the policy (with plenty of advanced notice and discussion) and begin using the data to make decisions, possibly collecting separate data focused on outcomes for decisions and maintaining a behavior-focused survey for development. Newcomers to the organization should be introduced to the process slowly, perhaps by collection of development ratings about them for 2 years before collection of outcomes ratings for use in making pay or promotion decisions about them.

Rater Effects

Mount and Scullen (2001) described the results from two large sets of 360-degree feedback data demonstrating that ratings from multiple sources are highly affected by idiosyncratic rating tendencies of the rater (see also Scullen, Mount, & Goff, 2000). In particular, raters neither distinguish between different performance dimensions very well nor agree with each other to a great extent. Capturing the rater's unique perceptions of the individual yields valuable information for guiding development, but not for distinguishing between people to make pay or promotion decisions about them. Fortunately, averaging across raters can provide a more reliable and accurate view of the individual's level of performance for administrative decisions. Also, raters (for 360-degree ratings, this essentially means all employees in the organization) can be trained to avoid rating errors by attending to, interpreting, remembering, and recalling performance information.

To be more specific, Scullen et al. (2000) studied the effects of five components of ratings and the impact of each on the rating. They looked at idiosyncratic rater effects such as the tendency to be lenient or harsh, the extent to which the rater forms a general impression on the ratee's performance, the extent to which the rater differentiates between different dimensions of performance in evaluating the ratee, the effects of the rater's role or perspective (e.g., as supervisor, subordinate, peer, or customer), and random measurement error. They found that idiosyncratic rater effects accounted for 56% of the rating. General impression accounted for 14% of the rating. Differences between dimensions of performance accounted for only 8% of the rating. The rater's role accounted for another 8% of the rating. Random measurement error accounted for 14% of the rating. Presumably, steps could be taken to reduce this random error by controlling the situation (e.g., being sure that the purpose of the ratings, instructions, and items are clear; training employees to observe behavior and rate performance; ensuring that the survey is administered under similar conditions to all raters). The primary benefit of multisource ratings is that averaging ratings for raters within each role can "average out" idiosyncratic rating, thereby increasing the percentage of variation in the ratings attributable to true performance. Averaging the ratings from two raters increases the amount of true performance (the combination of perceptions of general performance and performance on specific dimensions, as distinguished from rater biases attributable to idiosyncratic rating tendencies or organizational perspective) by approximately 50% (Mount & Scullen, 2001).

RECOMMENDATIONS FOR IMPLEMENTING MULTISOURCE FEEDBACK

There are ways to minimize rater effects and increase the value of multisource feedback. The way the process is introduced in the organization, slowly and with clear explanation, is meant to enhance its value. The very process of averaging ratings across multiple raters within roles is meant to provide more accurate evaluations than would occur if one rater (e.g., the supervisor alone) made ratings and provided feedback.

As I suggested earlier in this chapter, when a multisource feedback process is started, the information should be used for developmental purposes alone. Two or three rating cycles may be needed for raters and managers to become comfortable with the process, which means several years if the process is administered annually. After that time, the policy can be changed to incorporate the results into decision making about the managers rated. Generally, managers tend to be more accepting of multisource feedback when the organization provides training to help managers improve on the performance dimensions rated (Maurer & Tarulli, 1994).

The use of computer or telephone to administer a multisource rating survey is increasingly common. In computer administration, the survey comes on a disk or can be downloaded online. Raters complete the questionnaire on the computer and send the disk back or, in the case of an online survey, return the data directly via the computer. The telephone can be used also to record responses. In this case, the survey comes by mail. Raters dial a given number and then key in their numeric response to each question. Raters can request that a printout of their responses be sent immediately to their printer so they can check their answers. Of course, the questions can actually be delivered on the telephone by a computerized voice. These high-tech methods have many advantages over paper-and-pencil surveys. As technology develops, they are becoming increasingly cost effective. Results are computed automatically.

The following tables are a resource for designing and implementing a multisource feedback program. They summarize the points I made in London, 1995a, Chapter 10. Table 7.1 outlines guidelines for designing and implementing a multisource feedback program. Table 7.2 presents a sample upward feedback rating form. A sample feedback report is provided in Table 7.3. Table 7.4 gives excerpts from an interpretation guide to help feedback recipients use their results.

Use of Comments

Multisource feedback surveys usually have some space for open-ended comments. Managers often say that this qualitative information is the most useful, and they tend to rate them heavily in determining areas for improvement (Rose & Farrell, 2002). One reason for the compelling nature of verbatim comments may be that they are easy to interpret. They do not require digesting numbers and comparing scores. Recipients may feel that the evaluators wrote comments about areas that were of most importance to them, and that they thus deserve attention. Also, because the raters took the time to formulate and type in specific comments, the recipients will feel obligated to take them seriously.

If managers are going to place so much value on open-ended responses, then there should be ways to ensure that the comments are meaningful. Comments that are more behaviorally descriptive provide a better basis for figuring out what to improve. Rose and Farrell (2002) evaluated the usefulness of 1,324 open-ended comments from 312 multisource feedback surveys completed for managers at different organizational levels. The raters' written commendations were in response to two open-ended questions: what strengths of the leader do you admired most? and in what areas do you

TABLE 7.1
Guidelines for Designing and Implementing a Multisource
Feedback Program

Identifying item content

Performance dimensions rated should be derived from analyses of current jobs or top managers' beliefs about new behaviors they want to develop and reward in the future. Items should be worded in terms of behavioral frequency (how often . . .) or evaluations (e.g., 1 = poor, 5 = great). Ratings are likely to be most reliable when the items refer to objective or observable behaviors instead of individual qualities, such as trustworthiness and responsiveness.

Involving employees in program design

Employees should be involved in identifying and describing items that will be used in the rating process. They can flesh out performance dimensions set by top management and write comprehensible items to reflect these dimensions. Also, their involvement will increase their sense of ownership of the process. Furthermore, managers are more likely to accept the results when they know that the items reflect performance dimensions important to the organization and meaningful to the people making the ratings.

Scale format

Many scale formats are possible. One is a simple Likert scale, which asks for ratings of each item on a numeric scale ranging from, say, 1 to 5 points (see the description of a graphic rating scale in the preceding chapter). Another format asks raters simultaneously to rate and rank peers and themselves on the same scale. Richard Klimoski and I used a 20-point scale. Work group members listed their own name and the name for each of their peers next to a letter and placed the letter corresponding to each name on the appropriate place on the scales (one 20-point scale for each behavior rated, as indicated in the following example). Multiple letters could be placed on the same point so all group members placed on that point received the same rating. This method forced raters to compare themselves with their peers and to compare their peers with each other in a deliberate way.

Sample 20-point scale (letters stand for names of peers; "a" represents the self-rating)

```
                              a
                              d
                           b e   f c
Responsiveness . . . . . . . . . . . . . . . . . . . . .
          1              10            20
         low                          high
```

A disadvantage of this method is that it is more difficult to code than other formats, and it may be hard to computerize if the survey uses optically scanned forms, online computer ratings, or input on a computer disk that is returned for analysis, although software could be developed for this.

Raters' anonymity

The process should ensure raters' anonymity. This means guarding the ratings, probably by having an outside consultant code and analyze the data and prepare feedback reports. Such reports usually are computer generated, particularly if the survey is on an optically scanned sheet, on a computer disk, or on a computer program tied to a local area network server or mainframe. Handwritten comments need to be typed to disguise the handwriting. Managers should not receive subordinate ratings if there are too few peers or subordinates (e.g., four or fewer) because this may suggest the identity of the raters.

Rater training

All employees should be trained in how to rate accurately and what constitutes constructive comments. Also, recipients should be trained in how to use the data. Survey instructions

TABLE 7.1 (cont.)

should be clear. Employee briefings should be held to explain the reason for the ratings, how the data will be aggregated, and the nature of the feedback reports. Rater training should make raters aware of rating errors: leniency, central tendency, and halo (rating all elements of performance alike).

Uses

The use of multisource feedback is likely to affect employees' attitudes about the feedback process and possibly the favorability of the ratings. Respondents are more likely to be lenient if they know the ratings will be used to make decisions about the ratee than if they know the ratings will be used solely for the ratee's development and no one else will see the results other than the ratee.

believe the leader needs to improve. Independent judges categorized the items as to content (e.g., communication, customer service ability to work with others, organizational commitment, honesty) and in terms of usefulness for development (identifies problem and solution, identifies problem only, or is not useful).

The results showed that most (77%) of the responses to the "needs improvement" question were useful for development. Very few comments identified both the problem and the solution (25%). More than half (52%) identified a problem and were classified as only marginally useful. The most useful comments (with a statement of problem and suggested solution) were given for the areas of leadership/management skills and staff development. Among the least useful comments were those given in the area of integrity, perhaps because this an ambiguous concept about which raters find it hard to respond. Not surprisingly, the comments in response to the "strengths" question were not useful for development, as compared with the comments in response to the "needs improvement" question. One third of the responses to the "strengths" question were not useful for development, as compared with only 23% of the comments in response to the "needs improvement question." The content area most commonly cited as a strength was that of job skills and interpersonal characteristics. For this area, only 1.8% of the comments contained both a problem and solution. More than half (55%) of the comments in response to the "needs improvement" question specified behaviors rather than general characteristics. Even a larger proportion (63%) of the comments in response to the "strengths" question were behaviorally based.

Overall, the results show that the verbatim comments can indeed be valuable for development. However, most of the comments required further clarification to guide developmental activities. The results also suggest that comments about strengths can be helpful for development by, for example, creating increased self-awareness about behaviors the individual demonstrates well. The findings suggest that comments could be made more useful by providing raters with directions that ask for specific behaviors, problem areas, and solutions. It should be noted that the data were based on

TABLE 7.2
Sample Upward Feedback Survey

Instructions

An important aspect of leadership is the management of people. This survey focuses on your satisfaction with the relationship you have with your supervisor. Use the following numeric scale to rate your supervisor. Indicate the number that best describes your rating. Use "N" to indicate that you have had insufficient opportunity to gauge your degree of satisfaction accurately. Your responses will be averaged with those from other subordinates who also report to your supervisor.

Scale

    1 = very dissatisfied
    2 = dissatisfied
    3 = somewhat dissatisfied
    4 = somewhat satisfied
    5 = satisfied
    6 = very satisfied
    N = no opportunity to observe

_____1. Jointly sets performance objectives with you.
_____2. Supports you in developing your career plans.
_____3. Motivates you to do a good job.
_____4. Gives you authority to do your job.
_____5. Provides the support necessary to help you do your job (e.g., advice, resources, or information).
_____6. Understands the work to be done within your work group.
_____7. Is available to you when needed.
_____8. Encourages innovation and creativity.
_____9. Holds employees accountable for meeting performance objectives.
_____10. Keeps commitments.
_____11. Allows adequate training time for you.
_____12. Provides ongoing performance feedback.
_____13. Has provided a useful performance appraisal within the past year.
_____14. Conducts productive staff meetings.
_____15. Demonstrates trust and confidence in you.
_____16. Treats you with dignity and respect.
_____17. Informs you about issues affecting you.
_____18. Balances the work load fairly.
_____19. Communicates the reasons for his or her actions.
_____20. Supports and backs you up.
_____21. Has the subject matter knowledge to do the job.
_____22. Fairly evaluates your job performance.
_____23. Represents the group effectively to others (e.g., to clients, to management, or at meetings).
_____24. Ensures that you get credit or recognition for your work.
_____25. Encourages open, two-way communication.
_____26. Modifies his or her position on the basis of feedback from you (e.g., ideas, plans, or solutions).
_____27. Provides opportunities for you to develop new skills.
_____28. Strives for quality in spite of time pressure.

Adapted from Wohlers & London, 1989.

TABLE 7.3
Sample Feedback Report

	Mean		Range		No. of Subordinates Responding To Item	Norm*
	Self Rating	Subordinate Rating	Low	High		
Jointly sets performance objectives with you.	5	3	1	4	7	3
Supports you in developing your career plans.	4	4	2	4	8	4
Motivates you to do a good job.	6	5	3	6	8	4
Gives you authority to do your job.	5	4	3	5	8	3
Provides the support necessary to help you do your job (e.g., advice, resources, or information).	6	4	2	5	7	4

*The norm is the average of subordinate ratings for the item across all managers in the unit.

TABLE 7.4
Results Interpretation Guide

An interpretation guide asks the manager receiving the report to compare his or her self-ratings with the average subordinate ratings.

The number of responding subordinates is indicates the representativeness of the results across the work group. Data is not be presented if four or fewer subordinates responded to an item.

The "norm" provides a comparison with how managers overall were perceived by their subordinates.

The guide includes information about training and developmental experiences available that would be useful for each category of items.

independent judges' categorization of the comments. Research is needed to examine feedback recipients' perceptions of how useful comments are in interpreting feedback results.

PROCESSING MULTISOURCE FEEDBACK

In chapter 3 and Table 7.1 in this chapter, I discuss the value of feedback from multiple sources and show how a rating procedure can be developed to collect information from subordinates, peers, supervisors, and customers. The process of developing and administering multisource ratings is one thing.

Making it effective is another. The content of the ratings, how the feedback is delivered, and support for its use in setting goals for development and behavior change all are critical to making multisource feedback worthwhile. This is especially the case because multisource feedback can be difficult to interpret and opens the door to distorting or ignoring the information.

This section emphasizes the importance of having specific information, considers defensive reactions to multisource feedback, outlines alternative modes of delivering multisource feedback, reviews psychological processes that encourage the constructive use of multisource feedback, and suggests ways to make multisource feedback a part of the organization's culture.

Specificity of Information

The more the information is specific and reflects the nature of the task, the more compelling it is (Kluger & DeNisi, 1996). Information that reflects actual job behaviors is likely to be easier to understand and less threatening than descriptions of personal characteristics (Kluger & DeNisi, 1996).

In many rating systems, each rater makes ratings on the same set of performance items regardless of the source, whether peer, subordinate, customer, or supervisor. In some rating systems, different information (i.e., ratings on different items) may be collected from different sources. There also may be a common set of performance items rated by all sources. This is a way to provide comparative information while collecting information about which a given source has specific observations not available to other sources. Therefore, for instance, subordinates may rate their immediate supervisor on items specific to boss–subordinate relationships that they would know more about than raters from other sources. Customers may rate the manager on delivery of products or services. Peers may rate the manager on collegial relationships. All sources may rate the manager on organization and communication skills.

Feedback results may be accompanied by normative information: the average score for each item across all managers rated. This provides a basis of comparison of the individual ratings. For example, knowing that I received an average of 3.89 on a 5-point scale ranging from 1 (low) to 5 (high) from my subordinates on giving feedback would have different meaning if I knew that the mean rating received by supervisors in my organization (across say 50+ supervisors) was 2.75 or 4.66. I would know that I was doing better or worse than average.

Instead of presenting managers with data on how they were rated, a less specific form of feedback provides them managers with a summary of the average ratings across the department or the entire organization. Thus, these employees receive only normative information. Such information may be a helpful and nonthreatening guide to managers in considering issues in their own departments. It can be valuable as an icebreaker in a team meeting aimed at discussing ways to improve interpersonal relationships, whereby the team is asked to consider the extent to which the results applies to them. However, it lacks specificity, and it is easy to rationalize unfavorable results, arguing that they apply to others, not to the team's department.

Of course, feedback also may be informal, coming from others directly (through their statements of opinion about your performance) or indirectly (through hearsay or other evidence of how they evaluate your performance). Such information may be welcome and even sought, or it may be unwelcome. However, as discussed in the chapter 6, people may seek feedback for the purpose of creating an impression in others instead of learning how others feel about them. Moreover, informal feedback may be ambiguous, or it may focus on personal qualities (you learn you are "hard to get along with") rather than behaviors or actions (you "don't listen to others' ideas"). The more ambiguous and general the information, the less valuable it will be.

Toward an Impartial and Dispassionate Reaction

Recipients can easily be defensive when confronted with multisource feedback. In requesting informal feedback, recipients can ask only sources they know will be favorable. The recipient of multisource ratings can focus on the highest ratings regardless of the source and performance dimension. If the feedback report includes the range (lowest to highest ratings) as well as the average rating from each source, then it is easy to focus on the top of the range. External attributions can be made for the lowest ratings ("There will always be some people who are unhappy" or "Low performers can't be expected to be honest"). Alternatively, the recipient can concentrate on the source or performance dimensions providing the highest ratings, rationalizing that these sources and dimensions are the most important.

The most constructive way for recipients to use feedback suggests the following guidelines. Review all the information thoroughly and objectively. Examine each piece of information, considering the overall strengths and enumerating the most serious weaknesses. For each source of multisource feedback, list the five highest and five lowest ratings, comparing the list between sources and identifying the strengths that should be enhanced and the weaknesses that should be reversed. Diagnose whether the areas for improvement are motivational (there is a need to devote more time and energy to the area, a need to overcome discomfort or dislike of the behavior, or a need to reward the behavior as an incentive) or ability related (there is a need to learn how to do the behavior). Set goals for learning (target training courses or special job assignments). Make commitments for changing behaviors. Review the feedback and refine the performance improvement goals with your supervisor. Compare the feedback from the next rating period to that of the previous rating period to determine whether the changed behavior has had an effect on the ratings. Finally, evaluate changes in unit performance to determine their links to development, behaviors, and rating changes. These guidelines are easier said than done, given the tendency of people to be defensive.

Modes of Feedback Delivery

The way multisource feedback is delivered affects how much attention the recipient gives to it and the likelihood of defensive reactions. Consider the following possibilities.

One-on-One Delivery of Results From a Consultant.   The consultant, an expert in performance improvement (perhaps an industrial or organizational psychologist or a human resource specialist), ideally from outside the company, reviews the results with the individual. This minimizes threat and forces the recipient to consider all the results. The consultant also may help the recipient use the feedback to set goals for performance improvement.

One-on-One Delivery of Results From the Immediate Supervisor.   Knowing that your supervisor not only sees your ratings but also reviews them with you makes them highly salient. This enhances the threat and increases chances for defensiveness. However, if the supervisor knows how to review the feedback objectively and constructively by tying the results to directions for improvement, the outcome can be beneficial. If the supervisor attributes blame and merely demands improvement, then the subordinate may be particularly defensive.

Deskdrop.   The feedback may come in the form of a computer print-out or an online report. Written guidelines for using the feedback may be provided. However, whether the recipient reviews or uses the information is totally up to the recipient. When the feedback is meant solely for the recipient's development and no one else in the organization will see it, the only incentive for reviewing the information is performance improvement. However, the easiest defense is not to look at the information at all. If recipients know that their supervisor also will see the results, however, there is more incentive at least to know what they are in case the supervisor brings them up.

Group Session With General Discussion on Use.   The recipients convene in a group to receive their individual results, usually delivered in a sealed envelope, and to hear from a consultant or human resource specialist about ways to interpret and use the results. Recipients then have a chance to examine their individual results and ask general questions for clarification (e.g., "What does it mean if I rated myself lower than my peers and subordinates did?").

Group Session With General Discussion and Targeted Discussion About Each Individual. The proceeding procedure is followed except that each person is given everyone else's ratings as well as his or her own. This may occur after a leadership development simulation in a course whose participants all are from different organizations. The simulation is followed by a chance for the trainers to rate the participants and for the participants to rate each other. The results are shared as a means of starting a discussion about each individual. Fellow participants share their reactions as a way to help each other. This information is hard to deny at the time it is given, but easy to forget after the course.

Designing Survey Feedback With Psychological Processes in Mind

Attention to and acceptance of multisource feedback can be enhanced by building in reinforcement mechanisms. These rest in several well-understood psychological processes as follows:

Information processing: the questions asked (items rated) communicate what performance dimensions are important in the organization.

Reward mechanisms (expectancy that behavior change leads to valued outcomes): people pay attention to behaviors and outcomes on which they are measured and reinforced.

Impression management: people want others to think well of them. Knowing that others will be evaluating them explicitly drives attention to the behaviors evaluated.

Social comparison: people want to know their performance in comparison with others. The availability of comparative data (i.e., how others did on the average) makes the results more salient, but also may focus attention away from behavior to ones self-concept. Helping the recipient compare the results to his or her past results may be more productive.

Goal setting: goals and feedback are mutually supportive. Goals help feedback to work, and feedback helps goals to work. Using the feedback to set goals translates the feedback into action.

Frequent feedback: some firms, such as Motorola, use multisource feedback quarterly, collecting the data and generating reports via computer.

Social learning: people model the behavior of others when they see it is valued and rewarded. When top managers seek and use feedback, others will too.

Commitment mechanisms: people develop commitment to new behaviors when they are do-able (i.e., the individual sees the behaviors as possible and realistic), when rewards and valued outcomes can be anticipated. Also, and when rewards and valued outcomes are anticipated (a process known as prospective rationality). The rewards may be social and self-administered (e.g., a stronger sense of belonging) or material and visible to others (a salary bonus; an awards dinner). Also, people develop commitment to behaviors for which they are making a substantial investment of time and money to develop (a process known as retrospective rationality) (Salancik & Pfeffer, 1978). For instance, they express commitment to goals to which they agree in public (e.g., during a team meeting). To deny the commitment would be inconsistent with their self-image as an effective, rational person.

Making Multisource Ratings a Part of the Organization's Culture

Organizations need to support the use of multisource feedback for develop-ment. One study examined the extent to which multisource feedback led to development responses, such as participating in self-development activities, meeting with raters, targeting skills for improvement, and preparing a writ-ten development plan (Holt, Noe, & Cavanaugh, 1995). Managers' were more likely to engage in such development responses after feedback when development planning was required, development plans were complete, and the organization had a total quality management program that promoted continuous improvement. Sharing information publicly decreased the like-lihood that managers targeted specific skills for self-improvement.

The organization should strive to make performance information col-lection and use a constructive, normal part of doing business, part of the organization's culture. This will happen as multisource feedback or upward feedback ratings are collected at regular intervals (perhaps only annually); used to evaluate individuals and make personnel decisions about them (in-corporated into the supervisor's appraisal); fed back with organization-wide data for comparison purposes to establish organizational standards and track the accomplishment of these standards; and integrated into a human re-source system that selects, develops, sets goals, appraises, and rewards the same set of performance dimensions (elements of performance that have been determined through job analyses to be critical to the organization's performance).

How do you know when 360-degree feedback does not work or has out-lived its usefulness? The following trouble signs may occur after several ad-ministrations: low response rates, considerable data are missing (scores can-not be reported because of fewer than four respondents per item), follow-up use surveys asking about usefulness of the 360-degree feedback indicate that managers are negative about the process (even after several years of annual administrations), and ratings over time are lenient. These problems may be fixable through training, better instructions, clearer communications about the purpose of the survey and how the results are used, or rater training and management training in how to help subordinates use the results.

Eventually (over 3 or 4 years of annual administration), managers and employees may feel they have enough direct feedback from their coworkers without needing to rely on a periodic survey. Feedback discussions may be more common because managers feel more comfortable asking about their performance and giving feedback to others. This climate may have evolved as a result of the survey. This means it has been a rousing success, but it also means that the time and money invested in the survey itself may no longer be necessary. As a support tool, 360-degree feedback is meant to be part of an overall performance management process. The feedback instrument and results are supposed to enhance conversation about performance management, to help managers take responsibility for their own development planning, and, overall, to create a continuous learning, feedback-orientated environment. If this environment has been established, it may need to be reinforced through continuous support and role modeling by supervisors, but the survey itself may not be required, at least for several years.

This chapter has focused so far on multisource feedback surveys as a way to collect performance data and provide feedback reports to individual managers. Next, I consider the more general employee attitude survey. Although this may not provide feedback to specific individuals, it allows tracking of employees' perceptions across the departments. Managers can study these results and discuss them with their subordinates to identify means for improving the way the organization or department functions. This organization development tool is described in the next section.

SURVEY FEEDBACK

Another formal method of providing feedback involves the employee attitude survey. This process reports attitude survey results to managers and employees (London, 1988). It is called "survey feedback" when accompanied by a structured follow-through procedure to help work groups interpret and use the information (Nadler, 1977). Employee attitude surveys may be collected via paper-and-pencil questionnaire, one-on-one interviews, or interviews with groups of employees (termed "focus groups"). This is different from multisource surveys such as upward and multisource feedback because the survey items ask for general attitudes about different facets of the company, possibly including the supervisor. However, instead of averaging the results separately for each unit manager and giving the manager an individualized feedback report, a single report is generated for the entire department or even the entire company. Therefore, managers must evaluate the extent to which the overall results apply to them and their work groups.

Employee attitude surveys are less costly than analyzing and preparing reports for each manager separately, although the results are necessarily less precise. Nevertheless, survey feedback results can provide a useful way to stimulate discussion in the work group about issues that may be relevant to other parts of the company as well. Results may be reported to everyone in the organization or department in special bulletins. Supervisors should be encouraged to meet with their work groups to discuss the meaning of the results for the organization as a whole and the work group in particular.

The overall corporate survey results become a tracking mechanism to evaluate the effects of organizational policies on employee satisfaction. Also, the importance of the satisfaction measures can be determined by examining the correlations between employee satisfaction and outcome measures such as employee turnover and absenteeism.

CONCLUSION

Multisource feedback (ratings from subordinates, peers, supervisors, internal customers, and external customers or some combination thereof) is growing in popularity as a method for evaluating employees and providing them with input for development. It captures information from multiple constituencies and focuses the recipient's attention on his or her role from different perspectives. Multisource feedback processes are more palatable and constructive. They build on psychological processes that model, reinforce, and integrate feedback in employee development and performance improvement. Feedback of employee attitude survey results provides another way to stimulate discussion in the work group about how supervisory behaviors and organizational policies and programs influence employees' motivation and desire to remain in the organization. The main conclusions from this chapter can be summarized as follows:

1. Multisource feedback can be used to guide development, make administrative decisions, and, by results averaged across managers, evaluate organization change and development.
2. Most companies use multisource feedback solely for development. Increasingly, however, companies also are using the results to make administrative decisions about managers.
3. Multisource feedback is valuable for development because it provides comprehensive information from different perspectives. It builds self-awareness, which in turn increases self-reflection and suggests directions for behavior change.
4. Managers generally feel accountable to respond to others' ratings of them. That is, they want to demonstrate that they used the ratings and that, as a result, they improved their performance over time.
5. Multisource feedback is valuable for development because the ratings are provided anonymously. Raters are less likely to be lenient when they know their ratings will not be used to make decisions about the managers they are rating, and keeping the results confidential promotes psychological safety and reduces defensiveness.
6. Multisource feedback also can be valuable for administrative decisions. Important decisions should be informed by information from different perspectives, especially when supervisors do not have daily contact with the managers who report to them. Executives are likely to

gather information about managers from different sources before making decisions about them anyway. Multisource feedback formalizes and standardizes this process for all managers, not just for those executives who would like information for a special reason.

7. Ratings from multiple sources are greatly affected by idiosyncratic rating tendencies of the rater. Raters do not distinguish between different performance dimensions very well. Also, they do not agree with each other to a great extent.

8. Raters' unique perceptions of the individual is valuable information for guiding development, but not for distinguishing between people to make pay or promotion decisions about them.

9. Averaging across raters can provide a more reliable and accurate view of the individual's level of performance for administrative decisions.

10. Raters can be trained to avoid rating errors by attending to, interpreting, remembering, and recalling performance information.

11. Ratings can be improved by being sure the areas of performance rated are specific and clear, the raters and recipients understand how the results will be used, and the recipients are encouraged to review their results in detail and consider their implications (i.e., the feedback reports are delivered in ways that promote close attention, for instance, with the support of the recipient's supervisor or an external coach).

12. The multisource survey and feedback method should be designed with recognition of the psychological processes that influence the extent to which people attend to feedback, for instance, providing comparative data to demonstrate change in ratings over time and encouraging the use of the results to set goals for performance improvement and development.

13. Multisource feedback helps the firm to develop an organizational culture in which feedback is sought and welcomed and people are accustomed to discussing feedback results as they manage their own performance and help support that of their coworkers.

14. Although multisource feedback, when averaged across individuals, is a way to track organizational results, sometimes organizations do not use multisource feedback for this purpose, but rather use employee attitude surveys as a less personal, and hence less sensitive, way to collect perceptions about organizational effectiveness.

The next chapter continues the discussion of multisource feedback by examining whether it is in fact effective in changing behavior and improving performance.

8

The Usefulness of Multisource Feedback

The preceding chapter describes multisource ratings (360-degree and upward performance evaluation surveys) as a source of feedback. They provide a systematic way of collecting and delivering performance feedback that may be more broadly representative than relying on feedback from supervisors. The preceding chapter describes ways to enhance the value of multisource feedback, such as ensuring that raters and recipients understand the elements of performance rated and the purpose of the results. However, several critical questions need to be answered: What determines whether people use the feedback? and Do these ratings actually change behavior and improve performance? This chapter explores research that addresses these questions. As you read this chapter, remember that the results suggest how people react to and use feedback in general, not just multisource feedback. As such, the literature on multisource feedback has become a rich source for understanding how to make feedback more valuable in organizations.

The chapter begins by exploring whether people are motivated when they discover that they are evaluating themselves more favorably than others think they deserve. It then turns to consider whether feedback results improve performance. The chapter next reports the results of studies that suggest personality characteristics that affect the extent to which people are receptive to feedback. The chapter concludes with recommendations for evaluating a multisource feedback program and, more generally, for increasing the likelihood that people will pay attention to feedback and use it to set goals and track their improvements in their performance over time.

IS DISCREPANT FEEDBACK A CALL TO ACTION?

A number of studies have reported improvements in performance after multisource or upward feedback (Atwater, Rousch, & Fischthal, 1995; Johnson

104

& Ferstl, 1999; Reilly, Smither, & Vasilopoulos, 1996). On the other hand, a review of the feedback literature showed that in more than one third of the cases, negative feedback discouraged performance improvement, especially when the feedback focused on personal characteristics instead of task behaviors (DeNisi & Kluger, 2000; Kluger & DeNisi, 1996). Recipients of positive feedback are more likely to see the feedback as accurate, more likely to accept the feedback, and more satisfied with the feedback and the appraisal process than recipients of negative feedback (Facteau, Facteau, Schoel, Russell, & Poteet, 1998, Podsakoff & Farh, 1989, Stone & Stone, 1985). This is not surprising, especially for appraisal results used to make administrative decisions about the recipients (e.g., regarding their salary or chances for promotion). Self-enhancement theory (Schrauger, 1975) predicts that people will respond positively to more favorable ratings regardless of the purpose. Also, the question becomes whether negative feedback also can prompt constructive, corrective action.

Brett and Atwater (2001) tested the assumption that negative feedback or discrepant feedback (self-ratings higher than ratings received from others) creates awareness and motivates individuals to change behaviors. Studying 360-degree ratings provided solely for developmental purposes, Brett and Atwater (2001) hypothesized that receiving favorable ratings (including higher ratings than the people rated gave themselves, a condition called "underrating") would be perceived as more accurate and result in more positive reactions than receiving unfavorable ratings (including lower ratings than the people rated gave themselves, a condition called "overrating"), which would be perceived as less accurate and result in result in negative reactions. They also hypothesized that perceptions of accuracy would be related positively to positive reactions, and that, together, positive reactions and accuracy perceptions would be related to perceived usefulness. Moreover, they hypothesized that usefulness would be positively related to the recipient's developmental focus and negatively related to the recipient's defensiveness (as rated by a facilitator who met with the recipient to review the feedback). Furthermore, they hypothesized that the relation between being overrated or receiving negative feedback and negative reactions, including perceptions of accuracy and usefulness, would be stronger for recipients whose goal orientation was to prove their competence compared with those who view feedback as a means of learning and developing mastery (Dweck's, 1986, mastery versus performance proves goal orientation; see also Dweck & Legget, 1988).

Brett and Atwater (2001) studied 125 students enrolled in a master's of business administration (MBA) program who also had 2 or more years of managerial experience. They started the study while they were employed full-time, and before they left employment to pursue the MBA degree. Participants completed self-ratings and asked their bosses, peers, and direct reports to rate them on a leadership behavior assessment survey. When the ratings were received 6 to 8 weeks later, the participants were no longer working. They received their feedback report based on the ratings of their former coworkers in a facilitated group workshop setting, after which they completed a measure of their attitudes and reactions to the feedback, including perceived accuracy and usefulness. After another 2 weeks, 103 of the students participated in an hour-long voluntary individual meeting with the facilitator to discuss developmental plans. At the end of this meeting, the participants competed a second survey on their reactions to the feedback process, again including perceived usefulness. The measure of goal orientation was completed at the start of the semester.

The results showed that, as hypothesized, negative feedback and feedback that was lower than expected (self-ratings higher than ratings received from others) were not perceived as accurate or useful. Instead of resulting in increased awareness, the feedback generated anger and discouragement. Contrary to prediction, however, more positive feedback was not related to positive reactions, but merely to no negative reactions. Thus, those who need the feedback the most because they are not performing well or have an unrealistically positive view of their own performance are the least receptive to the feedback and perceive it as the least useful. Unlike the studies examined by Kluger and DeNisi (1996), the ratings in Brett and Atwater's (2001) study were solely for development. In fact, the participants no longer actually worked with the raters. Other research found that managers rated unfavorably by their current subordinates reduce their level of loyalty and commitment to their subordinates after receiving feedback (Atwater, Waldman, Atwater, & Cartier, 2000), and in another study, reduced their liking toward their subordinates (Atwater, Brett, Waldman, & Yammarino, 2000).

Goal orientation did not affect the relations between ratings and reactions or perceived accuracy. Brett and Atwater (2001) suggested that this may be because the 360-degree feedback process induces a situational "performance-prove" orientation. That is, the recipients are more concerned about their performance in comparison with others than about developmental aspects of the feedback because of the way the feedback ratings are presented in comparison with others' ratings and with normative results. However, once these situational cues subside, goal orientation may influence perceptions of the value of the feedback. Brett and Atwater (2001) found that after controlling for perceived usefulness immediately after the feedback report was received, learning orientation was related positively to usefulness, whereas performance-prove orientation was not related to usefulness.

Interestingly, ratings from different sources were perceived differently. The significant relations regarding accuracy held for ratings from bosses and direct reports, but not for ratings from peers. Higher ratings from peers were not seen as more accurate. Because raters selected the peers, they may have been less surprised by their ratings, or they may have believed that low ratings from peers are deserved. Another interesting finding was that feedback from bosses and peers was more highly related to reactions than feedback from direct reports. Specifically, low or discrepant ratings from direct reports did not result in negative reactions, perhaps because the recipients expected some subordinates to rate them low or lower than the recipients rated themselves. Thus, the value and relevance of feedback from different sources need to be considered in implementing a multisource feedback process.

Regarding implications for practice, Brett and Atwater (2001) argued that individuals who receive negative feedback may need different follow-up activities than those who receive positive feedback. Follow-up sessions with a facilitator or executive coach may help them confront and use negative results. Also, specific characteristics of the recipients, such as a high development orientation, may make them more susceptible to negative reactions. Those with a performance-prove orientation may need different coaching to help them digest the information than those with a learning orientation. In addition, because recipients view positive feedback as useful when it actually provides them with the least information about developmental needs, facilitators should focus recipients' attention on performance areas rated highly, which can help them feel good about themselves, thereby minimizing negative reactions to low ratings and motivating them to examine their developmental needs and follow-up with developmental activities. Overall, Brett and Atwater (2001) indicated that organizations implementing multisource feedback should invest in follow-up coaching and facilitation to help recipients perceive the positive points, and identify developmental needs. Saving money on a simplified feedback delivery method (e.g., simply mailing the report or delivering it electronically) may mean that the feedback will not be used and, even worse, could engender negative feelings and outcomes.

CONVERGENT VALIDITY OF MULTISOURCE RATINGS AND IMPROVEMENT IN RATINGS OVER TIME

Several studies support the validity of multisource feedback data. That is, they demonstrate its relationships to separate ratings of performance, promotion, and turnover. These are summarized in Table 8.1. For instance, Sala and Dwight (2002) found that earlier feedback ratings of competencies from supervisors and direct reports were most strongly related to the job performance measure. Self- and peer ratings of competencies were not related to the performance measure. These results suggested that direct reports and managers had a unique chance to evaluate competencies found to

TABLE 8.1

Research on the Convergent Validity of Multisource Ratings and Changes
in Ratings Over Time

Study	Method	Results
Convergent validity studies relating multisource ratings to other measures		
Sala & Dwight (2002).	Studied the relation between ratings of performance from different raters and separate ratings of performance in relation to meeting targets. Their sample consisted of 276 executives from a global technology company. The executives were assessed once during a 4-year period from 1996 through 1999 using a multirater instrument that collected self, manager, subordinate, and peer ratings on behavioral items measuring different aspects of leadership competence. Separate performance measures were collected in 1999 for all the executives. The business objectives established at the start of 1999 were classified by the executive's management based on end-of-year performance in degree of achievement on a 4-point scale: 1 (unsatisfactory), 2 (achieved some/most of commitment), 3 (achieved/ exceeded target), and 4 (excellent).	The earlier feedback ratings of competencies from supervisors and direct reports were most strongly related to the job performance measure. Self- and peer ratings of competencies were not related to the performance measure.
Halverson, Tonidandel, Barlow, & Dipboye (2002)	Examined the extent to which agreement measures between self-ratings and ratings from a 360-degree feedback survey were related to the promotion rate in a sample of Air Force officers.	Self–subordinate agreement was more highly correlated with promotion rate than self–peer or self–supervisor agreement in predicting promotion rate. Those who were higher in self–subordinate agreement had the highest promotion rates, although the promotion rate dropped as the favorability of the ratings dropped. Officers who underestimated their performance had lower promotion rates than those who overestimated their performance, and both over- and underestimators had lower promotion rates than those inagreement. Subordinates' perceptions of performance were more important in helping managers calibrate their own leadership performance.

TABLE 8.1 (cont.)

Reiter-Palmon & Haley (2002)	Examined the relation between multisource feedback ratings and turnover in a sample of 128 employees in a Fortune 500 transportation company. Half of the employees in the sample had left the company and half had stayed.	Those who left were rated significantly lower by their managers before leaving than those who stayed. Also, those who left inflated their self-ratings (i.e., had higher discrepancies between their self-perceptions and their managers' views of their performance). The relations between turnover and ratings from subordinates were not as strong, indicating that performance ratings from managers were a better predictor of later turnover. Ratings from peers and customers were not related to later turnover.

Studies of changes in performance over time

Studies with control groups

Hegarty (1974)	Studied supervisors of university staff employees. Performance was measured again 10 weeks after the initial feedback.	Employees who received feedback improved significantly more than those who did not.
Atwater, Waldman, Atwater, & Cartier (2000)	Studied police supervisors and their subordinates. Supervisors were randomly assigned to one of two conditions: either a group in which supervisors rated themselves and were rated by subordinates but did not receive feedback or a group in which supervisor self-ratings and subordinate ratings were both collected and reported to the supervisors. In both conditions, the performance ratings were collected 10 months apart.	Subordinate ratings did not improve in either of the groups. However, performance ratings improved in the group receiving feedback for supervisors who had a positive attitude about the feedback. They believed that the feedback was honest and valuable, helping them set goals.
Heslin & Latham (2001)	Compared managers who received subordinate ratings (upward feedback) twice in a 6-month interval with managers who received feedback only once at the second point in time.	Managers receiving feedback improved significantly over time and received higher ratings at the second point in time than the managers who had not received feedback previously. Managers who received feedback twice improved more when they were high in self-efficacy (the belief that they could change their behavior to bring about positive outcomes) compared with those who were low in self-efficacy.

(Continued)

TABLE 8.1 (cont.)

Smither, London, Flautt, Vargas, & Kucine (2002)	Studied the effects of feedback and coaching. In this study of bank executives, some received coaching and some did not, but all received feedback.	Executives who worked with a coach improved more than those who did not work with a coach in terms of ratings from subordinates and peers 1 year apart.

Studies without control groups (studied changes in performance of managers who received feedback but did not compare them to managers who did not receive feedback)

Atwater, Roush, & Fischthal (1995)	Studied student leaders at a U.S. military academy 18 weeks after they received feedback.	Follower ratings were higher, especially for over-raters (leaders whose self-ratings were initially much higher than the ratings they received from their followers). In other words, they received negative feedback.
Johnson & Ferstl (1999)	Studied managers receiving subordinate ratings 1 year after first feedback.	Managers received higher ratings. Overraters decreased their self-ratings over time, whereas underraters (those who initially rated themselves lower than others rated them) increased their self-ratings.
Smither, London, Vasilopoulos, Reilly, Millsap, & Salvemini (1995)	Studied managers over a 6-month period after they had received initial feedback.	There was a small increase in performance reported.
Reilly, Smither, & Vasilopoulos (1996)	Followed the same group as studied by Smither et al. (1995) for another 2 years.	Continued improvement in performance ratings was reported.
Walker and Smither (1999)	Followed bank managers who received upward feedback annually for 5 years.	Managers who were initially rated unfavorably improved significantly over the 5 years. Those who met with their subordinates to clarify their results and discuss the subordinates' ideas for how the manager could improve improved more than those who did not, and managers who sometimes discussed their ratings improved more in the years they discussed their ratings than in years they did not.
Hazucha, Hezlett, & Schneider (1993)	Examined performance ratings and self–coworker agreement for managers 2 years after receiving initial feedback.	Found improvement and higher self–coworker agreement, although there was the possibility that only managers who felt they had improved decided to participate at the second point in time.

TABLE 8.1 (cont.)

Bernardin, Hagan, Ross, & Kane (1995)	Studied assistant store managers in a retail clothing chain.	Subordinate and peer ratings increased over a 1-year period, but ratings from the boss and customers did not.
Johnson and Johnson (2001)	Studied managers studied over 26 months.	Supervisor, peer, and subordinate ratings improved.
Conway (1999)	Studied managers 7 months after they had received feedback followed by one-on-one coaching sessions of about 60–90 min to help managers identify strengths and weaknesses and create an action plan for development.	No improvement inperformance was found.

be associated with job performance. This implies that in trying to identify and develop behaviors that will be related to increased performance for senior executives, an organization should focus on data from managers and subordinates, perhaps because they have a better vantage point or more direct contact for observing and evaluating executives' performance. Another explanation may be that in this study, the executives chose the peers who would be invited to rate them, whereas they could not choose their subordinates and managers. They may have selected peers who they thought would be favorable, but who had limited access to the range of work behaviors. The study also suggested that some competencies (e.g., aligning systems to support strategy, developing new market opportunities rated by managers and subordinates, making decisions quickly to capitalize on new opportunities, and demonstrating a desire to achieve personal goals rated by subordinates) were more highly related to the performance measure than others. Such data can be used to pinpoint competencies that are especially important to performance and should be a prime focus for development.

A principal question executives want to have answered before they implement multisource feedback is whether it ultimately improves performance. Answering this question requires longitudinal research. Summaries of such studies are also included in Table 8.1. Multisource or upward feedback often, but not always, has increased performance (2 of the 14 studies showed no improvement). The data also indicate that people are sensitive to how their self-ratings compare with how others see them, and they change their self-ratings to match if they initially over- or underrated themselves. Self-efficacy and a positive attitude about the feedback increase it effects. Also, discussing feedback with the raters improves later performance, either because managers understand the feedback better and thus improve more, or because their subordinates or peers believe they are trying harder.

RELATIONSHIPS BETWEEN RECIPIENTS' PERSONALITIES AND THEIR REACTIONS TO FEEDBACK

Personality refers to a person's distinctive interpersonal characteristics evident from behavior across different situations (Hogan, Hogan, & Roberts, 1996). The personality of people will shape how they act and affect how their performance is perceived by others. It also is likely to influence how people react to feedback and use the feedback for their development. Personality can be defined in terms of five key constructs, often referred to as the "Big Five": agreeableness (cooperation, trust, warmth, empathy), extraversion (sociability), emotional stability (calmness, self-confidence, security), conscientiousness (responsibility, organization, persistence), and openness (curiousity, broadmindedness, intelligence, originality, and imagination) (Goldberg, 1990, 1992; Hogan et al., 1996; McCrae & John, 1992; Mount & Barrick, 1998). A number of studies have found that conscientiousness is related to performance in a wide variety of jobs (see Barrick & Mount's 1991 review of 117 studies). Similar results have been found for agreeableness and emotional stability (Brooks, 1998; Dalton & Wilson, 2000).

Smither, London, and Richmond (in press) conducted a longitudinal study to determine the extent to which personality predicts 360-degree ratings, reactions to feedback, and later use of the feedback. They studied 116 male leaders in an elite unit of the U.S. military who had completed the Jackson Personality Inventory (Jackson, 1997) 6 months before the underwent multisource performance measurement by subordinates, peers, and supervisors. The Big Five personality measures were derived from this instrument. Immediately after receiving a feedback report about the multisource ratings from a psychologist, these military leaders completed a self-report measure of their reactions to the feedback. The psychologists also rated the leaders on their reactions to the feedback. Six months later, 49 of the the leaders competed a survey investigating their participation in developmental activities.

Smither, London, and Richmond (in press) found that performance ratings were significantly higher for leaders who scored high on agreeableness. Sociable and socially confident leaders were likely to be rated highly by themselves and others. Less sociable and less socially confident leaders were likely to see themselves as poor performers, whereas others rated them favorably. Leaders high in emotional stability were rated by psychologists as motivated to use the feedback. Conscientious leaders, particularly those high in responsibility, were likely to indicate that they felt obligated to use the feedback. Six months after receiving the feedback, leaders high in extraversion were most likely to have requested additional feedback. Conscientious leaders were significantly more likely to have engaged in developmental activities and to believe that their performance had improved.

EVALUATING THE EFFECTIVENESS OF A MULTISOURCE FEEDBACK PROCESS

How do we know whether multisource feedback is worthwhile? (See Scott and London, in press, for a full discussion.) First, process by which the items were developed should be reviewed. The survey was introduced, and the results were presented to managers. The items should be written to reflect organizational goals or important organizational or job competencies. If goals change, the items should change, although there is value to retaining a set of core items with which results can be compared year over year to identify changes in performance. Second, employee attitude surveys can ask whether employees understand the purpose behind the company's multisource rating process. Confusion, misunderstanding, or distrust would, of course, indicate problems with how the rating process is viewed. Third, rating results can be compared across raters, and systematic rating errors can be identified and called to the attention of the raters, perhaps in training classes on how to avoid rating errors. Interrater agreement can be examined. Raters in the same role (subordinate raters, peer raters) would be expected to agree with each other. Average subordinate ratings may not agree with average peer ratings because raters in these roles have different perspectives (indeed, they may be asked to rate different sets of items reflecting their ability to evaluate different aspects of performance), but we would expect agreement within classes of raters. Fourth, analyses can examine the relation between the ratings and objective indexes of performance. Although we would not expect a complete overlap in results because the objective indexes may reflect outcomes that are influenced by a variety of factors beyond the manager's control, there should be some correlation. Fifth, experimental designs may be used to isolate the unique effects of multisource feedback from other interventions aimed at changing behavior and improving performance. Thus, for instance, an experimental design could compare managers who have completed a leadership development program with those who have not. Half of the managers in each group would receive multisource feedback and half would not.

In general, the organization should track the success of the multisource feedback process over time, recognizing that it is both multifactored (e.g., consisting of item development in relation to organizational goals, data collection, feedback, and interventions such as coaching to enhance the use of the feedback), and long-term, taking place over time, indeed years, across multiple administrations of the survey. Changes in performance should be evident over time. Also, employee attitude surveys should show that employees throughout the organization are more comfortable with the rating process and with feedback in general. Ultimately, the goal should be to eliminate the need for the ratings, at least for developmental purposes, by increasing the extent to which managers seek feedback on their own and prompt discussions about their own performance and that of their their peers and their subordinates.

IMPROVING THE VALUE OF 360-DEGREE FEEDBACK

Feedback interventions are more likely to be effective if they direct and maintain the recipient's attention to the task and avoid focusing attention on the recipient's personal characteristics (DeNisi & Kluger, 2000). Unfortunately, elements of multisource feedback often do more of the latter than the former. For instance, feedback reports often include comparative or normative information that allows recipients to compare their results with how others were rated (e.g., the average of managers at their level of the organization on each item). Links to goals and consequences for the evaluation (e.g., will it be used to make pay decisions and how?) often are unclear. The results usually do not convey direct information about how to improve. When rater sources disagree (e.g., average ratings from peers differ from average ratings from subordinates for certain items), there is no indication which source of information is correct. Because multisource feedback provides information from multiple raters, the results focus the recipients' attention on the "ought" self: what others feel they should be doing. This is especially true when the messages are inconsistent and the recipients need to make sense of different viewpoints from different perspectives.

The major issue is how to improve the quality of feedback. Ratings alone may not be very useful. We need to look at the quality of the feedback, for instance, charting changes in performance over time, comparing results with company norms, and evaluating the depth and specificity of narrative comments. DeNisi and Kluger (2000) offered a number of helpful suggestions: (a) Using 360-degree feedback for administration focuses attention on the "ought" self, and those who receive negative feedback are likely to feel threatened and stressed by the pressure to change. Many companies start out using 360-degree feedback for development and then, after several years, begin using it as input for personnel decisions. Changing the rules like this can breed distrust and generate anxiety. (b) If 360-degree feedback ratings are to be used for decision making, employees (both raters and ratees) must be informed in advance so they do not feel betrayed. (c) The feedback recipients should be helped to interpret and react to their results. Workshops, training for supervisors, and external coaches can help managers to digest and use their results. (d) The amount of data presented to employees should not be overdone. The information should be summarized if possible. Some feedback reports include means, ranges, norms (average results across all managers), and past results for each item in the survey. This increases the difficulty of interpreting the results. Recipients will not necessarily focus on what is most important, or they may pick what seems most palatable to them and ignore other results. (e) Raters should be asked evaluate what they know best depending on their relationship with the ratee as peer, subordinate, or boss. All raters do not have to rate all items. For instance, subordinates can evaluate their manager's supervisory behaviors, whereas peers can evaluate their colleagues' cooperation on team efforts. (f) A strong link to the formal goal setting process must be included. The survey should ask about performance in areas that are important to the organization. I know one company that asked managers to input three key goals into an information data base. From this, an online survey was developed so that subordinates, peers, and their supervisor could evaluate them on each one of their specific goals. (g) The 360-degree process must be made a regular procedure, whether quarterly, semiannually, or annually. Seeing results over time will help feedback recipients track their improvement. (h) The effectiveness of the multisource feedback survey process should be assessed to see whether behavior change has occurred and whether performance has improved. The results should be correlated with other performance indexes. The raters and recipients should be asked how they liked the process and what ideas they have for improvement.

Ghorpade (2000) noted that although multisource feedback is widely used and delivers valuable information, it has problems related to privacy, validity, and effectiveness. For instance, some programs are not linked to the organization's strategy. The performance areas evaluated and the development process are not tied to the organization's goals. As such, the survey feedback does not contribute to the company's competitive advantage. Another problem is that feedback for development gets intertwined with the appraisal process, creating the potential for confusion. This limits the usefulness of the data. Having data from multiple raters in different roles (supervisor, subordinate, peer, customer) broadens the information, but does not necessarily provide better feedback (i.e., concrete, actionable, behaviorally oriented information). Anonymous ratings may be more honest than signed ratings, but this does not make them more accurate. Evaluating someone is a complex cognitive task, and raters often simplify the process by focusing on the latest observed behavior or general impressions that could be distorted by untold biases. Raters are likely to think about how the ratings they give could benefit them, for instance, how the ratings may affect their friendship with the person they are rating or the way they will be treated by that person. Another problem is that quantitative data, although inexpensive, can be hard to interpret and may not be fair. Some raters may be lenient, others quite demanding. Thus the same rating may mean different things to different raters. Yet another problem is that senior executives should be involved in the design and administration of the process, but their involvement may cause suspicion that the survey's purpose is other than the expressed purpose.

Given these difficulties, Ghorpade (2000) recommended the following steps for the development and administration of a multisource feedback process that is appropriate for the organizational context. First, identify who will receive the feedback, who will provide ratings, and who will serve as subject matter experts (representatives of the raters and ratees) on the process and elements of performance evaluated. Second, working with subject matter experts, select the behavioral measures and be sure they reflect behaviors that the organization values. Third, format the survey, including rating scales and a place for open-ended responses that explain the ratings.

CONCLUSION

The chapter reports results about the effectiveness of multisource feedback. It addresses whether people are motivated by gaps between their self-ratings and other ratings, and whether people actually change their behavior and improve their performance as a result of feedback. Research suggests that recipients' personality affects how they react to feedback. Organizations implementing multisource feedback should develop ways to assess its effectiveness and enhance its effects. The following conclusions can be drawn:

1. Negative feedback is not necessarily perceived as accurate or useful. Instead of resulting in increased awareness, it may generate anger and discouragement.
2. People who receive negative feedback may need more support and attention from a coach or supervisor to help them confront the negative results rather than deny or ignore them. Companies using multisource feedback should also invest in follow-up coaching and facilitation to help recipients accentuate the positive and identify developmental needs.
3. A relation has been found between multisource feedback ratings and independent measures of performance, promotion rate, and turnover.
4. Most studies have found that 360-feedback or upward feedback often, but not always, increases performance.
5. Multisource feedback is more valuable to people who care about how others view them and generally have a positive attitude about feedback.
6. Discussing feedback with the raters improves later performance, either because managers understand the feedback better and thus improve more or because their subordinates or peers believe they are trying harder.
7. Personality may affect the feedback people receive in relation to their self-perceptions and how they react to the feedback. For instance, sociable and socially confident people may be more likely to be rated highly by themselves and others. People high in emotional stability may be more likely to use feedback than those who are low. Conscientious individuals may be more likely to feel obligated to use feedback. People high in extraversion may be more likely to seek feedback.

8. The effectiveness of multisource feedback should be examined in the organization. The company should not just assume that it works. Ways to evaluate multisource feedback include assessing how it was developed (e.g., the extent to which managers had input to the items and the extent to which the items reflect organizational goals). Interrater agreement should be studied. Controlled experiments can be conducted to determine the extent of behavior change and the performance improvement resulting from feedback as compared with groups that did not receive feedback.

9. Organization should track the success of the multisource feedback process over time, recognizing that it has multiple purposes and that the effects take time, often years.

Ratings are just one source of systematic feedback. The next chapter considers sources of performance feedback under controlled conditions, specifically assessment centers and business simulations.

9

Assessment Centers and Business Simulations

This chapter focuses on certain methods that give employees information about their skills and capabilities: assessment centers, computerized testing and assessment, and business simulations. These methods offer participants a chance to try new behaviors and learn about themselves. Some organizations use these techniques as part of a development program. Such programs are available in a number of forms to anyone who wants to enroll in them. They may be run by universities, leadership development institutes, or training firms. In other cases, firms have their own programs customized to the needs of their employees and the objectives of the organization.

ASSESSMENT CENTERS

Assessment centers rate employees' skills and abilities. Assessment centers are sometimes used to evaluate job candidates in the employee selection process. But they also are used to evaluate current employees, especially those being assessed for possible promotion. An assessment center also may be used solely for development purposes (Spychalski, Quinones, Gaugler, & Pohley, 1997). The results provide diagnostic information that will helps employees to identify directions for development in areas that will be needed in managerial positions at higher organizational levels. Often, managers already determined to have the potential to advance are nominated to attend a developmental assessment center.

The assessment center (which does not refer to a place, but a process) includes such exercises as the in-basket (written material requiring prioritization and responses), an interview, management games, a leaderless group discussion, and a variety of psychological and achievement tests (Munchus & McArther, 1991; Thornton & Byham, 1982). Assessment centers are expensive to develop and operate, and they cannot be implemented without a good deal of work and investment. They are a way to assess general managerial skills and then consider directions for development. This may cost several thousand dollars per participant.

The goal of an assessment center is to collect and integrate diverse information about an employee. The exercises represent typical job duties and are meant to assess dimensions of behavior important to job performance such as managerial skills for middle management positions. Multiple assessors evaluate the participants' behaviors in a variety of joblike situations, and multiple raters produce more reliable and valid results than can be obtained by any one method alone (Cascio & Silbey, 1979).

The first step in designing an assessment center is to identify the performance dimensions to be assessed through job analysis. Examples for general managerial ability are "organizing," "communication," "decision making," and "leadership." The next step is to identify relevant tests and behavioral exercises for measuring the performance dimensions. For instance, a sales assessment includes simulations of sales situations and measures relevant knowledge of marketing. A managerial assessment center includes techniques to evaluate behavior in boss–subordinate relationships.

Once the assessment methods have been determined, the assessment center is organized. As managers participate in the process, multiple assessors observe and evaluate them on the performance dimensions. Narrative reports are written, and tests are scored. These are then reviewed by the assessors during an integration session. The assessors rate the participants on each dimension and discuss their ratings, usually trying to agree within 1 point on, say, a 5-point scale.

Developmental Assessment Centers

Developmental assessment centers are those used primarily, if not solely, for development of the participants rather than input to decisions about them. The results are reported to the participants by an assessor or a psychologist. During the feedback session with the participant, the assessor reviews the meaning of the results and offers guidance for development. Suggestions for development may recommend building on one's strengths rather than eliminating weaknesses. Some elements of managerial performance, such as decision making, cannot be learned easily. Others, such as communication skills, are learned more easily.

Developmental assessment centers provide feedback that encourages people to engage in activities that make them more eligible for promotion into management. This process was demonstrated in a 10-year study of 151 insurance company employees who participated in an assessment center and received formal feedback and recommendations for development (Jones & Whitmore, 1995). They were compared with a similar group of 167 people who were not assessed. The assessment center consisted of eight exercises completed by six assessees at a time over a 2-day period. The exercises included a background information questionnaire, a standardized interview, a supervisor–subordinate discussion role play (with a trained middle manager playing the subordinate role), an in-basket, a writing exercise, a formal presentation, and two group problem-solving discussions. Assessors were upper level managers who had received 2 days of training on assessment methods. After the assessment, the assessors discussed each candidate, rated the candidate on seven performance dimensions, and considered specific developmental recommendations on each dimension. For instance, an assessee judged to be low in oral communication skills may have received a recommendation to attend a course on public speaking. Written feedback reports provided dimension-by-dimension evaluations. Assessees reviewed their feedback reports privately, then met with one of the assessment center administrators for a discussion. The assessees were encouraged to consider the causes and accuracy of the results and to describe their intentions of accepting the information and following the recommendations for development. The assessment manager also met with each assessee's manager to review the results. The goal of this meeting was to gain the manager's support for the assessee's development. Assessees were asked on a follow-up survey to rate their acceptance of the feedback (e.g., to indicate on a 5-point scale from 1 [strongly disagree] to 5 [strongly agree] their responses to seven items such as "The feedback I received from the center was accurate" and "The feedback I received adequately captured my performance at the center").

The results showed no significant average differences in career advancement between the assessees and nonassessees over the 10-year follow-up period. However, the assessees who followed up on the developmental recommendations advanced further. Interestingly, the assessors' ratings of the participants' career motivation, rather than performance, predicted subsequent developmental activity and career advancement. Thus, the assessment center information was valuable feedback for those with high career motivation who followed the assessors' recommendations for development. The results suggest that for people with a strong career motivation, feedback leads to developmental activities, and that these activities, rather than abilities at the time of assessment, contribute to advancement.

Summary

Assessment centers use activities and exercises to examine participants' behaviors under controlled conditions that are standardized for all participants. The advantage is that the behaviors are based on performance dimensions important to the job that cannot be measured easily through nonbehavioral methods such as paper-and-pencil or computer-based tests, for instance, communication, organizing, and interpersonal skills including resolving conflict, negotiating, and persuading. Also, assessment centers can be constructed to measure behaviors in situations that are typical of positions (e.g., higher level managerial jobs), so the results reflect potential to handle situations that may not be typical of the participants' current positions. In assessment centers, trained observers carefully record their observations during the exercises, then later rate behaviors and write in-depth qualitative reports on each exercise. These data are then combined across exercises and assessors to generate a useful report about the participant's managerial abilities and potential to perform well at higher levels. The data often are used to make selection or promotion decisions about people. However, they are valuable also for development. Indeed, some companies use assessment centers to provide employees with feedback about their strengths and weaknesses as input for development, not decision making. The next section explores the evaluation process in assessment centers and its implications for generating meaningful feedback.

Characteristics of Assessment Center Measurement

Just as the literature on multisource feedback discussed in chapters 7 and 8 tell us about how people perceive others, assessment center research shows how people perceive others in controlled conditions. This research speaks to the accuracy of the assessment center as a way to measure performance ability and potential. It addresses the effects of situational conditions on measurement. Also, it indicates whether assessment center results are valid sources of feedback that should be used as a basis for decision making and as a guide for development.

Do Assessment Centers Measure Distinctly Different Performance Dimensions? The assumption underlying assessment centers is that the exercises allow the assessors to observe behaviors related to different dimensions of performance. These performance dimensions may be reflected in different exercises. The assessors, then, should be able to combine their evaluations of each performance dimension across exercises to make an overall judgment of the assessee's ability in the dimension. However, considerable research on assessments has shown that ratings of different dimensions on a given exercise are highly interrelated, and that ratings of the same dimension from different exercises are not highly interrelated. Sackett and Tuzinski (2001) reviewed this literature and the methods used to overcome this problem. One approach is to treat performance dimensions as different within each exercise because the exercise represents a specific situation. Thus, for instance, decision making is considered as a dimension of performance. Decision making in a group setting may be different from decision making when an individual is alone.

There are several reasons for this exercise effect in assessment centers and the argument that performance dimensions should be rated separately for each exercise (Howard, 1997). Exercises are not meant to be equivalent situations. Performance dimensions are complex and multifaceted. Also, some exercises provide more opportunity than others to demonstrate a particular performance dimension. Exercises vary in the dimensions of performance that are rated. Ratings within each exercise may correlate simply because they are made by the same rater. Ideally, several different raters would evaluate each performance dimension in each exercise, and the same raters would be used for all exercises. This would allow determination of the extent to which intercorrelations among performance dimensions are the result of individual rater biases and the extent to which different raters agree in evaluating different dimensions and perceive differences between the dimensions. Also, it could be that well-trained assessors recognize that exercises vary in the extent to which they provide solid evidence of different dimensions, and that they consider this in providing overall ratings after listening to reports from each exercise. As such, Howard (1997) argued, overall dimension ratings may measure the intended dimensions well even though there is low agreement between dimension ratings across exercises and high intercorrelations among different dimensions within exercises.

Sackett and Tuzinski (2001) indicated that there is no getting around the fact that single raters seem to form overall impressions of an individual's performance on a given exercise, and that perhaps together with the rater's general response biases (e.g., tendency to be lenient across all ratings), there are likely to be strong exercise and rater effects. As a result, they argued that overall ratings for each performance dimension should not be collected. Also, they would not even average ratings of the same performance dimensions across exercises. Instead, they return to the arguments in earlier papers by Sackett and Dreher (1982, 1984) that assessment centers should be viewed as a series of exercises intended to evaluate effectiveness in different job roles, such as negotiator, counselor, fact-finder, and persuader. Job analyses should be conducted to determine the important managerial roles at a given organizational level and then to develop exercises that bring out behaviors reflective of these roles. Each exercise should be scored separately, and more than one assessor should rate the participant on each performance dimension for the exercise and then try to reach agreement. The dimension labels may be narrower (e.g., negotiation decisiveness in a negotiation situation, leadership decisiveness in a group situation, fiscal decisiveness in a budgeting process). Each resulting dimension then should be left alone as a separate predictor of ability, creating a profile of performance dimension ratings. Decisions about participants would be based on the pattern of results for the profile. Statistical methods (e.g., multiple regression) could be used to determine the extent to which the set of dimensions is related to ratings of performance on the job for a large sample of participants.

Are Assessment Center Results Related to Multisource Survey Ratings?   An important question in understanding the meaning and validity of assessment center results as a source of feedback is whether they are related to other measures of performance. One such measure is ratings of performance from other sources (i.e., multisource, or 360-degree, feedback described in the chapter 8).

Although their outputs are similar, assessment centers and 360-degree feedback surveys differ in several respects. Whereas assessment centers are expensive tools for selection and development, 360-degree feedback surveys are less expensive and often used just for development. Assessment centers measure competencies required in jobs for which the participant is aspiring, whereas 360-degree feedback measures current performance (Gordon, Mian, & Gabel, 2002). Assessment centers use specially trained assessors who should be aware of common rating errors and try to minimize them. Whereas 360-degree survey raters interact with the manager rated for considerable time, and continue to do so, the assessment center assessor may not spend any personal time with the manager. Given that both tools may be used to measure the same behaviors and competencies, research is needed to examine their relationship.

Hatten, Glaman, Houston, and Cochran (2002) studied whether assessment center ratings used for selecting first-level managers are related to 360-degree evaluations used for managerial development in the Boeing Company. In this study, 360-degree ratings were completed for 281 first-level managers who had been selected up to 2 years earlier for their positions, partly on the basis of assessment center scores. The assessment center, using a structured interview and a coaching simulation, produced ratings on the following performance factors: interpersonal skills, positive work orientation, working together, basic abilities, oral communication, planning and time management, and problem solving. The 360-degree feedback ratings were made solely for feedback to the managers to support their development (i.e., the results were not used to make administrative decisions about them, unlike the assessment center). Rater sources were self, the immediate supervisor, direct reports, coworkers, and customers. The items rated reflected behaviors associated with company values such as leadership, integrity, quality, customer satisfaction, people working together, a diverse and involved team, corporate citizenship, and enhancement of shareholder value.

Hatten et al. (2002) found high interrater agreement across the different assessment center exercises and within the different rating sources for the 360-degree feedback ratings. As expected, the factor of "working together" from the assessment center was positively related to the 360-degree feedback dimensions of "leadership" and "a diverse and involved team." The assessment center factor of "interpersonal skills" was positively related to "leadership." Managers' ratings and, to a lesser extent, coworker ratings from the 360-degree feedback survey were more strongly related to the assessment center results than the 360-degree feedback ratings from direct reports and customers. Even stronger relationships were found between the assessment center ratings and the average of manager, customer, and peer ratings on the 360-degree feedback survey than between other combinations of sources on the survey, indicating that averaging results across some sources may enhance the ability of the 360-degree feedback survey to capture the performance measured in the assessment center. This also suggests that assessment center measures can be valuable sources of early feedback, particularly for assessment centers used in the selection process. Feeding the assessment results back to the participants, at least to those managers selected as first-line supervisors, can pinpoint areas for their development. Their later success can be tracked on 360-degree feedback surveys, which in turn, can provide tracking information for the managers to calibrate the success of their development efforts. Because this was not done in the current study, future research should examine the effects of assessment center feedback on later 360-degree feedback results, comparing randomly selected managers who received assessment center feedback with those who did not.

In a second study, Gordon et al. (2002) collected data from a large wireless communications company that had gone through a change in leadership. The new CEO wanted senior executives to be evaluated using an "objective" method from outside the organization for developmental purposes. A 1-day assessment center with four simulations was designed by an outside consulting firm for this purpose. The four simulations included a coaching interaction (the participants prepared feedback and then met with a role player who assumed the role of the manager in need of coaching), a peer interaction (the participants prepared for and conducted a meeting with a role player who assumed the role of a peer from another division), a new product rollout (the participants wrote their recommendations for a set of new products and then discussed these with a role player who assumed the role of an assistant director), and a business plan presentation (the participants presented their findings and recommendations for a new product and an overview of the state of their region to two role players who assumed the role of board of directors members). The assessment resulted in an evaluation on 11 competencies. The participants received a summary report of their results in one-on-one feedback sessions.

Approximately 9 months after the assessment center, the senior managers participated in a 5-day training workshop to learn about and discuss the organizational vision and mission developed by the new CEO. As a prelude to this process, a 360-degree feedback survey was conducted for feedback to participants during the workshop to help them focus on their readiness to implement the behaviors needed for the new mission and vision. The survey was administered over the Internet. The same 11 competencies measured in the assessment center also were rated in the 360-degree feedback survey. Data were available for 53 senior managers who participated in both the assessment center and the 360-degree feedback survey. The results were fed back to the managers in one-on-one sessions with experienced executive coaches as a start to establishing a personal development plan.

The results of Gordon et al.'s (2002) study cast doubt on the relationship between assessment center dimension ratings and 360-degree feedback ratings. Only two competencies (high impact communication and people development) were significantly related between the assessment center and the 360-degree feedback survey. This suggests that the assessment center and 360-degree feedback survey were best at measuring some competencies, but not others. Ratings from the managers' supervisors correlated most highly with the assessment center ratings, similar to the findings of the Hatten et al. (2002) study. Overall, this suggests that managers' supervisors seem to be most accurate among the various sources of ratings, perhaps because they have the best opportunity to observe, because they have experience evaluating performance, and because they may not be influenced by political factors, leniency, or severity errors that may affect self, subordinate, and peer ratings. Subordinate ratings on the performance dimension, high-impact communication, correlated as highly with the assessment center ratings as the supervisor ratings on this dimension, possibly because subordinates have considerable interaction with the senior managers, as compared with peers, and are able to evaluate communication skills accurately. Peer ratings of organizing and planning were more highly related to the similar performance dimensions evaluated in the assessment center, perhaps because peers are directly influenced by the senior manager's organizing and planning skills.

Gordon et al. (2002) did not examine different combinations of rater groups from the 360-degree feedback as did Hatten et al. (2002). Possibly, an average of the data from different combinations may have been more highly related to the assessment center results. In general, however, the results of these two studies suggest that assessment center and 360-degree feedback results are most likely to coincide from the perspective of the manager's supervisor. The results also suggest that 360-degree feedback results should not be averaged automatically across all raters, but that results from different rater groups should be examined and their validity determined separately. Recipients of feedback results from assessment centers need to understand the perspective of the results, that assessment center results seem to reflect their boss's perspective, but may reflect subordinate or peer perspectives for certain dimensions. Recipients of 360-degree feedback need to understand the validity of the different rating sources and different dimensions.

The message for practitioners who want to use assessment centers for feedback purposes is that the assessment center needs to be designed to reflect actual job experiences (i.e., it needs to be content valid), and that the raters need to be well trained to observe behaviors and rate performance dimensions. Recipients need explanations of what the results mean, what they predict, and what they suggest for development. Feedback results should not be taken as absolutes, but rather as relative to the validity (i.e., how it relates to other measures and other raters' vantage points). Therefore, for example, if a person received a low score on the assessment center dimension of oral communications, this does not necessarily mean that he or she is not a good communicator, but rather may have problems in contexts similar to the assessment center. Because the assessment center may be particularly likely to reflect supervisors' viewpoints, the person assessed should think about how to improve his or her communications ability (e.g., perhaps in formal presentations or meetings with higher level managers).

Next, other assessment methods, particularly computerized assessment, business simulations, and organization analysis, should be considered as sources of feedback.

COMPUTERIZED TESTING ASSESSMENT

Another increasingly available and cost-effective method for identifying skills and proficiency levels is computerized assessment. This method uses computers to present items customized to the assessee's ability, to measure a variety of responses (e.g., time to respond to different situations), and, if appropriate, to provide feedback at various points in time. It uses computer technologies, including the CD-ROM with full-motion video (Drasgow, Olson, Keenan, Moberg, & Mead, 1993). For instance, managers being tested may be presented with several boss–subordinate video scenarios involving, say, the need for conflict resolution, delegation, or coaching. After watching each scenario, the managers are asked to answer multiple-choice questions. Their responses may indicate different styles of management, which in turn can be demonstrated on follow-up videos that show the outcomes of different choices. As such, the method presents realistic, clear information; allows people to see how others might react to their behavior and decisions; repeats similar situations across assessees; can vary the difficulty and complexity of the simulations; offers immediate and repeated feedback; and records precise information about the assessee's performance (e.g., it can determine whether the assessee responds to an issue before viewing other pertinent information). It is most valuable for assessment of skills not easily or inexpensively measured via traditional in-person exercises or paper-and-pencil tests.

BUSINESS GAMES AND SIMULATIONS

Business games and simulations often are incorporated into training programs as a way to communicate changing business strategies and directions and help participants assess and build their strengths and weaknesses in relation to these strategic directions. Assessment centers use short business games and simulations. In this section, I address in-depth simulations of a longer duration, sometimes several hours or even days. These techniques are sometimes referred to as "practice fields" in that they help individuals and the organization as a whole to learn and develop. They are valuable because managerial action in the real world may be too slow, ambiguous, and even risky to learn by doing (Drew & Davidson, 1993; Senge, 1990). Feedback from a simulation can be fast and clear. Moreover, a simulation setting is a safe place where managers may practice decision making and experiment with new styles of management. Managers have a chance to do, think, and feel, and feedback is an important part of the learning (Keys, 1994; Stumpf & Dutton, 1990). Of course, the simulation must be realistic enough to be engaging, but not so complex that it is threatening. Several examples follow.

A Computer-Based Simulation

A telecommunications firm engaged consultants to deliver a new leadership training and development program that would communicate a vision for the organization and encourage managers to take more responsibility for leadership and increase managers' knowledge and understanding of the industry (Drew & Davidson, 1993). The program was designed for the firm's 350 top managers. About 16 managers attended each 2 ½ day session, 1 ½ days of which were dedicated to a simulation that modeled new global alliances, joint ventures between cable and telephone companies, and linkages with computer network providers and other industries, such as publishing and entertainment.

The computer-based game (which took 18 person-months to develop) had four teams of usually four participants each enter decisions on new products, marketing, sales force, customer service, and operations. Participants were assigned roles, such as VP marketing and VP new product introduction. Each team could launch up to 12 products. Each team worked in a room with a PC networked to a central file server. Each team established its own strategic plan and goals at the start. Printable screens provided the teams with support data. Each round of the simulation required that the team search for data and decide about such issues as new products, pricing, and budget allocations between departments. Decisions were made about each function performed (e.g., marketing, customer service, operations), which in turn had implications for quality and market results. The teams could cooperate by licensing new products to other teams or investing in national advertising. At the end of each round, key results were summarized, and teams were encouraged to compare each other's performance. The simulation provided a shared experience and an opportunity for discussion. Participants received feedback about their behavior and also learned how to step back from situations and hold process discussions.

Group Simulations: Foodcorp and Globalcorp

Stumpf, Watson, and Rustogi (1994) developed behavioral simulations lasting 6 to 10 hours. The simulations assigned participants to senior management roles. Two simulated companies were developed: Foodcorp and

Globalcorp. Foodcorp was a fictitious international food manufacturing organization with three levels of organizational hierarchy, two product groups, and two subsidiaries. Its products were sold to distributors and retail supermarkets throughout the United States and 60 other countries. Globalcorp was a fictitious diversified international financial services conglomerate with $27 billion in assets and a consumer banking sector (composed of branch banking, credit card operations, and consumer credit) and a commercial banking sector (composed of investment banking, institutional banking, and transaction services). Whereas Foodcorp had homogeneous lines of business and cross-functional activities, Globalcorp involved active coordination and competition across its lines of business within sectors.

These were especially lifelike simulations in that participants adopted roles in a formal organizational hierarchy, dealt with realistic information, served on committees (with prescheduled committee meetings that could be attended, rescheduled, or ignored), and received and sent mail. Both simulations began with the following complex and ambiguous task: "Run the organization as you see fit." After 6 or more hours of operating, the simulation concluded with an address by the president and other key executives to the employees. Postsimulation questionnaires and observer evaluations were used in the feedback process during the debriefing session. Feedback covered how decisions were made, how formal and personal power were used, what climate was created and how it affects participants, and actions taken or not taken.

These simulations were applied by two different firms with different goals for development of their managers (Stumpf et al., 1994). Northern Telecom, a midsize telecommunications equipment manufacturer headquartered in Canada, wanted a practice field experience that placed their managers in a matrix organizational structure confronting a competitive, global marketplace with a line of products that had potential for rapid growth. Foodcorp fitted their needs. In contrast, Citicorp, a large, international financial services firm headquartered in the United States, wanted a practice field that reflected a decentralized, multiproduct-line firm that was diverse in its product offerings. It wanted a situation with a large number of profit centers in it parallel to the Citicorp organization. Globalcorp fitted their needs.

The simulations were incorporated into 1-week, in-residence leadership development programs. The programs covered skills related to global issues and a diverse workforce. Lecture-discussions set the stage for the simulation. Both programs used results of multirater feedback ratings from coworkers and subordinates as a start to help the participants recognize their developmental needs. Participation in the program was voluntary, but limited to middle and top managers responsible for managing other people or to people who had significant responsibility for a line of business or function.

Posttraining evaluations indicated that most participants thought the program's objectives were met. A total of 357 people who participated in 48 behavioral simulations gave ratings ranging from 4.2 to 4.7 on a 5-point scale,

with 5 being the most favorable. Postsimulation assessments completed by
the participants and observers showed that most participants used the simulation to practice new behaviors. These efforts were used as the substance
for hours of feedback discussion immediately after the simulation as the
participants met with observers individually and then as a group. During
the feedback discussions, the participants identified areas for further development and opportunities to transfer new knowledge and skills to their
work.

A Simulation for Research and Development Managers

Another simulation, called RADMIS, was developed for training research
and development managers (Bailey, 1990). Trained observers assessed task
behaviors and interpersonal styles, then fed back this data to the team after
the simulation. Also, the information could be used to help each team member develop more effective managerial behaviors. Players took the role of development group members employed by a firm that makes printing plates.
This firm had faced one primary competitor until recently, when that competitor began marketing a new printing plate. The new plate could overtake
the entire market within 6 months, putting the team's firm out of business.
The day-long simulation asked members to develop a product and launch
it in the market quickly. The simulation provided participants with ample
information about financial data, including marketing costs; environmental
concerns; and risk entailed in two possible new products. Team members
worked up data to support different possibilities and negotiated alternative
directions. The postsimulation feedback session focused on what it is like to
work with or for each team member. Each person received cogent feedback
from the other team members. The simulation worked well for managers in
development work whose primary training has been in technical, as opposed
to managerial, areas.

Looking Glass

Perhaps the best known realistic simulation, and the model for others such
as Foodcorp, Globalcorp, and RADMIS, is Looking Glass, Inc. Looking Glass
was developed by the Center for Creative Leadership (a nonprofit organization established in 1970 by the Smith Richardson Foundation to study
issues of management and leadership) with funding from the Office of
Naval Research (Kaplan, 1986). Looking Glass is a fictitious organization
in the glass business. The simulation assigns roles to as many as 20 managers
ranging from president to plant manager. After reading extensive materials on the firm (e.g., an annual report, financial data, job descriptions, and
recent memos), the participants interact as they deal with the more than
150 problems embedded in the material. The simulation is used as part of
a week-long leadership development program by the Center for Creative

Leadership. Managers can enroll in these programs as individuals or as part of a corporate group.

An example of one person's experience in Looking Glass is provided in the text boxes (abstracted from Kaplan, 1986).

Allen Bruce was a successful manager with a bright future in a growing firm. A bachelor in his mid-30's, he thought of himself as someone who was friendly and good with interpersonal relationships. He was shocked when he learned from an associate that he had a reputation of being "threatening" to work with, that others saw him as an ambitious, somewhat self-serving person with little concern for others. After a discussion of this discrepancy between how he saw himself and how others seemed to see him, his boss recommended that Allen enroll in the leadership development program run by the firm that incorporated the Looking Glass exercise.

At the start of the workshop, Allen suggested to the other participants that they have a presimulation meeting with other participants. After reviewing the materials, Allen came to the first meeting well organized with special interest in a memo from the company president that the three divisional directors of sales and marketing, of which Allen was to be one, get together to coordinate solutions to common problems. Allen's goal was to formulate a plan that would bring about dramatic improvement in Looking Glass's operations, and he planned to take the initiative to get things moving.

During the simulation, participants were assigned to office space. Phones rang, people talked, and mail was delivered. Allen began by calling the president as a way of making himself visible "upstairs." He then attended a products division meeting, but did not contribute much because he was preoccupied by his own plans. He later pigeonholed another participant, Carl, who played the role of Looking Glass's vice president, and suggested that all the company's problems were the result of inefficiency from lack of coordination, and he wanted to be given the authority to work with the other directors to develop a comprehensive plan to clean things up. Carl agreed, but during a subsequent meeting with the other directors, Allen had trouble convincing them that they really needed sweeping change.

Allen then worked in his office to draft an email to the president outlining a reorganization of the firm that would address the principal problem, as Allen saw it. But he received no response. The president had spent the day emphasizing cost containment, and had even sent a memo to the staff indicating that all recommendations should address cost cutting. Allen then shared his plan with the vice president, Carl, who suggested that Allen revise his plan limiting it to sales and marketing. This might make it more palatable to the management committee that would be meeting shortly.

Before the meeting, Allen telephoned one of his fellow regional directors, Wendy. She had seen Allen's plan and indicated she did not think there was any support for it in the management committee. In fact, she informed him that the committee members had already ruled out his plan. Allen did not see how Wendy would know this unless she had access to the president. Allen told her it was quite a shock to him to find that someone he trusted was a "back stabber." Allen felt better later when he learned from Carl that his reorganization plan had received "some consideration" from the management committee, and that the sales and marketing areas would be restructured in some way.

Allen later confronted Wendy with his feeling that Wendy and the other regional director had taken the essence of his plan for their own plan. Wendy was astounded that Allen would think she and others had spent their time plotting against him. Wendy said that she had been working on a "little agreement for transfer pricing," and that this is what Carl had referred to when he implied that parts of Allen's plan would be implemented. Allen was embarrassed and wondered how his imagination could have made him so paranoid.

The simulation ended in midafternoon. During the evening and the following day, Allen participated in three debriefing sessions. The first two were general sessions with all the participants to discuss the experience as a whole and the performance of each division as a unit. During the third session, each participant's individual performance was discussed. Four main points emerged with the help of a facilitator and the other participants. Allen realized that he had a tendency to manipulate people. He sometimes invested too much in his own plans at the expense of what others were trying to do. He was a skilled communicator and wanted to cooperate with superiors, but he was less concerned about building rapport with peers and subordinates. Finally, he discovered that he tended to attribute to others the same manipulative motives that he himself had as a way to justify his own actions.

Allen showed resilience in accepting this new self-awareness. He admitted that the messages were not easy to hear, but that they were useful. He felt that he got what he came to learn.

Looking Glass can be a vehicle for organizational change. First Union Corporation, a bank with headquarters in Charlotte, North Carolina, used

Looking Glass as a management development tool (Johnston, 1986). The company wanted to increase managers' understanding of the dynamic nature of managerial work, help the managers assess their own strengths and weaknesses, and encourage them to make developmental plans. The firm also wanted to enhance managers' awareness of the importance of training and development and to refine the training department's teambuilding and feedback skills. Looking Glass was used as the "catalyst experienc" in a 4-day management development program for 20 managers at a time. Although the managers initially questioned the relevance of the simulation's manufacturing environment for bankers, they found that the absence of banking-related issues helped them focus on aspects of their managerial behavior. The participants for each 4-day program were selected from a cross section of the bank's departments and levels, with management from first-line up to senior positions participating.

The program proved to be popular, with frequent requests from past participants for their subordinates to attend. Many participants made important career decisions soon after the program (e.g., deciding to change jobs, pursue further management opportunities, or improve their relationships with coworkers). Participants formed informal networks that continued to be useful to them long after the program. Some participants were assigned later to jobs that have them reporting to each other. They reported that Looking Glass feedback enhanced their understanding of each other.

CONCLUSION

This chapter and the preceding chapter consider standardized measurement tools that can be used as a source of feedback. Assessment centers are an excellent development tool because they provide in-depth information under standardized conditions. Increasingly sophisticated computerized assessments and business simulations also can provide meaningful feedback. The value of the feedback, however, lies in its use for setting development goals. These standardized, realistic methods may be particularly valuable at the start of a development process. Multisource feedback then can be a way to help managers track improvement in performance as they make progress in their development plans. The major conclusions from the chapter can be summarized as follows:

1. Assessment centers give employees feedback about their performance and suggest directions for their development.
2. Assessment centers aimed mainly at providing participants with information to guide development are most useful to participants who are high in career motivation (i.e., those who want the feedback and intend to use it constructively).

3. Assessment center ratings of different dimensions on a given exercise are highly interrelated. Also, ratings of the same dimension from different exercises are not highly interrelated. Exercises vary in the dimensions of performance that are rated. Ratings within each exercise may correlate simply because they are made by the same rater. These problems can be overcome by treating each exercise as a different situation and not averaging ratings across exercises. Assessment centers should be viewed as a series of exercises intended to evaluate effectiveness in different job roles. Each exercise should be scored separately, and more than one assessor should rate the participant on each performance dimension for the exercise and the assessors then should try to reach agreement.

4. Assessment center results predict later performance measured by 360-degree feedback ratings. The prediction may be enhanced when the 360-degree feedback ratings are averaged across certain rater groups, showing the value of obtaining job performance ratings from multiple perspectives.

5. The recipients of feedback results from assessment centers need to understand the perspective of the results, that assessment center results seem to reflect their boss's perspective, but may reflect subordinate or peer perspectives for certain dimensions.

6. Assessment results could be fed back to participants to help them determine areas for development. Then 360-degree feedback can help them track the effectiveness of their developmental efforts.

7. In addition to the assessment center, there are other methods for assessment and feedback about performance. Computerized assessment offers readily accessible, cost-effective, self-paced methods for self-evaluation. "Practice fields" are business games and simulations that allow participants to experiment with new behaviors in settings that are realistic and nonthreatening. These simulations often are incorporated into management development programs to provide feedback and stimulate learning.

8. Practice field simulations can be tools for individual and organizational change and development. They can give individuals information about their performance, and they can provide groups with information about how they work together.

9. Individuals can seek programs on their own that use practice field simulations, or organizations can commission the design of customized simulations to be used as an organization development intervention.

Now that I have covered formal sources of feedback, I turn in the next section of the book to how people use feedback and ways to help them do so effectively.

III

SUPPORTING THE USE
OF FEEDBACK

10

The Manager's Role As Feedback Provider

Performance data and evaluations are not much good by themselves. They must be communicated and interpreted. This chapter focuses on the role of the manager in providing feedback and facilitating its use. I describe the components of a meaningful performance review and offer steps and guidelines for a review that produces results. The steps and guidelines apply to conducting a formal review annually or semiannually or to holding an informal performance discussion. I include general guidelines to help managers respond constructively when a subordinate is defensive. I outline specific steps for conducting the review and then discuss some recommendations. Although many managers, like people in all walks of life, shy away from giving feedback, they can learn to make giving feedback a natural part of their management style. They can improve their observation skills, become more accurate raters, and be more supportive and constructive in giving feedback.

REACTIONS TO FEEDBACK AND READINESS TO CHANGE

Employees' reactions to feedback will depend on how the feedback is presented and on the readiness and ability of each employee to understand the feedback and change. Employees often are not sure why they are receiving feedback or what the manager intends by the feedback (Fedor, Buckley, & Eder, 1990). When a manager gives a subordinate feedback about his or her performance, the subordinate may be confused about the manager's purpose and goal and may not not know how to respond or realize what's at stake (e.g., the subordinate's pay or job stability). The subordinate may not be ready to change his or her behavior. Managers need to understand the stages

of change and be able to tell where their subordinates are in the change
process. This will help managers understand a subordinate's receptivity to
feedback, and can help them determine the approach to take in delivering
feedback.

Stages of Change

Prochaska's transtheoretical model of change (Prochaska, Prochaska, &
Levesque, 2001), suggests change management strategies based an individual's readiness to change. The model integrates stages of change, decisional
balance, and processes of change. The model posits 5 stages and 10 processes
of change. The model maintains that people progress through five stages of
change based on readiness to take action within designated periods (sooner
or later). During each stage, individuals vary in the extent to which they are
likely to modify their behavior on their own or with the support of others.

The first stage is *precontemplation*. This applies to people who do not
intend to take action within the following 6 months. The second stage is
contemplation. This applies to people who intend to take action within the
next 6 months. The third stage is *preparation*. Individuals in this stage intend
to take action within the next 30 days. The fourth stage is *action*. This applies
to people who are in the process of taking action or who did so within the
preceding 6 months. The fifth stage is *maintenance*. This applies to people
who made overt changes more than 6 months ago.

Prochaska et al. (2001) reported research that applied the model in different situations, from smoking cessation to changes job behaviors. They found
that across different settings and ranges of behavior, of the people who have
not yet taken action, approximately 40% are in precontemplation, 40% are
in contemplation, and 20% are in preparation. This means that when a supervisor attempts to implement change, expecting subordinates to listen to
feedback and then take action, most are not likely to be ready to do so
any time soon. This does not mean that the feedback will fall on deaf ears.
Rather, it may have effects on different change processes depending on the
recipient's readiness to change and the pressure for change in the context.
In organizations, feedback is part of an ongoing process within the context
of the organization's culture and circumstances. The 40/40/20 split may not
hold precisely. Still, supervisors and coaches trying to bring about change
need to consider that some employees may not be ready to change. They
should also consider ways to influence readiness before implementing the
change effort.

According to the transtheoretical model, a person's stage of change depends on decisional balance. Decisional balance refers to the employee's
perceptions of the pros and cons of change. In the precontemplation stage,
the disadvantages outweigh the advantages. In the contemplation and
preparation stages, the pros begin to outweigh the cons. To progress to
through the preparation stage to action, the pros must outweigh the cons.

Commitment to change should occur when the advantages outweigh the disadvantages.

Change Processes.   The processes that produce change are different for each stage of change, and this suggests the need for stage-matched interventions individualized to promote readiness to change in given individuals. During precontemplation, three processes encourage change. *Consciousness raising* refers to becoming more aware of a problem and potential solutions. Recognizing that the recipient of feedback is in the precontemplation stage, the supervisor or coach can use feedback to discuss performance strengths and weaknesses, examine areas for performance improvement, and suggest possible actions for development and behavior change. However, the supervisor or coach should not expect the employee to respond. Several iterations of feedback may be necessary, perhaps at 3- or 6-month intervals, before the employee is ready to see the benefits of change.

Another process during precontemplation is *dramatic relief.* The employee is likely to feel emotional arousal, perhaps pleasure from positive performance feedback, but also a threat from negative feedback and fear of failure, a foreboding that the attempt to learn and improve performance will not succeed. The supervisor or coach can offer inspiration for successful change, perhaps describing others who were successful under similar conditions.

A third change process during precontemplation is *environmental reevaluation*, with the employee recognizing that a change can have a positive impact on the social and work environment. That is, the employee recognizes that changing his or her own performance also will help the overall performance of the work group or department.

Overall, then, the goal of the supervisor or coach in working with employees in precontemplation is to help them recognize performance problems, deal with their emotions (especially their likely fear of failure, an emotion not likely to be expressed), and inspire them by pointing out the benefits of change and showing confidence in their ability to change.

The principal change process during contemplation is *self-reevaluation.* This is the growing appreciation that the change is important to one's identify, happiness, and success. The supervisor or coach can help the employee to recognize that he or she can change. The intervention needs to recognize the employee's current self-concept as a successful individual and level of self-confidence. People who believe they can bring about positive outcomes (i.e., those high in self-efficacy) are more likely to see the benefits of trying to change. Some self-reevaluation may be needed to tip the scales from the cons of trying to change to the pros, with the employee believing that change can indeed be accomplished and have positive results.

The change process during preparation is *self-liberation.* This is believing that a change can be successful and making a firm commitment to the change. This happens as the supervisor and coach reinforce the employee's self-reevaluation and squash any reason for self-doubt that may arise.

Four change processes work well during the action and maintenance stages of change. *Reinforcement management* is recognizing extrinsic rewards (pay, status, promotion) and intrinsic rewards (feelings of challenge, fulfillment, and professional growth) that result from the change. *Counterconditions* is substituting new behaviors and thought processes for the old habits of working. *Helping relationships* entails seeking and using social support for the change. *Stimulus control* is restructuring the environment to elicit new behaviors and limit old habits. An example of stimulus control is avoiding poor work habits, such as dropping by the break room to snack and chat or not taking work home to ensure time is available for the family. Supervisors and coaches can support each of these change processes. They are the source of extrinsic rewards. They can suggest new behaviors that substitute for the old. They can provide encouragement as new behaviors develop. They can restructure the environment, or suggest ways that employees can do so for themselves. The supervisor can respect the employee's nonwork time and not intrude on the employee's family and leisure pursuits.

Throughout all the stages of change, supervisors and coaches help with another change process: *social liberation*. This is providing the choices and resources that empower employees to change. In other words, supervisors, coaches, and other coworkers, not to mention friends and family, provide the resources that enhance the chances for change.

Of course, employees must assume responsibility for and commitment to change. They must recognize that, ultimately, they are accountable for resulting performance improvement. Short of establishing that commitment, they will remain in the preaction stages, and probably never really go further than contemplation. London and Smither (1999) referred to this as *empowered self-development*.

Stage-Matched Change Interventions.   The point of Prochaska's change model is that supervisors and coaches can intervene to enhance an employee's chances of changing, and that the way to do that is to recognize that the likelihood of an employee taking action depends on the employee's stage of change (Prochaska et al., 2001). The interventions need to be individualized to match the employee's readiness to change. This will reduce both stress and the time needed to bring about change.

In addition, stage-matched interventions recognize that all employees can participate in the change process, and that they are not failures if they are not yet prepared to take action. Thus, for instance, consciousness raising by communicating information about the need for change is valuable to employees in the precontemplation stage in helping them move to the contemplation stage. Pressuring these employees to take action would only cause resentment and provoke resistance. However, employees who are taking action to change can be helped by advice on overcoming barriers and rewards for improvement.

Dalton and Hollenbeck (2001) built upon the Prochaska model to argue that facilitating change after feedback requires understanding the change process and the conditions that contribute to lasting changes in behavior. Their simplified, four-stage model of change involves (a) becoming aware (developing within oneself an awareness of the need for change), (b) preparing for change and planning for development (making the commitment to change, setting goals, and developing an action plan), (c) taking action (doing whatever is required to develop new behaviors or discard old ones), and (d) maintaining the gain (developing processes to maintain the gain). Failure to change may result from starting the change process in the wrong place, for instance, taking action without adequate planning.

Summary

To target feedback so that their subordinates use it effectively, managers need to understand change processes. If subordinates are at the initial stage of becoming aware of their strengths and weaknesses, they need time and help to digest the information, accept it, and understand its implications. Then they will be ready to use subsequent feedback to prepare for change and plan a development strategy. Eventually, as they progress to take action and track their success, feedback will take on new meaning. Ultimately, feedback will become an integral part of ongoing change and adjustment. The trick to effective feedback is moving through the initial recognition stage to set challenging, realistic goals for development and track performance improvement in relation to these goals. The next section considers the importance of goal setting to making feedback worthwhile.

BEYOND FEEDBACK: GOAL SETTING

Goal setting is the means by which feedback motivates change. Feedback may have cognitive benefits such as showing a person what is wrong with his or her behavior and demonstrating ways to correct it, that is, creating awareness of feedback and coaching (as an Olympic ice skating coach would offer feedback and suggestions to a champion skater or as a ski instructor would demonstrate the correct method of downhill skiing to a novice). However, the individual needs to set goals to be motivated to improve his or her performance. The individual must be committed to the goals. For this to happen, it is helpful if the individual participates in setting the goals. Goals selected by others rarely have a positive effect, at least not in the long run (Dalton & Hollenbeck, 2001). The executive coach can bring problems inherent in multisource feedback results to the attention of the executive. Also, the coach can point out the risks of not paying attention to feedback results. However, it is up to the executive to recognize the value of the feedback in directing behavior change and the importance of actually changing.

Here, I examine the important link between feedback and goal setting. (This section of the chapter is from London, 1995c). Goals and feedback are mutually supportive. (Also, see Locke & Latham, 1990, chapter 8, for an extensive review of feedback and goal setting.) Goals make feedback meaningful, and feedback helps to improve goal achievement. Goals have little effect when feedback is not given. Similarly, feedback has little effect if it does not result in goal setting. Moreover, the combination of goal setting and feedback is more effective than either one alone (Locke & Latham, 1990).

To be more specific, goals are one of the key ways that feedback gets translated into action. That is, feedback motivates improved performance by means of goal setting. Research on goal setting and feedback indicate that feedback alone, without goal setting, does little to change performance. Similarly, when feedback is given for multiple aspects of performance, the areas that later improve are those for which goals have been set. Also, goals regulate performance more reliably when feedback is present than when it is absent (Locke & Latham, 1990). Goals focus attention on information that is significant, and they direct subsequent action. Furthermore, goal setting and feedback are important because they have positive and negative consequences. That is, they are followed by reward or recognition.

Internal and External Cues.   Goal setting and feedback are not necessarily explicit. Even when goals are not assigned or employees are not asked to set goals after feedback, they may do so anyway. Also, even if feedback is not provided explicitly, employees may use a variety of cues to get an idea about how well they are doing. They may use internal cues, such as how fast they are working or how hard they are trying. Although these cues may be inaccurate, they still play a role in the employee's cognitions about performance judgments.

Consider the process an employee goes through in evaluating his or her own performance and setting goals for improvement (adapted from Locke & Latham, 1990, p. 175). An employee's performance leads to feedback, probably from multiple sources. The employee detects, understands, and appraises (judges the accuracy and implications of) the feedback. The importance and value of the feedback is evaluated to determine whether it indicates good or poor performance, whether the performance level is significant or not, and whether the employee cares about it at all. The employee has an emotional response to the feedback and these judgments. If the employee believes the feedback is inaccurate, he or she may ignore it or seek more information. If the employee judges the feedback to be unimportant, he or she is likely simply to ignore it. If the employee believes the information is important and suggestive of favorable performance, he or she will set a goal to maintain or increase the level of performance (or, if satisfied with the performance, may switch activities). If the employee believes the feedback is important, but is dissatisfied with the level of performance, he or she will set a goal to improve, especially if the employee is committed to doing well and believes that he or she has the potential to do better. If the employee believes he or she cannot do better or is not committed to the task, the employee may lower the goal or give up altogether. If the employee cares about the task, but is unsure about his or her potential to do better, the employee may try to perform the task in a new way.

Locke and Latham (1990) summarized the relation between feedback and goal setting as follows:

> Feedback tells people what is; goals tell them what is desirable. Feedback involves information; goals involve evaluation. Goals inform individuals as to what type or level of performance is to be attained so that they can direct and evaluate their actions and efforts accordingly. Feedback allows them to set reasonable goals and track their performance in relation to their goals, so that adjustments in effort, direction, and even strategy can be made as needed. ... What gets measured in relation to goals gets done. (p. 197)

Comparing Locke and Latham's Goal-Setting Theory With Control Theory

Scherbaum and Vancouver (2002) delineated two contrasting explanations for goal-setting effects. One derives from Locke and Latham's (1990) goal-setting theory. Their approach, described earlier, focuses on what happens to motivate performance when people set goals. The other derives from Carver and Scheier's (1981) control theory. They focus on how it happens. Locke and Latham's (1990) theory indicates that specific, difficult goals have a positive effect on performance because they direct behavior, indicate the level of effort and persistence needed to achieve the goal, and help to establish constructive strategies for getting the task done. In other words, individuals calculate the amount of action required to achieve a goal, and then try to behave in a way that produces the goal. The goal and the belief that the goal can be accomplished (self-efficacy) are important. This is a linear, cognitive model of action.

Control theory's psychological (as opposed to cognitive) explanation, argues that people are motivated when they perceive a gap between their current behavior and where they or others believe they need to be. People evaluate their own performance or receive input about their performance from others. They compare these evaluations with standards of their own, others, or the organization. This is a model of dynamic interaction with the environment. Any gap suggests the degree of performance improvement needed. Hence, feedback is important as an ingredient for goals to be set and as a basis for evaluating movement toward the goal. The goal becomes the standard for evaluating performance. Negative feedback implies the need for more effort. Continuously monitoring performance and comparing it with this standard is important in control theory's dynamic model.

This suggests why self–other agreement in a multisource feedback survey is important to goal setting and performance improvement. The more agreement, the less the gap, and the less the need for change exists. A gap resulting from self-ratings lower than other ratings would suggest no improvement is needed, although data indicate that underestimation of one's own performance is associated with lower performance (Atwater, Roush, & Fischthal, 1995; Halverson, Tonidandel, Barlow, & Dipboye, 2002, Yammarino & Atwater, 1997). However, a gap resulting from self-ratings higher than other-ratings may suggest to the feedback recipient that there is a problem needing to be rectified.

The degree of goal accomplishment or the gap between performance and the goal is a subjective judgment. The gap may be presented in an objective way, but its meaning requires psychological interpretation. The same gap may be interpreted differently by different people. One person may interpret a gap as pointing to the need for even more effort, whereas another may say, "I'm almost there," and slow down. Locke and Latham's (1990) model is more static in that the nature of the goals set determines behavior, not perceptions of the gap between performance and the goal.

Of course, the two explanations for the effects of goal setting are not necessarily incompatible. Both indicate that goal setting is important to motivation. Scherbaum and Vancouver (2002) argued that control theory is a piece of the puzzle explaining how goal setting works. The process entails perceiving a performance gap, setting specific and challenging goals, evaluating performance in relation to these goals, and possibly revising the goals. Together, this is a dynamic, ongoing cognitive and psychological process requiring feedback.

Some Goal-Setting Principles

Goals for performance improvement and development should be initiated during the appraisal review session, but this should be only the beginning of goal setting and reviews of progress. Goal setting is a continuous process, with several meetings needed to suggest, negotiate, and agree on goals. Also, review sessions on goal progress should be held throughout the year, as well as quarterly, monthly, or even weekly depending on the job and the employee's experience (Meyer, 1991).

Outlining specific goals leads employees to higher performance than telling them to do their best (Latham & Wexley, 1981). When employees participate in goal setting, they tend to set higher goals than when the supervisor assigns goals without the employee's input. As long as an employee perceives a goal as reasonable and achievable, the higher the goal, the better the employee performs. Employees must receive ongoing feedback on how they are doing in reaching their goals. They must have control over the factors essential to attaining the goals.

Setting goals involves analyzing the gap between where one is and where one wants to be (Dalton & Hollenbeck, 2001). The supervisor or coach can ask the manager, "Where do you want to be in a year?" and "What do you have to do to get there from here?" Supervisors can convey their expectations for their subordinates, but the subordinates will not be motivated until they adopt these expectations as their own.

Dalton and Hollenbeck (2001) also pointed out that goals need to be few in number, clear, behavioral, and difficult (i.e., challenging but not unrealistic). Too many goals will dilute attention and reduce motivation. A clear, behavioral goal will specify what needs to be done. For instance, to encourage a manager to "pay attention to others' ideas," it may be necessary to ask the manager how he or she thinks this can be done. Asking for examples will reduce defensiveness and increase the chances that the manager will take heed. This may entail having a discussion about ways to elicit others' ideas (listening more than speaking, restating others' ideas for clarification, and acknowledging others' contributions). Goals should be difficult. Otherwise, they are not worth achieving and not intrinsically challenging. Stretch goals (those that are difficult yet doable) enhance the internal desire of employees to achieve them. Goals that are impossible, however, reduce motivation and prompt helplessness.

Dalton and Hollenbeck (2001) argued that developmental goals should be more about learning or mastery, not merely about performance improvement. Learning goals enhance persistence beyond achievement of a particular level of performance. Supervisors and coaches can help their charges recognize their increased degree of mastery by providing timely feedback, which in turn can lead to further persistence in learning even more, as opposed to stopping because a particular level of performance and the associated reward were achieved. Furthermore, a learning goal is not about merely taking a given course or completing a new type of task. Development and task performance should go hand-in-glove, occurring together and feeding on each other for continuous learning and continuous performance improvement.

Need for Goal Clarity

Kluger and DeNisi (1998) explained how two theories, control theory (Carver & Scheir, 1981) and their own feedback intervention theory (FIT; Kluger & DeNisi, 1996) help people to regulate their behavior by comparing the feedback they receive with the goals they set or with the standards set for them by the organization. Because people's attention is limited, they act on feedback–goal (or standard) gaps that receive attention. Feedback interventions change the focus of attention, and hence the behavior changes that result. That is, the feedback they happen to receive shapes their attention and causes them to change. If the feedback is not focused on what is important to performance improvement, or if there is no feedback at all, behavior is unlikely to change, or it could change in ways that actually diminish performance. On the other hand, if feedback is targeted to behaviors important to success and the individual detects a performance gap, he or she is more likely to be motivated to reduce that gap (i.e., to change his or her behavior and improve their performance).

Attention directed to the task at hand or the details of the task at hand (e.g., giving a subordinate ideas about the length of a presentation) is likely to be more constructive than feedback that threatens self-image (e.g., talking about the subordinate's speaking ability in general). As Kluger and DeNisi (1998) hypothesized, feedback interventions "that contain cures that direct attention to the self, or that are given in a self-threatening environment, will produce weak or even negative effects on performance" (p. 69). Even praise that directs attention to the self can result in lower performance effects than feedback that does not direct attention to the self (Kluger & DeNisi, 1996).

DeNisi and Kluger (2000) used Higgins (1987) self-regulatory model to explain that there are two aspects of the self: your ideal (what you want to be or do) and your ought (what others want you to be or do). Negative feedback focuses attention on what others want you to do and is likely to motivate you to work hard to avoid disappointing others. Positive feedback about tasks that others want you to do provides no incentive for further improvement. However, positive feedback that helps you bring about your ideal self ("be all that you can be") is likely to motivate you to continue to improve. But when you receive negative feedback about your performance on tasks you want to do, the gap between your desired and actual selves may seem too hard to overcome, so you give up.

Kluger and DeNisi (1996, 1998; DeNisi & Kluger, 2000) recommended that feedback interventions be used only in combination with goal setting. Feedback that relates to previously established goals is likely to direct attention to the task and not to the self. Goal setting augments the power of feedback effect on performance. These authors found that employees who say they want more feedback often are those who do not have clear goals. As such, effective performance management systems begin with need analysis (e.g., assessment of skill deficiencies in relation to organization requirements) and result in goals for development. Without clear goals, the feedback provider's focus may differ from that of the feedback recipient. These authors also discovered that feedback comparing a person's performance with that of others is less effective than information about degree of performance improvement over time. That is, interperson comparisons are not as good as intraperson comparisons over time and comparison of results with earlier goals. Comparison of a person to others is threatening (it diminishes the person's self-esteem), whereas comparison of performance over time focuses on the individual's own goals for improvement (what the individual can become, not what others want the individual to become) and behaviors needed to bring about further improvement. In general, human resource professionals should not assume that feedback is valuable in and of itself. In the design of a feedback intervention, such as a 360-degree feedback survey or an annual performance appraisal form, the intervention should be tied to previous goal setting and have implications for future goals. Then too, plans should be made to test the effectiveness of the feedback intervention to be sure it has the desired effect.

DeNisi and Kluger (2000) recommended that feedback interventions (a) focus on the task (i.e., behavior), not on the person's sense of self, (b) not threaten the recipient's ego, (c) be specific about how to improve performance, (d) link the feedback to prior goals and to future goals, and (e) minimize information comparing the recipient with others and maximize information about ways to improve performance.

Summary

Feedback provides direction for goal setting, and goals motivate behavior change. Goals need to be challenging yet realistic (i.e., accomplishable). They need to focus on behaviors that can be changed, not general personality characteristics that are difficult to define, let alone know how to change. Once goals are set, feedback needs to be sufficiently specific and targeted to behaviors that are goal focused. Otherwise it will be ignored. Next, we examine how managers incorporate an understanding of change processes (described earlier in this chapter) and goal setting into feedback discussions with subordinates. This usually begins with the formal performance appraisal and review process, but hopefully continues in ongoing performance discussions.

TOWARD MORE CONSTRUCTIVE
FEEDBACK REVIEWS

This section considers what managers should do to give more comprehensible information to their coworkers—feedback that will be accepted and used. The section also discusses how an effective feedback discussion can be conducted, a topic that receives more in-depth explanation in the next chapter. Here, I show how managers can incorporate self-appraisals into the performance interview, link feedback to goal setting, eliminate or reduce the threat of performance grades, and separate the discussion of salary and career development.

Some managers do not like to give feedback, regardless whether it is positive or negative (Hillman, Schwandt, & Bartz, 1990). They may believe that feedback is not useful or necessary, perhaps thinking that "no news is good news." They may believe that they are not competent to judge others. They may fear that their subordinates will react negatively to the feedback, that feedback may be used against them, as when subordinates defend themselves by blaming the manager.

We know from the chapter 2 that feedback is likely to be perceived more accurately and to be accepted when it comes soon after the behavior, it is specific and favorable, and it comes from a source the recipients view as an expert familiar with the work, trustworthy, and in control over valued outcomes. Also, feedback is likely to be perceived more accurately and to be accepted when it addresses behaviors the recipient has the competence and power in the organization to control, and when it tells the recipient what behavior leads to improved performance.

Helpful Hints

This section is an instructional resource to help managers conduct a formal performance review. I begin with guidelines adapted from Silverman (1991):

Avoid sweeping statements. Words such as "always" and "never" only make people angry and defensive. It is too easy for them to say, "That's not true. I don't *always* . . .!"

Focus on major responsibilities and performance standards. People want to know what is expected of them, not how they compare unfavorably with others.

Have employees identify causes for poor performance. Self-evaluation avoids defensiveness and gives the manager an alternative viewpoint to consider (see later discussion about the value of incorporating self-evaluation into the performance review discussion).

Provide feedback frequently. As noted already, performance feedback should not be saved up and dumped on the employee once a year.

Discuss behavior or results, not the person. Focusing on traits (e.g., "You are too passive") are likely to be seen as personal attacks. Supervisors should focus on the employee's observed behaviors or results.

Specify what needs to be done. Do not just tell employees what they did wrong. Help them establish a direction for improvement.

Use both positive and negative feedback. Positive feedback provides encouragement and enhances motivation. Provide negative feedback in a way that informs the subordinate instead of attacking the his or her self-esteem.

Coach rather than judge. A tenet of this volume is that the manager should help the subordinate to develop.

Fit feedback to the individual. As stated earlier, providing information enhances a person's insight into him- or herself and organizational expectations. Some people need more feedback than others, perhaps because of their experience or ability to discern their effectiveness in the organization. Some employees may not realize what is important in the department, perhaps because it was never discussed openly, or they may not realize the effect certain of their behaviors is having on coworkers' or the unit's performance.

Prepare for the review. Employees should receive at least a 2-week notice of the impending performance review. During this time, the employee should conduct a self-assessment, and the supervisor should review documentation on the employee (Cascio, 1986, p. 312).

Develop a structure for the review discussion. The supervisor should have a definite set of points to cover that focus on the subordinates' behaviors and results.

Agree on responsibilities and performance standards. After the review, the employee and supervisor should both review the employee's major responsibilities and performance standards. The cycle then starts again.

A Sample Discussion

Here's a way to start the review:

> "I'd like you to start the discussion. What do you think are the three most important things you accomplished during the past 6 months? "[later]" What are the areas in which you wish you had done better? What do you think needs improvement? What do you need to help you improve?"

Be prepared for defensive reactions: denying the problem, changing the subject, focusing on something else, or attributing external blame. Here are some possibilities:

> "That's not the way I see it at all! I tried my best, but there was nothing more I could have done. It was out of my control."
>
> "I don't know where you are getting your information, but that's not what happened."
>
> "Several people in the group just don't like me. But I worked as hard as anyone."
>
> "I'm doing my best. I did everything you wanted me to."
>
> "It's unfair to be telling me now you wanted something else. I would have been happy to change if you had only told me."
>
> "I've had plenty of experience, and I know how things work around here. This is the way we've always done it, and I see no reason to change now."
>
> "I agree with you that things didn't turn out as well as they could have. If we only had ... better information, a new computer system, more cooperation from other departments, and the like. Something should be done about this. Maybe I can work on it now that we all recognize the problem."

Avoid destructive comments in responses to defensiveness. Do not argue, debate, deny, insist, cite others as the source of the evaluation, generalize, or personalize. For example, do not say

"You're just going to have to see it my way. You really have no choice."
"You better think it over."
"It doesn't matter what you think."
"This isn't the way I feel. I'm just passing on what our boss thinks, and you better come to terms with that."
"How could that be?"
"Face it, you're not cut out for this job."

Here are some constructive responses to defensiveness. Recognize and diffuse the problem up front. Agree and move on. Be repetitive. Focus on facts (behaviors or outcomes) rather than personal characteristics. Suggest directions for improvement. For instance,

"I know you don't agree with me. I'm just asking you to hear me out."
"This is how I see it, and you need to know that. Now here's what I recommend."
"Here are some things you could do differently next time."
"Rather than debate the issue, let's work on what you can do differently next time."

These statements may have to be repeated several times before the employee hears.

Use Self-Appraisals

Self-appraisals should be incorporated into the performance appraisal discussion (Meyer, 1991). The subordinate takes the lead in the appraisal process. The supervisor's role is to give the employee recognition and suggest changes in behavior or activities. Supervisors are likely to need training in how to be a "counselor" and deal with problems, such as how to deal with an inflated self-evaluation, an unnecessarily self-deprecating appraisal, or an important issue not raised by the subordinate.

Meyer (1991) noted that the conventional approach to feedback is sometimes appropriate when then subordinate is dependent on the supervisor, as is the case for new employees, trainees, or people in highly structured jobs. Except for these, self-appraisal is extremely valuable. It increases the subordinate's dignity and self-respect, avoids defensiveness, and places the manager in the role of counselor, not judge. Also, self-appraisal is more likely to engender the subordinate's commitment to goals and development plans that emerge from the discussion.

However, there are some possible problems with self-review (Meyer, 1991). For instance, it violates traditional mores about the proper relationship between boss and subordinate. Employees have a self-serving bias that inflates self-appraisals. However, this "leniency error" can be minimized by orienting the self-appraisal toward development rather than appraisal for administrative purposes. Supervisors are influenced by subordinates' self-judgments because supervisors prefer to avoid confrontation that comes from subordinate defensiveness (Blakely, 1993). Supervisors therefore tend to be lenient when they know the subordinates see themselves positively.

Deemphasize Grading

Another recommendation is to deemphasize or even eliminate grading, that is, the practice of attaching a numeric score or overall adjectival grade (e.g., "satisfactory") to the review (Meyer, 1991). I introduced this idea in chapter 6 when describing ratingless appraisals. Grading is demeaning, and any administrative actions, such as a salary increase or promotion, communicate an overall appraisal better than a grade.

Learning to Give Constructive Feedback: A Behavior Modeling Approach

Behavior modeling encompasses four steps: explaining principles, demonstrating principles, providing a chance for trainees to try the new behaviors and receive feedback about their performance, and transfer to the job (Goldstein & Sorcher, 1974). These four steps may have the following applications for learning how to give constructive feedback:

Learning the Value of Feedback.   Constructive feedback is defined, and its potential value is described (as reviewed in chapter 2).

Observing.   Trainees are shown a video tape (or in-person role plays by the trainers) with several scenarios acted out: examples of constructive feedback, benign but worthless feedback, and destructive feedback. The scenarios are interspersed with opportunities for discussion, during which the trainers ensure that the trainees understand the differences between the desired and undesired behaviors.

Practicing Giving Feedback and Receiving Feedback on Feedback Behavior. Trainees are given several role-playing exercises. For instance, one person may take the role of the subordinate and another that of the supervisor giving feedback. Each would receive a paragraph describing their point of view. Trainers or fellow trainees would observe the role play and give the "actors" feedback. Each trainee should have several opportunities to play different roles and receive feedback.

Applying New Behaviors on the Job.   Trainees are expected to apply their newly learned behavior on the job. They may return to the training center at some later time for a follow-up description and postmortem of their behavior and effectiveness. A second way of giving feedback for on-the-job behavior is to be sure that higher level supervisors are trained in the same behavioral principles and know how to evaluate behaviors and give feedback. A third way is to ask those receiving feedback to describe the feedback process. The limitation here, of course, is that the recipient's views may be biased by the favorability of the feedback. Nevertheless, the extent to which they view the feedback as constructive likely is indicative of how the feedback was presented. A fourth evaluation technique involves examining changes in behavior of those receiving feedback. Positive changes in behavior would be expected from constructive feedback, although, admittedly, short-term improvements in performance can occur from coercive or destructive feedback. Consequently, a multipronged approach should be taken by gathering a variety of evidence for how feedback is being given and using that as a basis for "feedback on feedback."

Summary

Managers play a key role in the feedback process. Whereas assessment centers or multisource feedback surveys may provide useful data, an employee's supervisor is the key source of performance feedback, usually operationalized in the annual formal appraisal. The appraisal is inevitably accompanied by the performance review. This is the manager's opportunity to turn a bureaucratic and potentially threatening event into a coaching relationship. Managers can learn to be good observers and reporters of behavior and guides for changing behavior and improving performance. The recommendations in this section are a resource to help managers in being sensitive to employees' reactions to feedback and readiness to change.

CONCLUSION

This chapter explores conditions for enhancing feedback acceptance and use. The employee's readiness to change is important to acceptance of feedback. The use of feedback to set goals is important to making feedback worthwhile. The formal performance review and informal performance discussions can target behaviors, track goals, and motivate further accomplishment. Here are points to remember:

1. Information is likely to be perceived more accurately and to be accepted when it follows a number of conditions, for instance, when it comes from a source whom the recipients view as knowledgeable and trustworthy, when it comes soon after the behavior, and when it is positive, frequent, and specific.
2. Managers should deliver feedback that matches employees' readiness to change. This will reduce stress and reduce the time needed to bring about change.

3. Stage-matched interventions allow all employees to participate in the change process, even if they are not yet ready to change. The participation may be limited to discussing the pros and cons of change when it is in the precontemplation stage. Supervisors should have different expectations for these employee's than they do for those who are embarking on change. Employees in the precontemplation change should be expected to become more aware of the need for change. Employees already taking action should demonstrate their commitment to change and work on overcoming barriers to change.

4. A goal is the gap between where one is and where one wants to be. Goal setting is the means by which feedback motivates change. Ongoing feedback helps individuals calibrate their degree of goal accomplishment and the level of effort needed to reach the goal.

5. Individuals must participate in setting their own goals. Participation leads to commitment to the goals. Assigned goals do not work.

6. To motivate learning and behavior change, goals should be few, clear, behavioral, and difficult.

7. For continuous development, goals should be focused on learning and mastery, not on performance improvement.

8. Feedback interventions should focus on the task (i.e., behavior), not on the person's sense of self. Also, feedback should be specific about how to improve performance, link the feedback to prior and future goals, minimize information comparing the recipient with others, and maximize information about ways to improve performance.

9. In conducting a formal performance review discussion, a supervisor should focus on major responsibilities and performance standards and identify causes for poor performance. The supervisor should explain the purpose of the review meeting, ask the employee to summarize accomplishments and developmental needs, summarize accomplishments and development needs from the supervisor's perspective, reach agreement about what developmental steps should be taken, and initiate goal setting.

10. Principles for goal setting include encouraging employee participation and agreeing on specific goals. Employees do best when they perceive their goals as challenging, under their control, and achievable.

11. Observation skills can be improved by communicating performance standards, giving raters feedback on the accuracy of their ratings, and giving them a chance to practice observing, integrating, recalling, and evaluating behaviors.

In the next chapter, I turn to the coaching process as a critical adjunct to feedback. I describe the role of external executive coaches and the role of manager as coach and developer.

11

Performance Management, Development, and Coaching

The feedback process doesnot end with the performance review and setting goals for improvement. Performance management is an ongoing process that includes monitoring and supporting performance and development. An important part of the job of manager is supporting employees' performance management, encouraging and providing resources for their development, and being a coach. This chapter explains what it means to be an effective coach and developer. Unfortunately, these are low priorities for some managers. Instead of focusing on their subordinates' performance improvement and career development, they work to maximize their current performance because that affects their own performance and rewards.

In this discussion, I describe the manager's role in the performance management process. I describe how to create a corporate environment that supports development. I describe the role of the external executive coach, a consultant who works with senior managers to help them deal with feedback. In the process, executive coaches are coaching role models, encouraging senior managers to coach their subordinates. They, in turn, coach their subordinates as coaching cascades down the organizational hierarchy. Organizations that educate and reward managers for performance management and for being coaches and developers are more likely to be organizations that can adapt to changes in the business environment.

PERFORMANCE MANAGEMENT

Performance management is the process of monitoring employees' performance, holding frequent feedback discussions (conversations, not one-way monologues), and suggesting ways to improve performance. Performance management should not be left to chance or the assumption that it will "just happen," that employees will take care of themselves. Managers need to encourage and cultivate performance management (Hillman, Schwandt, & Bartz, 1990). Certainly, there are many good reasons for paying attention to employees' performance. For instance, it demonstrates a commitment to excellent management, accomplishes your group's objectives, maintains high-quality relationships, and develops critical job skills. It also increases employees' satisfaction, competence, and effectiveness. Furthermore, it helps employees understand how they can better contribute to the firm's success and improves employees' morale and quality of work life.

Although the value of performance management may seem obvious (a "no brainer," as they say), unfortunately it is not done well. Consider some common problems that subordinates cite about their managers. They may say that their managers do not face up to performance problems. Such managers need training in how to give negative feedback and make it constructive. The subordinates may believe that their managers do not explain the performance rating process, so employees have little understanding of the "system" (salary grades, rating procedures, salary treatment, and career opportunities). They may fault their managers for giving too little attention to helping them with career planning. They may feel that managers "micromanage," not leaving employees alone to do their jobs, and that managers do not know what employees want or expect from them.

Subordinates also may complain about organizational factors that contribute to poor performance management. They may say that the company's top executives do not believe employees are motivated by money. They may perceive that managers have little discretion about important decisions regarding employees' careers, and that managers are not rewarded for developing subordinates. In addition, they may believe that there are no clear career paths for advancement.

These show the kind of negative conditions that can and do occur. They happen because in many organizations, the role of managing people is not given enough attention. This is an important part of the reason why managers do not try to give meaningful performance feedback. Thus, some of what must change for feedback to improve has to do with the culture of the organization.

The role of managers in performance management, development, and coaching is largely dependent on their relationships with subordinates. A good way for you, as a manager, to understand your role as coach and developer is to complete the questionnaire in Table 11.1. Try it. Better yet, give it to your employees. The items ask about your relationship with your subordinates, particularly, the extent to which you support their performance improvement. Then across all the items in the questionnaire consider the following: What do you do most frequently? What do you do least frequently? Are these behaviors important to your organization? If you did these behaviors more often, would your unit perform better? What's stopping you?

TABLE 11.1
Manager Self-Assessment

Rate how much you do the activity now. Use the following scale for each rating:

1 = very infrequently/never
2 = infrequently
3 = a moderate amount
4 = frequently
5 = very frequently

____1. Facilitate and support my employees' efforts in meeting their goals
____2. Provide ongoing coaching and counseling on ways to improve each employee's effectiveness
____3. State and demonstrate my commitment to customer satisfaction
____4. Clearly articulate performance expectations to my employees
____5. Set clear performance goals
____6. Provide my employees with all relevant information for doing their jobs
____7. Create an environment in which candid communication is the norm
____8. Create an environment in which teamwork and collaboration is the norm
____9. Create an environment in which each employee feels valued
____10. Treat all employees equally regardless of their individual characteristics
____11. Be sensitive to the personal needs of my employees
____12. Own up to the commitments I make to my employees
____13. Encourage and value my employees' ideas
____14. Provide opportunities for my employees to make decisions on their own
____15. Provide meaningful and timely performance feedback to my employees
____16. Highlight episodes of good performance
____17. Explain areas for performance improvement
____18. Address developmental needs of marginal performers
____19. Explain career opportunities available in the organization
____20. Coach employees on what they need to do to achieve their career goals in the company

CREATING A CORPORATE CULTURE THAT SUPPORTS DEVELOPMENT

According to Maurer, Mitchell, and Barbeite (2002), three factors are important in determining the extent to which managers participate in development: favorability of feedback level (particularly from peers and subordinates), belief that development and improvement are possible, and a work context that supports skill development. This section focuses on creating an environment that supports development. Some organizations recognize that being a coach and developer is an important part of the manager's job. Others do not.

Consider two organizations. One expects employees to do their current jobs as assigned. Managers' attention is on the current performance of the department and each individual in the department. Occasionally, people are promoted, but these promotions are limited to young managers in a special program for high-potential managers. Even for this select group, there are few opportunities for job movement.

Another organization in the same industry in the same region of the country has a culture that is very different. The CEO talks about the importance of development to the organization. All the employees are expected to know their current jobs well and perform their best. Also, they are expected to think ahead and be aware of anticipated changes in the industry and the company that may change their jobs. They are encouraged to take courses, read, and in other ways stay ahead of the curve as much as possible. All the employees are expected to understand the changing and emerging technologies affecting their industry, at least in general, conceptual terms, even if they do not know every technical detail. Also, they are expected to be alert to changing market conditions, including elements of globalization, competition, and the economy that affect their business. The company supports this learning in a number of ways. It provides frequent updates through newsletters about the firm's progress and directions. It holds regular information forums with managers, and managers are expected to communicate this information to their work teams. Also, managers are expected to work with individual subordinates to plan their development activities in relation to what they need to know to do their current jobs better now and in the future, and in relation to other jobs that they might like to have in the firm. Although the company does not have rigid career paths, because department structures and job functions change frequently, it does have logical career paths that serve as guidelines to help employees prepare for career moves. These career paths show how one job can help an employee prepare for one or more other types of jobs. The company encourages job movement for the sake of development. That is, job moves are initiated by managers because they have subordinates who are ready for developmental experiences, not just because there happens to be a vacancy that must be filled. Human resource policies support this philosophy by providing ample training opportunities in competencies important to the organization, by using appraisal and pay systems that reward the manager's role as developer, by encouraging managers and subordinates to work together on career planning and development, and by making it easy for managers to help their subordinates move to new positions and, in turn, for managers to find the right people to fill vacancies in their units.

Although both firms are doing well financially now, officials in the second firm believe that their company will be better positioned for new developments in the future. This has proved true in the past as the firm found it easier to adapt to new products, markets, and distribution channels. Whereas the first other company responded to similar conditions by downsizing and to restructuring, the second company was able to respond to changes faster and to reorganize with no layoffs. As a result, the second company has more cash on hand for new ventures. Moreover, whereas the surviving employees in the first company have been traumatized by fear of insecure employment, the employees in the second company feel competitive as individuals and as a firm. They recognize the importance of understanding their strengths

and weaknesses in relation to changing organizational needs and environmental demands. They know how to learn, and they look forward to new
developmental experiences. They are poised for change.

In the first organization, there are some managers who believe in developing subordinates regardless of an unsupportive corporate policy. They have
developed reputations as good managers to work for, and as a result, they are
able to attract the best people to their units. Unfortunately, these individuals are not rewarded for their supportive development efforts. In the second
organization, some managers are not good at developing subordinates. They
feel uncomfortable talking with subordinates about their performance, and
they do not like disrupting the daily flow of activity to worry about what
might happen in the future. These managers wonder why they are rewarded
as well as others who have comparably good bottom lines. Some have been
encouraged to take advantage of an early retirement incentive.

In summary, companies vary in their support for employee development
and the extent to which they expect and encourage managers to spend time
supporting their employees' performance management and career development. Development-oriented companies provide resources for development, educate managers in their role as developers, and offer avenues for
career growth. Companies that focus on immediate business return without
investing in the employees' future development make it difficult for managers to build a coaching relationship with employees. Next, I turn to the
relationship between the manager, as source of feedback and support for
development, and the employee.

EMPLOYEES' PERCEPTIONS
OF MANAGERS' INTENTIONS

When employees receive feedback, they do not necessarily accept it at face
value, but instead may look for the intention behind why it was given. They
may search to find reasons for the feedback that extends beyond their own
behavior, perhaps because they would just as soon discover a viable alternative explanation that does not require them to take responsibility for their
own performance. Managers' intentions in providing feedback do, in fact,
vary, affecting the quality and frequency of the feedback they provide, their
sincerity, and the value of time spent to support their subordinates' performance and development. For instance, managers' relationships with their
subordinates may be affected by daily swings in work pressure, the managers' mood, the understanding between the managers and their employees
about fair exchange (reward for performance), and the relationship (mutual
understanding and trust) between the subordinates and their managers. In
one study, business students (full- and part-time) and faculty were asked to
recall all the "constructive" and "not so constructive" reasons they perceived

concerning why managers had given them feedback about their performance (Fedor, Buckley, & Eder, 1990). The intentions fell into four major groupings: manager dominance, attentiveness to unit expectations, subordinate nurturance, and exhortation to increase subordinate performance.

When managers are using feedback to increase their dominance, they demonstrate their power or authority. They bolster their own self-image at their subordinates' expense, and have a tendency to belittle the subordinates to whom the feedback is directed.

When managers are attentive to department expectations, they ensure that their subordinates' performance meets departmental standards. They explain standards that their subordinates should use to evaluate their own performance. They provide subordinates with information on progress toward the department's goals. They help subordinates perform their jobs more efficiently and with less effort. Also, they encourage the work group to perform as a team.

In contrast, managers may give feedback to nurture subordinates and help them feel more relaxed about their work. These managers try to bolster their subordinates' self-image and ensure that they do not store up feelings of dissatisfaction.

Managers who exhort subordinates to increase their performance, expect them to work harder. They may encourage subordinates to the point of demanding that they take initiative.

In short, it is possible for subordinates to perceive their bosses as having other than the best intentions in giving feedback. This perception is likely to affect their reactions and responses to the feedback (Fedor et al., 1990). Of course, the subordinate's perception of the manager's intent may not match the manager's actual intent. Managers should be aware of not only the feedback information they are providing, but also their underlying reasons or intentions for providing that information and the feedback recipient's interpretation of their intent. However, managers are only partially in control of subordinates' conclusions about their intentions. In part, perceptions of manager intentions are in the eye of the beholder. Therefore, managers should try to be explicit about their intentions. They should explain to their subordinates the purpose for the feedback. Also, they should consider other organizational occurrences in choosing when and under what conditions to provide feedback. For instance, providing unfavorable feedback when there are rumors of downsizing may be perceived as a warning or a way to build a rationale for laying off the subordinate.

Manager Biases

Managers' behavior toward subordinates may be biased in favor of or against individual employees. Considerable research shows that this bias influences the attention and support employees receive to enhance their performance.

The *Pygmalion effect* occurs when a manager has high expectations about a subordinate's potential, which in turn often result in an increase in the subordinate's performance. This is a special case of the self-fulfilling prophecy (Fedor et al., 1990). The *Golem effect* ("Golem" is "oaf" or "dumbbell" in Hebrew slang) is the Pygmalion effect in reverse. In this case, low manager expectations depress subordinate achievement, causing either absolute decreases in subordinate performance or smaller gains in performance than could have been achieved otherwise (Rosenthal, 1991; Rosenthal & Jacobson, 1968).

Interventions to Correct Biases

Interventions can restrict or enhance the effects of the aforementioned biases. They can have the following effects.

Reduce the Golem Effect.   To study the Golem effect, military squads were randomly assigned to an experimental or control condition (Babad, Inbar, & Rosenthal, 1982). In the experimental condition, subordinates who received low test scores on a physical fitness test were targeted for de-Golemization by affecting the leader's low expectations toward all low-scoring subordinates in the squad. Squad leaders in the control condition were not treated. The treatment consisted of an explanation to squad leaders designed to prevent them from forming low expectations toward their low scorers. They were told that "research on the . . . test, as well as past experience in many . . . units has shown that low scores do not predict performance well" (Oz & Eden, 1994, p. 746). The explanation continued by saying that men with low scores often achieve as much or more than those who have scored considerably higher. Several possible reasons were given (e.g., perhaps the test is unreliable for low scorers, or low scorers were not motivated to do their best). During biweekly follow-up meetings, squad leaders were asked specifically how things were going with the leader's low scores and how the leader was handling them.

Repeats of the physical fitness test showed that initially low-scoring subordinates in the experimental squads improved more than those in the control squads. Moreover, these initially low scorers in the experimental groups maintained their improved scores, rated their squad leaders more favorably, and were more satisfied than initially low scorers in the control group.

Induce Pygmalion.   Earlier experiments showed that interventions could induce the Pygmalion effect (i.e., that managers get the performance they expect; Eden, 1992). Subordinates designated as having high test scores reflecting high achievement potential scored higher on achievement tests after training. The subordinates designated as having high potential had been randomly assigned to this group. The Pygmalion effect works in part because managers who expect high performance communicate these expectations to their subordinates and unwittingly treat these high-potential subordinates differently, which is likely to raise the subordinates' own expectations. This stems from the expectancy theory of work motivation, with its prediction that people exert greater effort when they expect to succeed.

Manager–Subordinate Relationships and Ways to Increase Feedback

Ways to improve feedback depend on the nature of the relationship between manager and subordinate. Consider the three types of relationships (described in chapter 2) based on the manager's primary need: control-dominated, reward-dominated, and relationships-dominated. Each has implications for improving feedback.

In control-dominated relationships, managers should be trained in self-management skills to help them understand the control they have over their own behavior and its effects on others. They should be taught how to understand the importance of building a power base such that their subordinates view feedback from them as coming from an expert, attractive, and trustworthy source (Hill & Corbett, 1993). Once this more positive relationship is established, subordinates are likely to react constructively to unfavorable feedback in order to reduce dissonance from receiving such feedback from a trusted source of feedback. Also, controlling managers should learn counseling techniques, in particular, how to recognize, clarify, and accept subordinates' expressed feelings, with the result that the recipient's feelings will become more positive. Consequently, subordinates will develop an understanding of their own feelings and initiate positive coping actions (Hill & Corbett, 1993). However, if controlling managers are reluctant to change their behavior, management actions may be necessary to remove them from the situation, for instance, by transferring them to another group with different capabilities and work demands or by firing them.

In reward-dominated relationships, managers should learn how to alter the reward structure to link subordinates' performance to outcomes they value. Both managers and subordinates should receive skills training that will increase their chances for excellent performance. Managers should learn behavioral modeling and reinforcement principles (so they can help subordinates understand how their behavior resulted in valued outcomes. Managers should learn how to raise the value and size of behavioral outcomes or rewards, for instance, by combining outcomes, withdrawing from the situation before having a chance to say something destructive, increasing the recognition and other rewards from giving constructive feedback, and highlighting the long-term negative implications of destructive feedback (Logue, 1995). Managers should learn how to change outcome contingencies, for instance, by being sure that the they do not give destructive feedback after withholding it for awhile, and recognizing outcomes that result from destructive and constructive feedback.

In affiliation-dominated relationships, managers should learn observation and social management skills. They should model constructive feedback. Managers who receive constructive feedback from others are likely to be constructive when giving feedback to others. They might benefit from sensitivity training and various individual and group therapies that help them understand how others react to them and how they react to others.

Feedback and Support for Marginal Performers

Marginal performers are employees who lack the ability or motivation needed to perform well (London & Mone, 1993). Doing "marginal work" does not mean that the employee has failed. Rather, the employee is doing the minimum necessary to get by. The potential for marginal performance has increased because of pressures on organizations to reduce costs and improve efficiency. Different types of marginal performance include underutilization (high ability and low effort), misdirected effort (low ability and high effort), and a combination of the two (low ability and low effort). Underutilization stems from inadequate goal setting, misunderstood subordinate skills, oversupervision, or poor boss–subordinate communication. Misdirected effort may occur because of a poor job match or changing job requirements. People who lack both motivation and capability are likely to withdraw from work because they do not live up to increasing standards.

The way to address marginal performance problems depends on whether the problem is motivational or ability related. The following are some ways to improve marginal performance.

Underutilization. Employees with high ability but low effort may benefit from performance management (honest and direct feedback about the subordinate's marginal performance), rewards (what will result when goals are accomplished), *role models* (public recognition of deserving employees), job enrichment and empowerment (increased autonomy and responsibility), team building and conflict resolution (improved interpersonal relationships through communications skills assessment and training, group meetings for sharing perceptions, and problem-solving sessions), counseling (better insight into skills and interests in relation to the current job and available opportunities in the organization, and burnout prevention and management (encouraging completion of work during regularly scheduled hours, recognizing employees for meeting performance goals rather than rewarding them for working overtime, and recognizing burnout when it occurs and dealing with it by reducing work load or providing some extra time off).

Misdirected Effort. Employees with low ability who try hard may benefit from goal setting (setting and clarifying goals in relation to the employees' capabilities and insight into job requirements and expectations), coaching (suggesting behavior change; frequently giving performance feedback and reinforcement for desired behaviors), *delegation* (assigning clear tasks; coordinating the work to reduce the employee's work load and increase the department's productivity), temporary assignments for *skill development* (transferring the employee to a less demanding job or to a job in a related department), *restructuring of the job assignment* (restructuring the job in line with the marginal employee's strengths).

Low Ability and Low Effort. The solutions to this situation may require more drastic steps, such as no financial rewards (withholding merit pay and cost-of-living pay adjustments), transfer or demotion (moving the employee to another job that would be more suitable for the marginal performer), outplacement (inviting the employee to leave the organization voluntarily with rous severance pay and assistance in finding employment elsewhere), or outright firing (removing the marginal performer from the organization on the basis of properly documented marginal performance over time, such as that of performance appraisals during the last 3 years).

Summary

Managers' intentions in giving feedback and the nature of their relationship with their subordinate affect feedback and performance management. Managers need to consider how the message they are delivering in giving feedback could be influenced by the intention they are conveying to subordinates. For instance, some managers are viewed as dominant and controlling, others as caring and nurturing. Mangers should also recognize that their biases and expectations may affect the attention and support they give to different employees. Furthermore, managers should consider that the type of relationship they have with subordinates may affect how they can improve the value of feedback. Finally, managers are likely to be challenged by needing to give feedback to marginal performers. Ways to turn around their performance, or at least to try, will depend on the reason for the marginal performance: ability, motivation, or a combination thereof.

THE APPRAISAL AND DEVELOPMENT CYCLE

Performance appraisal and feedback should not be merely annual events, nor should attention to development. Rather, they should comprise a "systematic and continuous process of improving employee performance" (Silverman, 1991, p. 128). Moreover, this process of performance appraisal and feedback should involve the subordinate every step of the way and, as such, establish and reinforce the subordinate's commitment and motivation to improve.

The process changes the relationship between manager and subordinate by requiring clear communication, collaboration, and follow-up assessment on goal accomplishment and performance improvement. Also, the process engenders a climate of support for development and continuous learning in the organization. The process can be viewed as a five-step cycle (adapted from Silverman, 1991, pp. 129–149). The cycle is repeated as the employees' capabilities grow and new responsibilities are added.

The cycle begins with clarification of the employee's capabilities and major responsibilities. The manager and subordinate should have a clear idea, and the same idea, of what is needed and what the subordinate is able to accomplish on the basis of the subordinate's capabilities and the situation. Vague communications about job requirements and expectations can lead to frustration on the part of the manager and subordinate. This does not mean that a rigid, written job description is necessary. Companies such as Computer Associates do not use formal job descriptions because jobs are highly fluid. Assignments and responsibilities change constantly, and job descriptions impose unnecessary limitations, engendering a civil service mentality (i.e., employees may decline to do activities that are not clearly part of their job description). At Computer Associates, however, managers work with subordinates to generate a common understanding of expected work activities and outputs.

The next step in the appraisal and development cycle is to develop performance standards. Expectations are refined further in the process of developing performance standards through goal setting and rewards (see chapter 10). Standards might be expressed in terms of behaviors (controllable and observable actions that employees exhibit on the job) or results (accomplishments that are under the employee's control and depend on the employee's actions) expected on the job (what the subordinate does to earn his or her salary). Rewards (e.g., a bonus or promotion) may be specified for special accomplishments or an accumulation of accomplishments. A philosophy developed by AT&T and expressed in performance management guidelines held that managers should set goals in terms of outputs, not activities (London & Mone, 1987). This did not mean that it mattered not how employees accomplished a task as long as they got the job done. Certainly, they would be held accountable for their actions. However, it meant that goal setting should focus on the end result. Goal setting did not have to specify every action needed to accomplish the goal.

Once standards are developed and goals are set, managers should provide subordinates with periodic performance feedback. Frequent communication between subordinate and manager about performance is vital to the success of the performance management cycle. Once-a-year performance reviews have questionable value unless they are accompanied by ongoing discussion about performance.

Part of feedback is helping subordinates diagnose performance difficulties. Managers should also provide coaching on ways to improve performance.

When performance improvement is indicated, the manager and subordinate need a clear understanding of the discrepancy between current and expected performance, a discussion and common understanding of the causes for the performance discrepancy, and the development of action plans to enhance the employee's performance.

The last step in the appraisal and development cycle is to review overall performance. This should not be a surprise to the employee if the first four steps were conducted adequately. This requires preparation and follow-up evaluation.

Learning How to Be a Developer

Some firms offer explicit training in each step, with videos to demonstrate points and activities such as behavior modeling, a training method that presents learning points, showing how they apply; role playing for practice and feedback; and on-the-job review of the new behaviors (Goldstein & Sorcher, 1974). Managers can incorporate the steps in their appraisal process even when the company provides little support and expects much less from the performance review. Managers can still show their personal concern and commitment to performance management and employee development. Even if managers are not rewarded directly for coaching subordinates, coaching should enhance the department's performance, increase employees' motivation, and attract the best people into the department.

Training and Practice. The appraisal–development cycle and performance review steps require practice. Managers should consider each step in the cycle:

1. Think about characteristics of effective and ineffective performance.
2. Understand major responsibilities and performance standards.
3. Observe and document employee performance.
4. Consider what is required to diagnose and coach employees on their performance.
5. Review elements of the employee's performance that you want to discuss during the review.

Some Corporate Examples

The performance management cycle may be implemented differently depending on the organization's needs and preferences. Consider two firms: Sovran Financial Corporation and Metro Information Services, Inc. These cases were described by McAfee and Champagne (1993). Sovran is a financial holding company with major offices in Maryland, Washington DC, Virginia, and Tennessee. It has more than 15,000 employees and assets exceeding $50 billion. Metro provides computer consulting and information services implementation to clients through the Southeast. It has more than 450 people with sales exceeding $25 million.

Impetus. The need for the program at Sovran came from one regional manager in a retail division who wanted a new performance appraisal form. A consultant hired for the project suggested that the form per se was not the answer. The regional manager therefore worked with the company's head of training and organization development to create a new system that asked managers to meet with each employee annually to develop jointly a development plan, performance goals, and standards along with expected completion dates. The training and system was implemented one region at a time.

Metro's program emerged from a similar need. The company hired a team of three consultants to design a performance management workshop and introduce the process. The workshop reviewed each program area (performance planning, managing performance, and performance review) with a lecture, cases, and role plays.

Performance Planning. At Sovran, a competence rating form was used as a basis for discussion of the employees' competencies in such areas as decision making, planning and organizing, and teamwork skills. The system was integrated into the company's overall strategic planning program in that each employee's goals and development plan were established after review of the firm's overall goals, business plans, and department direction.

Metro's approach was a bit different. Annually, managers completed a personal assessment development form, which requested two strengths and two areas for development and suggested actions. Employees completed the same form for themselves. Managers and subordinates met to discuss their evaluations and arrive at an agreement for development in areas of technical skills, professional competence, and/or management abilities.

Managing Performance. At Sovran, managers were expected to follow four key steps: (a) observe and document performance, (b) provide periodic feedback, (c) offer coaching and counseling, and (d) revise goals and developmental plans if needed on the basis of changing business or economic conditions. Metro did much the same thing. The company trained managers to write specific and behavioral statements of performance accomplishments with sufficient details for determining the extent to which the employee was accountable for the results (versus events beyond the employee's control).

Reviewing Performance. Sovran employees were encouraged to complete a self-evaluation and come to the feedback discussion prepared to review it. Managers prepared their evaluation by considering what was expected, how much was done, when it was done, and how it was done in reference to each performance goal. During the discussion, the employee explained his or her self-assessment, and then the manager made his or her presentation. Areas of disagreement, if unresolved, were noted on an Employee Comments section of the appraisal form. A separate meeting was set to establish a new set of goals and development plans. The process was similar at Metro, except the firm expected that 80% of the performance discussion would focus on "where do we go from here." This was because both the employee and manager were expected to know already what had and had not been accomplished by the time they reviewed annual performance, if have had conducted an ongoing series of performance reviews.

Implementation.   When these cases were reported, Sovran's program had been in operation for 6 years and Metro's for 4 years (McAfee & Champagne, 1993). Metro used the program in all its offices. At Sovran, managers using the program reported few problems, and most viewed it positively. Some indicated that it was more time consuming than the more traditional appraisal system that preceded it. Some employees expressed frustration with developing a specific list of goals that later needed to be revised or changed completely as a consequence of organizational changes. The company's director of training and organization development argued that just telling employees what is or is not important results in major performance improvement.

Components of a Systematic Program Evaluation

Metro and Sovran did not systematically review the success of their performance management programs. At least, such a review was not reported. Indicators that might be used for such a systematic evaluation range from determining whether the program was used, to collecting perceptions of the program's use, to measuring changes in performance that resulted from the programs. Data for evaluation would include the reported use of the program. Another indicator would be an examination of forms maintained in a central human resource office. Such forms may be copies of actual reviews or merely certification by each manager–subordinate pair that the process was completed for the performance period. Attitude survey questions could ask specifically for satisfaction with different elements of the program. In upward feedback surveys, employees could be asked to rate the extent to which their manager complied with elements of the program. Managers' self-ratings were compared with those of their subordinates' to determine any gaps in perceptions about how the program was being implemented.

Such measures can be used to hold managers accountable for their implementation of the management program. Any unsolicited complaints or reactions to the program could be collected. In addition, performance could be tracked over time, perhaps comparing units using the program with those not using it while accounting for other factors that might contribute to any performance differences.

Summary

In summary, performance management is an ongoing cycle of specifying and clarifying performance standards, evaluating performance, identifying performance gaps, and supporting development to close the gaps and set new, higher performance expectations. Organizations implement human resource development programs to institutionalize and support this cycle. These programs, which include managerial training, need to be evaluated to determine their effects on performance improvement. Just as performance management itself is not static, so the programs that support performance management need to evolve as organizational conditions and associated performance standards change and as standards for performance and employees' capabilities increase. Next, I expand this discussion of performance management and development to advance understanding and foster coaching as a method for managerial development, and to develop oriented manager–subordinate relationships.

COACHING

What Is Coaching?

Executive coaching is "a practical, goal-focused form of personal one-to-one learning for busy executives" (Hall, Otazo, & Hollenbeck, 1999, p. 39). External coaches can offer honest feedback. Executive coaching has become an increasingly popular trend in organizations (Graddick & Lane, 1998). There have been numerous popular books on coaching (Kilburg, 1977), but few empirical studies of its effectiveness. Hall et al. (1999) and Edelstein and Armstrong (1993) have found that executives are generally very satisfied with their coaching experiences.

Executive coaches may enhance the impact of multisource feedback on behavior change in five ways: (a) setting appropriate goals, (b) encouraging executives to discuss feedback with raters (e.g., the feedback recipient's manager or direct reports), (c) increasing executives' feelings of accountability for using the feedback results, (d) strengthening the organization's feedback culture, making feedback a way of doing business in the organization, and (e) helping the feedback recipient navigate through the stages of change (London & Smither, 2002).

As an example, a company offered its senior managers executive coaches as part of a leadership development initiative. The managers could select coaches from a list provided by the human resources department. The list described each coach's background including education, corporate managerial experience, and experience coaching managers in different corporations. During the first 3- to 4-hour meeting, the coach explained the purpose of the coaching and discussed the manager's job as well as current business and departmental issues. Follow-up sessions were scheduled. Coaches tried to arrange for meetings away from the manager's office (e.g., in a conference room) so that the manager would not be disturbed or distracted. Some coaches met with the manager's subordinates or other coworkers to obtain additional input. Multisource feedback survey results were available, and the manager could ask the coach for help in understanding the results. Some coaches asked the manager to complete measures of leadership style and personality that might be helpful in understanding how the manager handled interpersonal relationships. The coaches worked with managers to set development goals and formulate a plan for meeting those goals. The human resources department paid for the first four sessions—the amount of time usually required to review needs and set developmental goals. After that, managers could elect to continue with the coach, paying the bill from the their departmental funds.

Managers can also be coaches to their subordinates (Fournies, 1999). External coaches can model excellent coaching skills and encourage executives to be coaches to the people who report to them. They, in turn, can do the same for their subordinates, and so on down through the organization. Human resource managers and organization development specialists who work in the organization also can coach executives. Internal coaches need to distinguish the coaching role from their other roles. That is, subordinates and other employees need to understand clearly when their managers or human resource professionals are engaging them in a coaching session as opposed to directing or monitoring performance. Managers must learn to be coaches and developers, and organizations need to make this a valued and rewarded dimensions of managerial performance. Coaching sessions may be formal talks, with meeting times scheduled to set them apart from the grind of daily activity. They may also occur in the moment, perhaps immediately after an event or critical incident. The manager needs to state explicitly that the session is meant to be a coaching, experience, and the employee needs to agree that he or she is willing to participate in a coaching session. If this is an informal, spontaneous meeting, the manager might say: "Let's have a coaching session." "What did you think happened in the meeting?" "How did people react to you?" "Here's what I saw." "Do you agree with my assessment?" "How could you have responded differently . . . more constructively?"

Drawing on humanistic and transpersonal psychology, Whitworth, Kimsey-House, and Sandahl (1998) defined the concept of "coactive coaching." This is coaching that focuses on the whole person and aims to enhance feelings of fulfillment, life balance, and effective processes for living.

Coactive coaching focuses on building an alliance between two equal parties: the coach and the client. The agenda stems from the client and the needs of the organization, of course, so the focus is on the client's strengths in relation to organizational requirements (skills needed, business problems to be resolved). The principal client is the manager who is coached, and the organization paying the bill is also the client. The coach does not aim to "fix" the client per se, but assumes that the client can work through his or her problems and discover alternative behavioral strategies. The coach is not an expert consultant, but rather a guide who helps the client form the questions and sift through alternative approaches in a nondirective way. Managers are more likely to be committed to actions they have discovered for themselves.

Elements of Coaching

Support from coworkers, especially the manager, encourages the employees' motivation and resilience in the face of daily job pressures. The following eight behavioral dimensions of coaching within organizations were developed by Kahn (1993):

1. *Accessibility*: Remain in the employee's vicinity, allowing time and space for contact and connection.
2. *Inquiry*: Ask for information necessary to prove the employee's emotional, physical, and cognitive needs; probe the employee's experiences, thoughts, and feelings.
3. *Attention*: Actively attend to the employee's experiences, ideas, and self-expressions; show comprehension with verbal and nonverbal gestures.
4. *Validation*: Communicate positive regard, respect, and appreciation to the employee.
5. *Empathy*: Imaginatively put oneself in the employee's place and identify with the employee's experience.
6. *Support*: Offer information (about salient issues and situations), feedback (about the employee's strengths and weaknesses), insights (about the coaching relationship), and protection (from distracting external forces).
7. *Compassion*: Show emotional presence by displaying warmth, affection, and kindness.
8. *Consistency*: Provide an ongoing, steady stream of resources, compassion, and physical/emotional/cognitive presence for the employee.

Coaching is useful for a number of reasons (Smither & Reilly, 2001). External coaches have the advantage of being an objective, outside party with whom the executive can share information in private and from whom honest feedback can be received. A coach can be almost a therapist, perhaps the only one who will give the manager a straight, honest answer. Executives can describe their feelings and test reactions to various ideas in a supportive, no-risk environment. Coaches can help the executives they coach become coaches to the managers who report to them. These managers, in turn, can become coaches to their subordinates, cascading the coaching role throughout the organization.

Coaching Stages

A number of authors have delineated the steps needed for effective coaching (Graddick & Lane, 1998; Harris, 1999; Kilburg, 1996). For example, Smither and Reilly (2001) outlined a five-stage model for effective coaching: (a) establish the coaching relationship, (b) assess the executive's needs relative to evidence of performance (e.g., 360-degree feedback survey ratings of the executive's strengths and weaknesses), (c) engage in goal setting and development planning, (d) implement actions to achieve goals, and (e) evaluate progress in learning, performance improvement, and the value of the coaching relationship. Often, coaching is stopped after the first three steps. The coach helps the executive collect or interpret performance feedback and set goals for development and performance improvement, but does not follow the executive further. This is partly a cost issue. Companies may pay for several coaching sessions from a central human resource department fund, but the executive then needs to absorb the cost from the executive's departmental budget if he or she wants to continue working with the coach.

Smither and Reilly (2001) outlined the social psychological processes that occur during each stage of the coaching process. During the relationship establishment stage, executives are likely to be cautious about accepting coaching. The coach needs to explain the purpose of coaching. Both the coach and the employee or manager being coached need to agree on the coach's role. Coaches can explain the value of feedback as a way to become more self-aware and discuss how being aware of the way others see you can improve your performance.

During the assessment stage, coaches need to examine the situational constraints facing the manager being coached. The coach may interview the manager's subordinates or other coworkers in hopes of getting more information. The coach may have trouble garnering unbiased information, and may need to interview enough people to obtain as complete information as possible. Understanding the client's situation may require a bit of empathy as the coach tries to comprehend what it would be like to be in the executive's place. The coach should determine the executive's self-perception. People generally have a fixed self-concept, and they are resistant to changing it. The coach works on opening the executive's mind, unfreezing the executive's self-concept, and encouraging the executive about new ways of looking at him- or herself. This is why building rapport and confidence in the first stage of the coaching relationship is so important.

During the goal-setting and development-planning stage, the coach needs to focus the executive's attention on ways of attaining success rather than avoiding failure. This focus on success can enhance the executive's motivation to succeed. The coach can help the executive set goals that are challenging, yet achievable. Also, the coach can help the executive frame goals in terms of learning rather instead of demonstrating a particular skill or achieving a particular performance outcome. As such, the executive can concentrate on continuous improvement and self-directed learning.

During the implementation stage, coaches break up the learning task into smaller successes, express confidence in the executive's ability, and encourage the executive's accomplishments. Executives are influenced by others' expectations for them, and having a coach's encouragement can bolster the executive's ego and lead to a self-fulfilling prophecy of learning and performance improvement. The coach can encourage the executive's persistence in constructive courses of action and discourage the continuation of ineffective action. When executives give excuses for poorer than expected performance, coaches can discuss the credibility of their explanations and rationalizations, detecting excuses early on and not letting the executives persist in self-handicapping.

During the evaluation stage, coaches help executives to process what happened instead of glossing over events that may be emotionally difficult to face. Also, coaches can guide executives in evaluating the coaching relationship, asking what the executives learned and how this demonstrates the possibility of greater accomplishment.

Steps for Effective Coaching

Coaching is harder than giving feedback. It is easier to say what is right or wrong with performance than it is to identify ways to correct a performance problem (Hillman et al., 1990). An important managerial skill for effective coaching of subordinates is problem solving, because coaching is essentially problem solving applied to a performance problem (Stowell, 1988). The following steps for effective coaching discussion were adapted from Hillman et al., (1990, p. 26):

1. *State the purpose.* Be direct (e.g., "I want to talk about the report you gave me yesterday.").
2. *State the performance problem.* It helps to have observations or measures. Describe the expected performance, the actual performance, and the effects of the actual performance on the job (e.g., "The vice president wanted the report to include a time series analysis of the company's financial performance, but you didn't do that."). Also, admit that there are multiple perspectives. This results in greater liking for the information and better memory of it (Langer, 1992).

3. *Get reaction from the subordinate.* Ask for the subordinate's view ("What do you think?" "Do you agree with me?"). Keep the discussion on track. Do not get sidetracked by ancillary issues (e.g., a response such as "Other reports don't include the information, and I recall that their authors were given a chance to present the results in person to the vice president. I hope you'll let me have that chance.").

4. *Analyze the causes for the unsatisfactory performance.* Explore with the subordinate possible causes of the performance problem. Ask the subordinate to identify factors over which he or she has control that may be causing the problem (e.g., "Maybe you don't know enough about the database or software to get what we need here."). Consider external factors that may have caused the performance problem (e.g., "The computer systems were down.").

5. *Seek a collaborative solution if possible.* Ask the subordinate for ideas about how to solve the problem (e.g., "How can we fix this?"). Be patient, and consider all ideas. Offer your own course of action if the staff member is uncertain what to do. Summarize the agreed-upon course of action. (e.g., "Okay, so we agree. You'll ask Bill for help in analyzing the data, and you will revise the report this weekend.").

6. *Provide assistance and follow-up evaluation.* Establish assistance that the subordinate will need in the future. Determine what each of you will do for follow-up evaluation and subsequent performance review (e.g., "Let me have the revised report on Monday morning. I'll read it right away, and we can discuss it right after lunch.").

Evaluating the Effects of Coaching

Few studies have systematically examined the effects of coaching on performance change. Coaches may be used to improve performance, prepare for career advancement, or establish an agenda for major organizational change (Hall, Otazo, & Hollenbeck, 1999; Witherspoon & White, 1996). Coaches may use a wide variety of behavioral techniques and methods to help the executive achieve a mutually identified set of goals (Harris, 1999; Kilburg, 1996). Coaches help executives to interpret their 360-degree feedback, prepare to discuss the feedback with others, absorb the feedback in a constructive manner, and develop an action plan for enhancing performance (Graddick & Lane, 1998). Coaching too often is evaluated by anecdotes rather than research (Hollenbeck & McCall, 1999). When asked to evaluate the coaching experience, executives tend to be quite positive (Hall et al., 1999). Consider the following studies:

Olivero, Bane, and Kopelman (1997) studied the effects of executive coaching in a public sector municipal agency. Before coaching, 31 managers participated in a 3-day management development program. This program together with executive coaching resulted in a significantly greater increase in performance than that achieved with the management development program alone.

McGovern, et al. (2001) studied the impact of executive coaching on 100 executives from 56 organizations. In this study, 86% of the participants and 74% of the stakeholders (immediate managers or HR representatives) reported that they were very satisfied or extremely satisfied with the coaching process. The participants estimated that the return on coaching was nearly 5.7 times the investment in coaching. Note that this was a survey, and the estimates are subjective guesses.

Conway (1999) studied the combined effect of multisource feedback and coaching on 23 midlevel managers in a large state agency. Self-ratings and ratings from others did not change over 7 months, although 2 years later, the managers reported that both the multisource feedback and the coaching had been helpful.

Smither, London, Flautt, Vargas, and Kucine (in press) studied the extent to which executives can benefit from feedback and coaching. In particular, they studied 1,361 executives in a large, global company. All the executives received feedback from their boss, peers, and subordinates at time 1, and then set two to four goals for improvement. About one fourth of these executives worked with external coaches (consultants selected by the human resources department) to help them interpret their feedback and set goals. The executives were not assigned randomly to the coaching condition, but were in departments that participated in the coaching process. Human resources managers matched coaches to executives on the basis of the coach's prior experiences in management and work with clients in similar situations. Each executive worked with a coach for three or four sessions over a period of 6 weeks or so. The coach was given the executive's feedback results before the first meeting with the executive.

Approximately one half of the executives who were coached completed a brief online questionnaire about their reactions to the coaching soon after it took place. The company administered a "mini-360" survey 8 months after the first survey to obtain ratings of the extent to which the executives had made progress toward their goals. Both executives who had been coached and those with no coaching were rated in this survey. The survey actually listed each executive's specific goals and asked for ratings of improvement on each one.

Then, 1 year after the first survey, another survey was completed by most of the original sample of managers. The results showed that 86% of the executives who had the chance to work with a coach wanted to work with a coach again, and 78% wanted to work with the same coach. The executives generally believed that their coaches had done a good job. Those who had worked with a coach were more likely to set specific goals, share their feedback, and solicit ideas for improvement from their managers than those who had not worked with a coach. Contrary to prediction, the executives who had worked with a coach were rated lower in goal progress by their peers and managers 8 months after the first survey than those who had worked with a coach, but there was no significant difference for subordinate ratings. This could have occurred because the expectations were higher for those who worked with a coach, or because the coach actually slowed down performance improvement in taking more time to set the goals. After 1 year, the executives who had been coached improved more in ratings from their subordinates and managers than executives who had not been coached, but there was no significant difference for peer ratings. The number of meetings with the coach was not related to changes in performance ratings.

In this company, the 360-degree feedback ratings were used by senior executives to make decisions about all managers and executives. Also, all the executives were asked to record their development goals, and these were entered on a database maintained by the corporate headquarters human resource department. As a consequence, the executives may have concentrated on using the results to set goals whether they were coached or not.

Another finding from the study showed that there were differences between coaches. That is, some coaches produced more positive effects than others. Coaching was not a uniform process. Although the company had worked hard to identify competent coaches, train them in the purpose and content of the feedback survey, and match them with executives, the coaches varied in their approaches. Some began their coaching by reviewing the feedback results with the executive. Others spent time asking the executive about current business issues and challenges, then related the feedback results to coping with these current problems. (This was a way to capture the executives' attention by focusing on business issues at hand rather than general development needs.) Still other coaches asked the executives with whom they worked to complete various personality measures (e.g., measures of the tendency to be introverted or extroverted). These coaches may have spent less time on the 360-degree feedback results than on the particular personality measures they favored. Overall, idiosyncratic coaching styles are likely to influence the value of coaching.

Summary

Coaching is a management development process targeted to the specific developmental needs of the manager being coached. It often starts with a multisource feedback report. External coaches frequently are hired to help senior managers work through feedback and establish development plans. This coaching relationship may continue as the manager uses the coach as an objective sounding board for ideas, a counselor to help with work relationship problems, or a sage advisor. Managers can become coaches to the people who report to them. As such, they go beyond formal performance reviews to provide guidance and resources for the performance improvement and career development of those they coach. Being a coach does not mean giving up other more directive aspects of the managerial role, such as delegating work and making tough staffing decisions. In other words, the manager and the subordinate need to understand the boundaries of the coaching role, recognizing when the manager is acting as a coach providing individual and interpersonal support and when the manager is acting as a decision maker providing direction and control. This can be a fine line that the manager may need to clarify explicitly at the start of one-on-one feedback and performance management discussions. In general, the research on coaching suggests that it is a valuable adjunct to feedback, but more extensive research is needed in this area if we are to understand the effects of different approaches to coaching and the conditions under which these approaches are most likely to be successful.

CONCLUSION

This chapter explains what it means to be an effective coach and developer. It outlines reasons for supporting performance management and some reasons why managers do not face up to performance problems in their units. I argue for a supportive corporate culture that trains and rewards managers to be coaches and developers of their subordinates. Managers' intentions and biases are considered along with ways of encouraging managers to have high expectations for their people. Ways to be an effective coach are described. Finally, I review elements of an effective appraisal and development cycle. The chapter's central points can be summarized as follows:

1. Managers should learn to be effective coaches and developers by starting with self-assessment. Review your style of management, including how you support your subordinates' career planning and development.
2. Unfortunately, managers often fail to face up to performance problems. Performance management needs to be encouraged and cultivated. Doing so demonstrates your commitment to excellent management as well as your desire to accomplish your group's objectives and enhance employees' satisfaction, competence, and effectiveness.
3. People who receive feedback try to evaluate the source's intentions, and this influences their reactions to the feedback. Managers want to communicate their desire to consider seriously the best interests of their subordinates and the organization. In general, managers who have positive expectations for subordinates' performance provide more support to encourage the subordinates' success. Conversely, low manager expectations restrict subordinates' achievement.
4. Managers can learn to give more constructive feedback. How they give feedback should depend on the nature of the relationship they have with each subordinate. For instance, in control-dominated relationships, managers should learn self-management skills to help them

understand the control they have over their own behavior and its effects on others. In reward-dominated relationships, managers should learn how to alter the reward structure to link the subordinate's performance to valued outcomes. In affiliation-dominated relationships, managers should improve their observation and socialmanagement skills. A manager who has different relationships with different subordinates may have to learn all three approaches.

5. The appraisal and development cycle is a continuous process of improving employee performance that involves the subordinate. It rests on a foundation of clear communication, collaboration, goal setting, follow-up on goal accomplishment, and performance improvement. It involves clarifying the employee's major responsibilities, developing performance standards, giving periodic performance feedback, diagnosing performance problems and coaching in ways to improve, and reviewing overall performance.

6. There are five stages to coaching: (a) establish the coaching relationship, (b) assess the executive's needs relative to evidence of performance (e.g., 360-degree feedback survey ratings of the executive's strengths and weaknesses), (c) engage in goal setting and development planning, (d) implement actions to achieve goals, and (e) evaluate progress in learning, performance improvement, and the value of the coaching relationship.

7. External coaches have the advantage of being an objective, outside party with whom the executive can share information in private.

8. Managers can be coaches to their subordinates, but they need to distinguish the coaching role from their other roles so that subordinates will understand clearly when their managers or human resource professionals are engaging them in a coaching session as opposed to directing or monitoring performance.

9. Managers must learn to be coaches and developers, and organizations need to make this a valued and rewarded dimension of managerial performance.

10. Coaching sessions may be formal talks, with meeting times scheduled to set them apart from the grind of daily activity.

11. In-the-moment coaching can be a very effective way to change behavior because it is immediate and closely tied to actual behaviors that can be discussed.

12. Most executives who have a chance to work with a coach want to work with a coach again, and most of them want to work with the same coach.

13. Executives who work with a coach are more likely to set specific goals, share their feedback, and solicit ideas for improvement from their managers.

14. Coaching increases the positive benefits of 360-degree feedback. Executives who have been coached are likely to improve more in ratings

from their subordinates and managers than executives who have not been coached, although this effect may be lower in organizations that require feedback recipients to set goals after receiving feedback, whether they are coached or not. Having to use the feedback, either reviewing it with a coach or setting goals for development, may be key to increasing the value of 360-degree feedback.

Now answer the questions in Table 11.1 again, this time indicating the type of behavior you want to exhibit in the future. What do you have to do to make this a reality? Develop a plan for becoming a better coach and developer. Then read the next chapter on holding managers accountable for giving and using feedback.

12

Holding Managers Accountable for Giving and Using Feedback

We assume that people treat performance feedback seriously, learn from it, and change their behavior to improve their performance. Much of the literature on feedback has focused on how to collect information and deliver it to employees. For instance, the literature on multisource upward and 360-degree feedback has concentrated on the methods and process for collecting survey feedback and providing participants with the results (Tornow, 1993). In this chapter (based on London, Smither, & Adsit, 1996), I argue that attention should be paid to how employees apply the feedback and interventions that encourage its effective use. The chapter focuses on giving and receiving multisource feedback. Increasing rater and feedback recipient accountability will improve the value of the performance feedback, increase the recipient's sensitivity to the information, and increase the likelihood that the feedback will improve performance. I describe structures that increase managers' accountability for giving and using feedback. This leads to suggestions on how to enhance accountability.

ACCOUNTABILITY PROCESSES

Typically, if a manager does a good performance appraisal or a bad one, there are no consequences. Also, recipients often are not accountable for using the feedback. Yet accountability is critical to the effective use of feedback. For instance, raters try to be more accurate or more lenient when their identity is known by the recipient of the feedback (Antonioni, 1994). Revealing the raters' identity to feedback recipients is one way to hold them accountable for their ratings. Also, recipients say that they value the feedback more when they know the names of the raters. Whereas the identity of the rater is generally known in traditional performance appraisal (because the supervisor makes the ratings), this is not the case in multisource feedback processes,

179

which generally emphasize to raters that they will remain anonymous. Raters fear retribution from the supervisors and coworkers, and not protecting the raters' identity may destroy the integrity of the process. Therefore, other methods are needed to increase rater accountability in multisource feedback programs.

Consider the viewpoint of the manager receiving multisource rating results. When the ratings are collected solely for the development of managers, they can take the results or leave them unless they are encouraged through some means to use the information. When the ratings are collected to make decisions about the manager (e.g., how much merit raise he or she should receive), then the manager may feel compelled to pay attention to the results. However, this does not mean that the manager will. Managers as recipients may not value the feedback because they know that the raters were not accountable for providing the most accurate judgments possible.

To increase supervisory accountability in performance appraisal, supervisors can be expected or required to explain or justify their evaluations. For instance, supervisors may meet to review and explain how they evaluated their subordinates, possibly developing a combined ranking or grouping (e.g., top performers, good performers, marginal performers, and unacceptable performance). Supervisors may be asked by their peers to justify their evaluations as the group compares subordinates. Similarly, in upward rating programs, top managers may hold skip level meetings with lower level subordinates to review how the subordinates evaluated their supervisor. A difficulty with these ways to increase accountability is that raters may be more lenient so that they do not have to explain negative evaluations. In addition, they may use their ratings as an attempt to influence how top managers or their peers view them. For instance, some raters may want to show that they are tough. Others may want to give an evaluation they think the top manager wants to hear, or one that they believe conforms to the top manager's opinions (Klimoski & Inks, 1990; Tetlock, 1983).

In general, rating processes are likely to be more complex and the ratings more accurate when the raters are accountable for the outcomes (Tetlock & Kim, 1992). Even if the rater does not have to provide direct feedback to the recipient, having to justify the rating to someone who cares about the quality of the evaluation (perhaps a top manager or a group of peers) also enhances accountability (Beach & Mitchell, 1978). Having to justify ratings to others can influence the judgment process and the ratings themselves (Tetlock, 1985a, 1985b). Raters who know that they may have to justify their ratings think longer and more carefully about their evaluations (Ford & Weldon, 1981). They mentally prepare a justification that matches the other party's expectations. This is called "preemptive self-criticism" (Tetlock, 1983). Raters in this situation criticize their own judgment processes and the favorability of the ratings in light of what they think others expect.

Definition of Accountability

Accountability may be defined generally as being held responsible for one's actions in terms of expectations and obligations. Responsibility means there is a consequence: The behavior is either rewarded, accepted, or punished. Pressures to make people accountable come from law, conscience, or society. We assume that the person who is accountable for an action or decision usually is the one taking the action or making the decision. The accountable individual also may be someone who supervises the person taking the action of making the decision. The accountable person in a given situation and the responsibility for which the person is accountable should be specified by the person who holds the individual accountable. Moreover there should be some way to track, evaluate, and impose consequences for the person who is accountable for the action or decision. In performance appraisal, we can talk about the accountability of the rater (or more generally, the source of the information) and the recipient (the receiver of the information).

Accountability works because people want to be seen favorably by doing what they are supposed to do (Baumeister, 1982; Blau, 1964; Carnevale, 1985; Deutch & Gerard, 1955; Jones, 1964; Simonson & Nye, 1992). They are concerned about having to justify their views or actions because they are concerned about how others will evaluate them. They want to appear competent, to make a good impression. They also want the approval of others. Evaluation apprehension focuses attention on the task (Geen, 1991).

The objective of an appraisal affects how raters find and process performance information. If raters know their ratings will be used for development, they are more observant and evaluate performance behaviors more carefully. They are more likely to be lenient if the ratings are used for administrative purposes (Williams, DeNisi, Blencoe, & Cafferty, 1985). However, if the ratings are used for administrative decisions and the raters must justify their ratings, the rating process has personal consequences for the raters, and the raters are likely to be more observant and accurate (Murphy, Balzer, Kellam, & Armstrong, 1984). Creating an appraisal situation that uses the ratings to make decisions about people and requires that raters justify their evaluations increases accountability and improves the quality of the ratings (Mero & Motowidlo, 1995).

> Requiring justification essentially makes raters accountable and should cause them to wonder how they might be affected by the ratings they make. This is the point at which feelings of accountability and cues from the motivational context merge to influence performance ratings. (Mero & Motowidlo, 1995, p. 518)

A study of rater accountability in upward feedback (wherein subordinates rate their supervisor) showed that managers who receive feedback from named raters feel more positive about the upward feedback process than managers who receive results from anonymous raters (Antonioni, 1994). When raters were identified, the managers receiving the results felt that subordinate raters were more objective. However, the subordinate raters felt less comfortable and were more lenient when they were identified than when they were anonymous. In other research on upward feedback, I found a similar result. Employees would rather be anonymous, and they report that they would feel compelled to give more favorable ratings if they were identified (London, Wohlers, & Gallagher, 1990). People usually do not like to give negative ratings, particularly if they know that the recipients are aware of who they are (Fusilier, 1980).

Accountability is enhanced when there is a system or structure in which feedback information is used. That is, top managers devote resources to support employee development and assess changes in performance that result from the feedback. Simply dropping feedback reports on a manager's desk is insufficient for multisource ratings to be taken seriously.

Stated simply, there are four necessary ingredients for holding raters and ratees accountable: (a) establishing clear duty or expectations, (b) preparing people to meet that duty (e.g., training and supporting), (c) obtaining reports of performance (e.g., justification of the ratings, agreement among measures of performance, correlations with objective performance indictors, subordinates' evaluations of feedback and support), and (d) attaching consequences to the report results (e.g., pay increases or promotions for managers who are excellent developers of their people). These ingredients are summarized in Table 12.1.

Think about how accountability varies depending on the way a multisource feedback program is implemented. In traditional employee attitude surveys, managers may have a choice about whether to receive a special report based on analyses of only employees in their department. However,

TABLE 12.1
Structure for Rater and Ratee Accountability

Structure	Rater	Ratee
Duty/expectations	Accurate ratings and honest feedback	Use the feedback to set development goals
Preparation/support	Rater training, instructions on the purpose and use of ratings, role models	Coaching from an external or internal source
Reports of performance	Justification of the ratings, interrater agreement, correlations of ratings with objective indexes of performance, subordinate ratings of the value of feedback	Participation in development activities
Consequences	Positive evaluation as coach and developer of people incorporated into pay and promotion decisions	Performance improvement and resulting rewards

the managers have no obligation to use the information, and there is no follow-up to see if they did. In many applications of upward and 360-degree feedback, managers receive a feedback report. The raters are anonymous, the feedback is confidential, and the management provides no support or resources for using the feedback.

Ways to hold raters accountable can involve several different strategies, such as requiring them to report and explain the evaluation to their peers or higher level managers. Another involves training supervisors to understand the value of accurate ratings and clear feedback. Yet another is to survey subordinates' perceptions concerning the quality of the supervisor's evaluations and feedback. Items about these behaviors are likely to be included in upward feedback surveys. Supervisors who receive low ratings can be questioned, sent to training, or rewarded for excellent results. Another strategy is to make supervisors more sensitive to others' perceptions and feelings (Mitchell & Klimoski, 1984). For example, raters who anticipate having to give negative feedback in person to a subordinate tend to be more lenient than raters who remain anonymous (Fisher, 1979; Ilgen & Knowlton, 1980). However, having to provide feedback directly to the recipient increases the importance of the rating task (Klimoski & Inks, 1990). Raters who have to give negative feedback often delay the performance review discussion. When they do hold the discussion, they are very specific about what they say and provide clear justification for their views. However, sometimes raters who have to give negative feedback simply distort the information so that it is less threatening. If the rater knows that the recipient thinks highly of him or her, the rater may actually distort the information so that it conforms to what the rater thinks the recipient wants to hear (Larson, 1984). To guard against this, raters need to be sensitive to how their ratings might be affected by anticipating the subordinates' feelings.

Consider how people cope with accountability. This applies to raters held accountable for their ratings and recipients held accountable for using the feedback results (Tetlock, Skitka, & Boettger, 1989). People who know what those who hold them accountable expect are likely to conform to these expectations, a phenomenon called *social attitude shift*. People who do not know what others expect and who have no prior commitment to conform to others' expectations use more complex judgment processes, are more certain of their cognitive processes, and are more careful about basing their evaluations and actions on available information (Mero & Motowidlo, 1995). This is the phenomenon of *preemptive self-criticism* mentioned earlier. People who already have committed themselves to a particular viewpoint make judgments and take actions that conform to their viewpoints and develop rationalizations for their judgments and actions, a phenomenon is called *defensive bolstering*.

Multisource feedback programs have three key sources: the manager who is rated, the raters (peers, subordinates, the boss), and top managers. None of these sources wants to be accountable. Rather, they want the other sources to be accountable. The managers who are rated want confidential feedback (low accountability). Also, they prefer that the 360-degree feedback not be used for to make decisions about them. Raters do not want to be identified. They are more lenient when they anticipate giving feedback in person or when they have to identify themselves on the rating form. Top managers expect feedback recipients to use the results to change their behavior and improve their performance. However, management may not provide the support needed to help recipients interpret and use the results.

What then does the organization communicate when raters are guaranteed anonymity and recipients are guaranteed confidentiality? The organization may fear that the managers will punish raters who gave unfavorable ratings. Furthermore, the organization may be concerned that negative performance results will be used against recipients when the purpose of the feedback is to help the recipients improve. Also, an upward or 360-degree rating process may make raters feel that there is no need for honest and direct communication about performance issues. Thus, not holding raters and recipients accountable may be symptomatic of a distrustful or fearful environment.

When multisource feedback results are used for formal performance appraisal, recipients should be held accountable for using the information to improve. If they do not achieve a certain level of performance, or do not compare favorably with their peers, they may fail to receive a merit increase in pay or a promotion. However, the feedback report still is dropped on managers' desks in the hope that they will do something with it. Top management may or may not provide resources to support personal development. Raters are anonymous and not accountable for the quality of their ratings.

Sometimes multisource feedback is incorporated into a training program. Before attending the training, managers are asked to distribute questionnaires to their subordinates, peers, customers, and supervisor. These raters provide anonymous feedback. The managers receive confidential feedback during a 1-week training program that focuses on the skills being rated. For example, Monday may deal with training in conflict management, so on Monday morning participants receive their upward feedback about conflict management. Recipients are encouraged to share their development plan with the boss. Although rater accountability still is low, recipient accountability to use the feedback is increased. The accountability of top management is high in that the company is providing a developmental resource to go along with the rating program.

Perhaps the highest levels of rater, recipient, and management accountability occur when the multisource feedback report is supported by a facilitator or counselor who guides the manager through the process. Raters provide anonymous feedback. The feedback results are sent to a facilitator, who reviews the feedback and presents it to the target manager. Together, they formulate some initial reactions and plans. They set up a meeting attended by the facilitator, target manager, and raters. The target manager shares initial reactions and plans. Raters offer additional guidance and specific, constructive suggestions. The facilitator meets with the target manager 1 month, 3 months, 6 months, and 9 months after the target manager receives feedback to help formulate goals and action plans, share approaches others are using, and direct the target manager to appropriate resources.

Summary

Accountability applies to raters and recipients of feedback. As applied to raters, accountability refers to feeling responsible for making careful judgments that reflect the rater's views of the ratee's performance as accurately as possible. Raters who take this responsibility seriously may keep their own notes about their observations as critical incidents occur, then draw on these notes when asked to make ratings, write comments, or write an extensive performance evaluation. Admittedly, however, this is rare. Managers and employees generally respond to the rating task when it occurs, especially in the case of multisource feedback, which asks subordinates to rate supervisors and peers to rate each other. Supervisors should expect that they will be asked to evaluate their subordinates. They should take preparatory notes and keep documentation over time to support their judgments. Although these ratings are anonymous, raters, as committed team and organization members, should still feel responsible for providing ratings that are useful.

Recipients who take responsibility for using the feedback seriously may seek additional information; may ask for assistance from the raters, their supervisor, or a coach in interpreting the information; may incorporate the feedback into planning for their development; and may follow up by tracking changes in their behavior and, hopefully, improvement in their performance over time. The feedback process itself and associated support from the organization and supervisor in the form of coaching, training, and job assignments will help todrive home the value and importance of the feedback to raters and recipients.

TOWARD A THEORY OF ACCOUNTABILITY

Figure 12.1 outlines how accountability works. It depicts how forces of accountability drive being and feeling accountable. The term "actor" in the figure refers to either the rater or the recipient.

Components of the Model

The components of the model are (a) the objective (expected behavior or performance), (b) the characteristics of the actor (the person being held

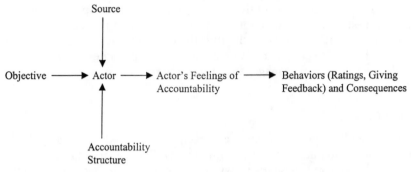

FIG. 12.1. A model of accountability processes.

accountable), (c) the sources of accountability (e.g., coworkers, the boss, organizational policies, or the actor him- or herself), (c) the accountability structure (internal or external accountability forces used by the sources to affect the actor's feelings of accountability, for example, internal forces such as the desire to gain recognition or avoid embarrassment, and external forces such as clear expectations, training, reports of performance such as accuracy of ratings, attention to feedback, and consequences), (d) the actor's feelings of accountability, and (e) the resulting behaviors and consequences.

The sources of accountability stem from oneself (in that people often hold themselves accountable for decisions and actions), others (e.g., one's boss), the social situation, norms, organizational policies, and task demands. The sources initiate, monitor, and enforce accountability. They influence the actor's feelings of obligation, and they impart implicit or explicit behavioral or material consequences.

The elements of the accountability structure are the reasons (essentially the power behind) why people feel accountable. Some elements of the structure are internal such as feelings of morality, efficacy, and self-control; the desire to gain approval and recognition (or avoid embarrassment); and the goal of meeting an obligation. Other elements are external, such as a valued outcome (e.g., money or job security). The structure may be implemented in different ways such as giving feedback; asking for, listening to, and accepting justification; having goals that are known to others; clearly attributing behavior (and not being able to diffuse responsibility or blame others); facing clear measurements and consequences; and dealing with few intervening variables or factors beyond one's control. Just as these are ways to hold people accountable, other mechanisms avoid accountability, such as scapegoating, procrastinating, and passing the buck.

Characteristics of the actor may influence the extent to which accountability forces successfully induce feelings of accountability. These may include achievement motivation, need for power or control, and need for affiliation or acceptance (McClelland, 1965). These needs increase the extent to which people are susceptible to holding themselves accountable or being held accountable by others.

Consider the sources of accountability:

- *Internal sources.* These may be the desire for feedback (knowledge of results) and the desire for positive outcomes brought on by the forces of self-regulation and the need for achievement, all regulated by internal self-control mechanisms. Facilitating factors include social norms that suggest the importance of others' views and meeting others' expectations.
- *Society.* People feel accountable to society. Norms and peer pressure are the social forces that encourage and reward the feeling of accountable to society. This feeling may be increased when comparative information is available about others' actions, and when there are strong, clear expectations for appropriate behavior.
- *The task itself.* Task requirements specify standards for evaluating oneself and others and setting goals for improvement. A moderately difficult task can create in an individual the sense of challenge and achievement for task fulfillment. This can be enhanced by specific measurements and a clear link between the individual's contribution and the task performance.
- *Interpersonal sources.* People want to be seen positively by others, and they are susceptible to others' views. They want to avoid embarrassment and maintain their pride. Therefore, face-to-face meetings, public displays of behavior, and announcements of outcomes are mechanisms that promote interpersonal accountability. These can be enhanced by task characteristics, mentioned earlier, that strengthen the relationships between individual behavior and task performance.
- *The organization.* People feel accountable to their employer. Forces include organizational rewards and punishments (e.g., employment security, pay increases) through the consistent application of performance appraisals and their implications for valued outcomes. This is encouraged when goals are clear, performance measures are objective, and, again, there are strong links between behavior and valued outcomes.

Applying the Model to Multisource Feedback

Consider the recipient as the actor. In one organization, the boss could be a source of accountability, and the recipient's desire for improved performance and financial rewards could be the accountability force. One accountability mechanism may be a requirement that the recipient share his or her development plan with the boss. Another might be an agreement with the boss to measure the extent of performance improvement by comparing the results from two consecutive administrations of multisource feedback 6 months apart. The behaviors and reactions may include the recipient's participation in a training program and persistence over time toward achieving performance goals.

Next, consider the rater as the actor. A source and associated mechanism of accountability could be coworkers' expectations that raters will provide candid, unbiased feedback. An internal accountability force may be the rater's desire to do what is right (i.e., provide fair ratings). An external accountability force may be negative outcomes controlled by the source (e.g., the work group does not respect raters whose face-to-face feedback to a recipient is different from anonymous feedback). An accountability mechanism may be the requirement or expectation that each rater will provide constructive comments during facilitated feedback sessions. The consequence of these accountability sources, forces, and mechanisms would be raters who provide candid, unbiased, fair, and accurate ratings as well as constructive feedback in person.

People manage their own accountability through motivation for high performance, sensitivity to the views of self and others, and a desire to conform to others' wishes. Self-ratings along with feedback from others allows self–other comparisons and improvement tracking. Facilitating factors include requiring that each person explain his or her own feedback to someone else (the supervisor or a counselor) and make commitments for improvement. Knowing that the survey is repeated over time also makes the results more pointed because there will be a chance to show improvement. Being confronted by data about their self-monitoring tendencies and sensitivity to others' views may influence recipients' receptivity to feedback.

Supervisors, subordinates, peers, and customers are interpersonal sources of accountability associated with multisource feedback. Supervisors enforce accountability through reward power and their ability or desire to control their work group members. Friendship also may motivate an employee's sense of accountability to the supervisor. Ways of increasing the extent to which the performance results are used include giving the supervisor access to the feedback results and the discretion to use them as a basis for salary bonuses and nonfinancial rewards. Another mechanism for accountability may occur when supervisors intentionally or unintentionally establish a tightly knit in-group of subordinates on whom they rely and have confidence. Such mechanisms of accountability can be facilitated by requiring that supervisors conduct performance review discussions with subordinates during which the multisource feedback is examined jointly. Training should be available to help supervisors conduct meaningful performance reviews. Also, organizational policies should evaluate and reward supervisors for developing subordinates.

Subordinates are a relevant source. Their ratings suggest the manager's obligation to the work group as a whole and to individual subordinates. The obligation of managers to their subordinates is based on mutual dependence and the desire for positive interpersonal relationships. These forces operate as subordinates cooperate with each other and with their supervisor to accomplish work group goals. This occurs through such mechanisms as subordinates' responsiveness to instructions and task demands, their effort, and ultimately their good performance. Also, subordinates can foster the manager's reputation as an excellent supervisor. Facilitating mechanisms include encouraging or requiring that the supervisor hold a group discussion with subordinates to review the results of upward or multisource feedback. In addition, the importance of subordinate ratings may be highlighted to the manager when the subordinates have a chance to participate in the development of the survey items. In this way, the items reflect what is important to subordinates. This is reinforced by top management's willingness to include these items in the survey.

Peers can be another source of obligation, and hence a valuable source of feedback. Employees value their friendship and viewpoints as role models and bases for comparison. The obligation of employees to their peers operates through mutual liking and engagement in social activities. Employees feel a greater sense of obligation to their peers when the peers show them respect and seek out their expertise. These mechanisms can be enhanced by the availability of normative multisource survey results showing how other employees were rated on the average. Teambuilding initiatives, such as joint participation in leadership development or conflict resolution workshops, may promote mutual support among peers, emphasize their obligation to each other, and increase the value of peer ratings.

Employees also are obligated to their internal and external customers, those who use the product of their efforts. Employees are dependent on customers for business, rewarded by them, and may develop friendships with them. This occurs through repeat business, an enhanced reputation for quality products or services, and involvement in social activities. Obligation to customers and the value of customer ratings can be enhanced when customers are involved in writing multisource feedback items, and when customers receive a report of the feedback results. In this way, customers become a direct part of the evaluation process, and knowledge of their opinions can foster improved customer relationships.

A multisource feedback program may be started by top management, the human resource department, or the members of the work group. In encouraging the process, the organization should promote a climate that supports development and continuous improvement. Thus, the process itself encourages an obligation for to provide accurate ratings and to apply the feedback. This is enhanced when the results are used for evaluative and administrative purposes (i.e., as criteria for promotion and pay decisions), and when the organization offers training programs and development opportunities linked to specific performance dimensions. In addition, raters and recipients will pay more attention to the rating process and results when the items are known to reflect organizational expectations. For instance, they may be based on a model of desired management behavior that guides selection, training,

appraisal, compensation, and outplacement policies. Also, the feedback results become more salient when the organization rewards continuous improvement and customer satisfaction, and when facilitators are available to
help employees interpret the feedback and incorporate it into development
plans.

This model of multiple accountability sources, forces, and mechanisms
makes several assumptions about how these components work together.
One assumption is that there are multiple ways to achieve the same end.
Different sources operate to drive feelings of accountability, and each may
affect the actor's behavior. One source is not, a priori, necessarily better than
another source. As a result, interventions to enhance accountability should
focus on accountability to the supervisor, to subordinates, to peers, to the
organization, and to oneself.

Another assumption is that different forces and associated mechanisms
are mutually reinforcing. They work together to enhance the salience of obligation to sources. Internal and external mechanisms may be important at the
same time. An additional assumption is that the actor may see functional
and dysfunctional outcomes resulting from the same accountability sources.
Therefore, for instance, having to share reactions to multisource feedback
with one's supervisor and justify them may raise the recipient's feelings of
accountability but increase the recipient's defensiveness, especially if he or
she feels that the ratings are in some ways inaccurate. Also, survey items may
focus attention on how work is done rather than the outcomes of performance. Accountability mechanisms in multisource feedback may be most
effective when they focus on means and ends (behaviors, process, and outcomes).

Using the Model to Enhance the Effectiveness of Multisource Feedback

In performance appraisal and multisource feedback, raters should be accountable to recipients to provide accurate meaningful information, and recipients should be accountable to raters, management, and themselves to use
the information. Multisource feedback can be made more valuable by establishing structures that reinforce accountability to oneself and others. These
interventions influence raters by holding them accountable for the accuracy
of their ratings, even if they do not identify them to the raters. Other interventions hold recipients accountable for using the results by requiring them
to justify, explain, or demonstrate how they benefited from the feedback.
We know, for instance, that managers respond positively to anonymous upward appraisals by improving their supervisory behaviors (Hegarty, 1974).
But they respond more positively when a consultant reviews the upward
performance ratings with them, encouraging them to use the information
to improve their performance (Nemeroff & Cosentino, 1979).

Consider facilitating mechanisms that apply to different sources in the multisource feedback process. Giving raters the results of personality tests that suggest their interpersonal sensitivity may increase their self-reflection. Asking raters to participate in designing performance appraisal items may increase their understanding of and commitment to multisource feedback.

For recipients, the frequency of self-assessment (e.g., regular surveys) may increase the salience of self-reflection. Asking recipients to make an explicit public commitment to use the feedback results for goal setting and performance improvement builds on the recipients' sense of integrity and desire to make a good impression. Such a commitment may be made during the course of a training session, in a meeting with a counselor or supervisor, or in a group discussion with subordinates. Work groups that spend time discussing their boss's feedback results increase subordinates' involvement in and commitment to the results. It should do the same for the managers who are the subject of the feedback. Incorporating peer ratings into teambuilding exercises and workshops enhances peer cooperation and learning from each other.

Recipients' accountability to use performance information also may be increased when the performance review session is conducted by the supervisor in a constructive manner (e.g., nonthreatening, behaviorally based). The availability of average ratings across work groups may increase accountability by highlighting comparisons and encouraging a discussion of standards. Training and rewarding supervisors' feedback and development behaviors support the importance of employee development in the organization and encourage employees to work seriously with the supervisor on learning from feedback.

CONCLUSION

Understanding how accountability develops and affects behavior suggests ways to enhance the value of feedback. Accountability structures may require the feedback recipient to explain and justify use of the feedback, may encourage employees to recognize the varying expectations of different sources, may foster expectation for raters to provide accurate and meaningful ratings, and may reward improved performance. Unfortunately, rating methods may not hold raters accountable for the accuracy of the information they provide or recipients accountable for using the feedback. The major conclusions from the chapter can be summarized as follows:

1. Increasing rater and recipient accountability improves the value of the information, enhances the recipient's sensitivity to the information, and increases the likelihood that the feedback will improve performance.

2. Accountability motivates the rater. People who feel accountable by having to justify their ratings to someone else generate more accurate ratings.
3. Accountability makes raters more susceptible to others' perceptions and feelings.
4. Accountability sources stem from the individual (e.g., the desire for feedback and positive outcomes), society, the task, other people, and how one is viewed by others and the organization (e.g., through performance expectations and rewards).
5. The value of multisource feedback can be enhanced by establishing structures that reinforce accountability to oneself and others (expectations, preparation/support, reports of performance, and consequences).
6. Multisource feedback can become part of the organization's management culture through interventions that support the use of the feedback.

The next chapter turns to reasons why feedback will continue to be an important part of successful management in the future.

IV

FUTURE DIRECTIONS

13

Feedback in Teams and Cross-Cultural Organizations

This section of the book focuses on new horizons and future directions. It discusses emerging areas for feedback because organizations are changing, doing work differently. This chapter is about feedback in teams and cross-cultural organizations. Both are important because of the increasing prevalence of teams as a means of getting work done and the increasing diversity of organizational members in expanding global enterprises. The next and final chapter describes how new technology has influenced feedback and development, and more generally, how work is changing and organizations are becoming feedback-oriented, continuous-learning environments.

Teams or groups (the terms are used interchangeably) involve people with diverse expertise and backgrounds bringing their knowledge, skills, and experience to bear on problems and projects. Often, team members work together in the same office, or can easily come together for periodic meetings, even if some travel is involved. The group members are sometimes separated by wide geographic distances, and modes of meeting and communicating other than meeting face-to-face and in person may be necessary. Examples include teleconferences, conference telephone calls, e-mail, Internet chat rooms, and combinations thereof. The teams may come together for short periods to accomplish specific, limited tasks, such as selecting a new CEO or designing a new data system. In other cases, the team may be responsible for an ongoing process or function, such as product advertisement or worldwide distribution of a product.

The complexity of these tasks requires that the team members work interdependently. The importance of these tasks requires that members share responsibility for the work and the accountability for meeting the organization's performance goals. Effective teams should have their own goals, criteria for success, and means of evaluation. Methods to facilitate team interaction in relation to these goals, the group process, and success tracking will enhance team performance and effectiveness.

Business is global. Many organizations have departments, subsidiaries, or partners around the world. This raises questions about whether there are cultural differences in the way people evaluate performance and give and receive feedback, and in the competencies people need to manage effectively across cultures. This is an area ripe for research to guide the development of performance management programs in global enterprises.

This chapter examines the issues and existing research results, offers a case study, and suggests directions for training to sensitize managers to cross-cultural differences and cultural biases that influence their judgments about people. The first part of this chapter examines feedback in different types of teams and in relation to changing group dynamics, focusing on the group and the individual within the group. It describes how group members develop a shared mental model that enhances cooperation and mutual trust. Ways of facilitating feedback in groups are suggested. The use of feedback in virtual teams (those with geographically dispersed members who communicate using a variety of communications media) and negotiating teams is discussed. The chapter then turns to research on the cultural effects of performance ratings in cross-cultural teams and organizations.

TYPES OF SPECIAL PROJECT GROUPS

In organizations, groups may be task forces, quality circles, or quality improvement teams. Such groups occur with increasing frequency in organizations (Hackman, 1990; Saavedra, Earley, & Van Dyne, 1993). The group becomes more productive as the members begin coordinating tasks and sharing information about themselves and others (Luft, 1970). Therefore, it is important to consider the effects of self and interpersonal insight on group interaction processes and performance. (For more information on this topic, see London, 1995a, chapter 7).

Consider how interpersonal feedback occurs in different types of work groups (Sundstrom, De Meuse, & Futrell, 1990). There are teams that give advice or provide an avenue for employee involvement (e.g., committees, review panels, and quality circles). There are teams that produce a product or service (e.g., assembly teams, flight attendant crews). Some teams work on a project (e.g., research groups, planning teams), whereas others engage in action or negotiation (e.g., sports teams, entertainment groups, expeditions, negotiation teams, surgery teams, and cockpit crews).

Teams that give advice, produce a product or service, or work on a project benefit from fluidity and loose coupling. Teams that engage in action and negotiation must perform as tightly coupled systems most of the time. Ensembles are groups that produce a particular effect or product (London & London, 1996). The members of ensembles are highly interdependent. Therefore, unrestricted, mutual feedback from everyone on the team, leaders and members alike, is particularly important to the development of the ensemble as a tightly coupled system (Gersick & Hackman, 1990). The product of the ensemble has a distinctive quality or synergism beyond any one of the individual members. Having highly expert ensemble members does not mean that the ensemble's performance will necessarily be excellent. Although coupling is a function that derives from the nature of the work, the members must work at achieving a tightly coupled system.

GROUP DYNAMICS AND THE USE OF FEEDBACK

In general, there are several key uses for feedback in a team (Hallam, 2001). Feedback can to identify team development needs and help the organization to identify teams that need help, such as teams that are floundering and not getting tasks done. This information, in turn, can be used to channel limited resources (e.g., for training) to teams that can benefit the most. Feedback can be an occasion to increase member involvement and control over team outcomes by asking the team members to analyze their own feedback data and prioritize areas for improvement. Having to face concrete feedback and support from a facilitator encourages the group to deal with problems directly rather than ignore them or blame them on outside forces. The organization must be used to collecting and using feedback (e.g., survey feedback surveys with results aggregated at the team level). Also, the organization must support team building by, for instance, providing team process consultants or training team leaders.

Group task demands and interaction patterns among group members mean that members must respond to stimuli from multiple sources. People generally have a common understanding about appropriate group behavior, the essence of a group norm (Gersick, 1988, 1989). This is a basis for the development of habitual behavior patterns. In fact, different groups have similar patterns of behavior. Groups develop these interaction patterns early in their "lives," and they maintain these patterns even after the situation changes. For example, one study found that groups in which a tight time deadline was assigned early in their limited existence maintained a fast rate but with low quality and with an interaction pattern that was highly task focused (Kelly & McGrath, 1985). The pattern continued into later trials although the groups no longer had the tight time deadline. Conversely, groups that began working against a less stringent time deadline worked at a slower rate but with higher quality and with an interaction pattern that was more interpersonally focused. This pattern continued in later trials despite shorter time deadlines. Under task conditions for which early trials yielded an experience of qualitative difficulty, groups tended to slow down in later trials, and may thereby have increased the quality of their work.

Group members can give each other feedback that helps them understand the emerging behavioral patterns. Also, newcomers to the group may receive feedback quickly. This helps them understand how to be an effective group member in relation to other members' roles and abilities. Through various means of socialization and social control, group members convey their expectations for the new member.

Feedback can be important to group process and performance, just as it is to individuals. Groups that receive feedback on their task achievement or interpersonal behaviors that do not match an ideal are more likely to change their behavior and improve group performance, whereas groups that do not receive feedback are not as likely to change their behavior and improve performance (McLeod, Liker, & Lobel, 1992). Whether feedback leads to performance improvement will depend on many factors, including the group members' defensiveness and willingness to accept the feedback.

Group feedback is a potentially threatening experience for the supervisor or facilitator responsible to give the feedback and for the group members. After all, the supervisor or facilitator providing the feedback has to look all group members in the eye. (This is not the case when the feedback is an impersonal computer printout of data.) The group members hear the same thing, and later will compare their views of the feedback. As such, the supervisor is on the spot publicly. In this case, the supervisor should focus on providing information about group performance, not each individual member's performance. This works well when there is group-level information (e.g., the total number of units produced by the group or the projects completed). It also works well when the group members are interdependent and the group's output is a function of a team effort.

Process feedback focuses on elements of how the group members interact with each other (Wells, 1992). Consider three major elements of group process based on interaction process analysis (Bales, 1950, 1988). The first is *dominancy*, the amount of group members' talkativeness, leadership, and influence at one extreme, and submissiveness, quietness, and obedience, at the other. Large differences between the most and least dominant people in groups should be detrimental to group process and task performance (McLeod et al., 1992). The second element of group process is *friendliness*, the amount of cooperation and loyalty at one extreme, and withdrawal and antagonism at the other. Behaviors should be primarily group oriented and friendly as opposed to individually oriented and unfriendly. The final element of group process is *expressiveness*, the amount of joking, nurturing, and affection at one end of the continuum, and emotional control, task-orientedness, and attention to rules at the other end. Groups should have a reasonable balance of task-oriented and socioemotional behaviors, although task-oriented behaviors should dominate.

One study had teams of observers make systematic ratings of each group member's behavior on these three performance dimensions (McLeod et al., 1992). The groups received the observers' ratings of group process along each dimension with a set of norms against which to compare their results (e.g., for dominance: "Group discussions should not be dominated by one or two people. There should not be more than an 8-point difference be-tween the most dominant and the most submissive group members"). Each group member knew his or her own score on each dimension. After the feedback, the groups had time to discuss their process feedback and deter-mine how they could improve during a subsequent task. The researchers found that small behavior changes could be manipulated using the feedback and information about ideal ratings on process dimensions compared with those of groups receiving only task performance feedback followed by an unstructured discussion.

Reacting to this study, other researchers suggested that stronger effects might occur by concentrating on specific goals given to the group as a whole and on each members' personal goals (Locke & Latham, 1992). Specific goals should be assigned rather than merely ideal ranges. Groups assigned difficult goals perform better than those assigned moderate or general ("do your best") goals (Whitney, 1994). The group's overall goals and each mem-ber's goals (and commitment to these goals) could actually be measured to be sure the goals were internalized before group performance. Group members' perceptions of the group's ability to do the task (induced by pro-viding the group with norms of excellent performance before the task is performed) also enhances performance. Furthermore, group feedback may be differentially relevant to group members depending on their results. Thus, for instance, only members at the extremes on dominance would need to act differently to change the distribution of dominance behavior in the group. However, the group process discussion about dominance differences gives everyone a chance to participate and influence the most and least dominant members.

Public feedback in teams can have a positive effect on team members' learning goals and the regulatory responses (e.g., group member's confidence in the team's ability to accomplish its goals) and ultimately performance. Kozlowski, DeShon, Schmidt, and Chambers (2002) studied 131 teams of three college students each engaged in a simulation. Team members who received public feedback were more likely to indicate that they wanted to learn for the sake of mastery (e.g., to acquire knowledge and improve their skills). This, in turn, was positively related to positive regulatory processes and performance outcomes for the team.

In summary, feedback can be as important to team functioning as it is to individual performance. Information about group performance can identify team development needs and assist the company in pinpointing teams that need facilitation or leadership. Feedback in groups comes from a supervisor, the team leader, or group members. Process feedback refers to information about how the team is functioning, for instance, how well members are interacting with each other, whereas task feedback refers to the work that gets done and the outcomes produced. Attention should be given to how process feedback is used. Members should be asked whether they found feedback to be valuable. The interplay between the effects of feedback on individuals and on the group should be considered. For instance, positive feedback to one team member in front of others may disrupt group identity.

TEAM DEVELOPMENT OF SHARED MENTAL MODELS

Fiore, Salas, and Cannon-Bowers (2001) argued that team effectiveness is a function of team members developing a shared understanding or mental model of expectations about team members' abilities and behaviors, common knowledge, and mutual interpretations of events. This requires group members to know each other well and to communicate their expectations, observations, and intentions. They may do this explicitly or implicitly as the group progresses. The overlap between team members' expectations is positively related to the speed with which group norms affecting performance develop (Gersick, 1988). In effective teams, members share a set of knowledge that facilitates interaction. According to Fiore et al. (2001), this knowledge set includes a shared understanding of the teammates' roles, a shared understanding of the team task and required interactions, and a shared understanding of the potential situations they may encounter. These shared understandings help the team members to coordinate their behavior explicitly or implicitly in response to situational demands. Implicit coordination refers to coordination without explicit communication that articulates plans and behavioral routines. Explicit coordination involves direct communication among team members about their interactions and performance. The more team members have worked together and are familiar with each others' common modes of behavior, the less they may need to communicate explicitly. However, when the need arises, they will be willing to ask for and accept assistance and performance feedback (Smith-Jentsch, Campbell, Milanovich, & Reynolds, 2001).

Feedback is the flow of the information that affects a mental model's speed of development and the extent to which the contents are accurately shared. When a team is first formed, coordination is affected by the prior experience of the members, the nature of the task, and the perceived demands for interaction. This is the start of a shared mental model. Feedback is the mediating process for forming mental models. If perceptions are accurate, the team is likely to make progress quickly. If perceptions are inaccurate, the team may spend time in early meetings sharing ideas and expectations and developing a shared understanding of the task and each other's capabilities. Alternatively, the team may forge ahead without forming a shared understanding, and the result may be frustration, disappointment, and wasted time. Therefore, unless team members know each other well at the outset, sharing information will be important to members remaining in the team and to the team's effectiveness. When team members do not know each other well, they need to be highly sensitive to the responses of each other, for instance, the extent to which they are agreeable or disagreeable or their degree of knowledge and skill.

The team members need to be motivated to care about each other and to send messages that they all can understand. This is more likely when team members are aware of each other's level of knowledge, which would be likely if they received the same training together or had a chance to talk about the team's goals. Moreover, information transmission must be accurate and accepted. The team members must trust each other to provide meaningful feedback untainted by ulterior motives or individual agendas. Inaccurate information will prevent coordination (Fiore et al., 2001; Hardin & Higgins, 1996). This is likely if there is a low level of trust, disagreement about the team's purpose and goals (e.g., what has to be done by when), or misunderstandings about the level of each team member's knowledge and skills.

In summary, teams develop a shared mental model of expectations about team members' abilities and behaviors, shared knowledge, and shared interpretations of events. This shared model helps the team to function effectively. Group members get to know each other well, communicating their expectations, observations, and intentions. Early in the team's formation, the members' prior experiences and the structure and demands of the task influence the degree of coordination and initiate the shared mental model. The team is more likely to do well from the start if the group members have had common experiences that lead them to share expectations. If not, the members may quickly hit roadblocks, such as a lack of communication or the emergence of conflicts, because they do not share common expectations or have different goals, and because they do not raise these differences. A facilitator can assist the group in communicating issues that affect the group process and help the team members establish common understanding and expectations for behaviors and goals that become a shared mental model and that establish mutual trust. (I say more about group facilitation later in the chapter.)

COLLECTING FEEDBACK DATA IN GROUPS

Unlike individual performance, the performance of the group may refer to issues of process, such as cooperation and conflict resolution or to outcomes or achievements, such as the quality of the team's products and the speed of production. Feedback for groups may focus on a team's process, development, or achievement. There are several ways to collect and deliver team performance data. Supervisors can evaluate their team as a whole and provide the group with periodic feedback about how the group operates as a team. The supervisor must take care to address team behavior and deal with individual members' performance in one-on-one private meetings with each member. Special performance surveys can be used to gather data from key observers, constituents, or customers about the operation and effectiveness of the team as a whole. Performance surveys (e.g., multisource surveys) may be used to collect data on each member individually. The group members then can discuss the average and variation (range from low to high score) for each performance item or dimension. Although this average does not nec-essarily reflect the performance of the group as a whole, it provides useful information for team discussion and development.

Data about a team's general effectiveness and working relationships can lead to group discussions about the group's strengths and weaknesses and areas for improvement. As a consequence, the team may participate in de-velopmental or team-building activities, such as experiential training, to understand the value of effective teamwork and how it can improve, for instance, ways to open lines of communication, face problems, and teach team members about collaboration (Hallam, 2001). In general, feedback data can help the team commission training that is customized to the team's needs. The feedback also can help the team members prepare for the train-ing, for instance, in recognizing why it is needed and being open to learn-ing.

Use of Multisource Surveys in Teams

Multisource surveys can be used by teams to assess team-level strengths and weaknesses (Hallam, 2001). Survey items can ask whether the team has the right mix of skills, manages conflict well, and meets objectives. The survey also can ask about the team leader (e.g., about the clarity of the leader's goals and directives). Customers, coworkers, and supervisors can complete the survey. Team members can rate the leader, and the leader can rate the team as a whole as well as the individual members in the team.

Summary

There are several ways to collect and deliver team performance data. Multi-source feedback surveys, with ratings from team members, supervisors of the team members, and the client or clients of the team, can evaluate strengths and weaknesses of the team. In addition, a survey can ask questions about whether the team has the right mix of skills, resolves conflicts, has clear goals, and meets objectives. The data can be averaged within different rater sources (e.g., all team members, all customers, all supervisors), and the team can discuss the results, perhaps with the assistance of a facilitator. Users of the team output can evaluate the output's quality and timeliness. Team members, the supervisor, or a process facilitator who directly observes the team in action can evaluate the team process to determine, for example, whether time is wasted on side-bar issues that detract from the task at hand, perhaps because of poor communication or disagreements about leadership or scheduling.

FACILITATING TEAM FEEDBACK

There are several ways to help ensure that the team uses the feedback constructively (Hallam, 2001). The facilitator may work with the leader individually to present the results and to suggest different behaviors the leader can try to help the team members work together better. This could be very helpful if the results show that the leader is a cause of the team's problems. Alternatively, the facilitator may work with the team as a whole by leading a discussion about the results, the reasons for them, and what the team can do about them. Note that the facilitator may be a professional in the field of organization development called in by the leader or a top executive to work with the team. In the absence of a professional facilitator, the team leader or even a team member may assume the facilitator's role, taking responsibility for designing a method to review and interpret the results with the group members, and for leading a joint effort to design a plan for development and improvement. When team leaders take on this role, they must be willing to acknowledge their own shortcomings to the team and to create conditions that allow participation without fear of retaliation.

Feedback is likely to work best when the issues addressed are within the control of the team members. On the one hand, if the problems arise from other organizational issues (e.g., lack of timely or accurate data or lack of cooperation from other parts of the company), then the team members are likely to be frustrated. On the other hand, if the problems arise from issues about which the team members can do something, and they are going to remain together long enough to make the required changes, they are likely to feel ready to try different courses of action that will make a difference. Moreover, they are likely to develop a shared commitment to become a better team (Hallam, 2001).

The Tendency for Groups to Overevaluate Their Performance

Jourden and Heath (1996) and Heath and Jourden (1997) discovered that group members develop a "positive illusion" about their group's performance, estimating that their group's performance is above the 50th percentile. There are several reasons why members of a group may overevaluate the performance of their team. Members may encourage each other when the group seems to be doing poorly, affirming each other's value and giving each other helpful suggestions. As the group's task progresses, they may convey to each other how much they are learning together.

Ross and Allen (2002) studied the relation between the extent to which group members report this type of information exchange and postperformance evaluations of the group's performance. The subjects were 55 undergraduate psychology students randomly assigned to 1 of 11 three-member groups or 5 four-member groups to work on a model bridge-building task. Before the task, the members ranked how well they expected their group to perform on the task relative to a hypothetical set of 10 other randomly selected groups. After the task, they ranked their group's actual performance on the same measure. They also completed a 14-item measure of the degree to which they experienced information exchange behaviors in their group (e.g., "The group made me feel as if my ideas made sense" and "We gave each other constructive feedback on our ideas"). The items were averaged to form a reliable information exchange measure. The measure of information exchange was positively correlated ($r = .37$, $p < .01$) with the postperformance ranking after a control had been used for the preperformance ranking. The results indicate that group members who perceive more information exchange are likely to rank their group's performance higher than those who perceive less information exchange.

Group Goal Setting

A team should establish group goals for each performance period. The group should discuss potential goals, and the supervisor should facilitate the goal setting in relation to organization-wide objectives. The goals should be challenging, neither impossible nor too easy. The members' involvement in formulating the group's goals should enhance their commitment to the goals. Members' public declaration of willingness to work on the goals and achieve them should enhance their feeling of obligation to accomplish them.

If group goals are set and group performance is reviewed, it stands to reason that there should be a group reward. As with individual performance review, the group award should be discussed and distributed some time after (preferably soon after) the group performance review. The tie between performance achieved as a group and the reward should be explicit. Also, a policy should be established for how the group reward is to be distributed.

Assuming that supervisors have discretion in compensation policy, some supervisors may agree at the time group goals are established to split a monetary award equally among all group members. Other supervisors may say they will split the group award according to each team member's contribution. Team members may be asked to rate each other's contribution as a basis for the distribution. Such a policy has the potential to destroy group unity, and an equal distribution probably is the most equitable. Keep in mind that group performance review and reward should be coupled with individual performance review and reward. As such, the supervisor can recognize outstanding individual performance and reward it accordingly after appropriate review. Such review may include collecting information from coworkers (e.g., as part of a multisource rating system, as discussed in chapter 4).

Individual Feedback in Groups

The group setting also can be valuable for giving feedback to individuals if it is done with careful facilitation. This is common after business simulations in management development programs.

For example, take an appraisal session that stems from a team-building process and feeds back peer ratings on a behavioral observation scale initially outlined by Locke & Latham (1990). Job analyses are conducted and behavioral observation scales constructed. Hence, the behaviors rated reflect specific job behaviors and requirements. Also, the scales are developed by employees for employees, so the raters and ratees understand the items as critical job behaviors. Another advantage of the process is that the behavioral scales remind raters about what behaviors are important to consider in providing their ratings. Open-ended questions ask what the ratee should continue doing on the job and what the person should start doing, stop doing, or do differently. Group sessions then are held. Each person's appraisal is given in a 1- to 2-hour period. A psychologist or a person skilled in group process facilitates the feedback by first asking the individual if he or she has any questions regarding his or her colleagues' evaluations. Colleagues are requested to offer comments regarding the evaluations. Peers are coached by the facilitator on how to emphasize what the person is to do differently in the future. The person assessed is then asked to summarize what was "heard" and to set specific goals as to what he or she will do differently as a result of this feedback. Subsequent discussion focuses on another individual in the group until every person has received feedback and has set goals.

Summary

A facilitator can help the group to focus on certain feedback, particularly areas about which the group can do something. Also, the facilitator can help the team leader to determine strategies that will help the group stay on track. Facilitators or team leaders serving in the role of facilitator can help group members accurately to calibrate the performance of the group, avoiding the tendency to believe the group is better than other groups. They also can help the group to set goals and conduct discussions of individual members' behavior in the group and contribution to group goals.

FEEDBACK IN VIRTUAL TEAMS

Many organizations do much of their business in team environments. This is because complex work distributed across regions, often across the country or across the globe, requires input from different disciplines and functions. The advent of new communications technologies, such as wireless telephone, e-mail, and Internet connections, has allowed people to work in virtual or geographically distributed teams. These teams may rarely, if ever, meet face-to-face. Members interact with each other in real time (synchronously) or at different times (asynchronously). Avolio, Kahai, Dumdum, and Sivasubramaniam (2001) recognized that the shift toward using virtual teams in organizations raises several fundamental questions, such as how do interpersonal perceptions evolve; how does trust develop; and how are leaders perceived by team members? More particularly, how do leaders of virtual teams learn about and develop their members' needs, show consideration, inspire, create innovative thinking, and act as role models for team members? The virtual team, similarly to the face-to-face team, has to establish norms of interacting, agree to a mission, appreciate each member's capabilities, share feelings, develop mutual trust, and gain a sense of cohesiveness. Members of a virtual team have less opportunity to interact face-to-face, so group development becomes a significant challenge. However, because virtual teams typically have much less opportunity to interact with each other face-to-face, developing a high performing team becomes a significant challenge.

Virtual teams face substantial problems (Avolio et al., 2001). Because they cannot take advantage of social and nonverbal cues, developing deep interpersonal relationships among team members takes substantially longer if it occurs at all. Team members have trouble establishing a common image in their mind of what is required of them, their roles, and how they must work together to accomplish the team's mission. They have trouble developing the interpersonal perceptions that are the foundation for building trust.

Elements of transactional and transformational leadership can help virtual teams to develop norms and expectations to guide their future interactions (Avolio et al., 2001). For example, transactional leaders clarify acceptable and unacceptable team behaviors, specify the team's goals, and provide feedback. By setting goals and rewards for accomplishing them, transactional leaders motivate the team members to achieve agreed-upon levels of performance. The leader and group members share information with each other about their task objectives, about who is responsible for what, and about who deserves recognition. This contributes to members' initial sense of conditional trust.

In contrast, transformational leaders develop unconditional trust by augmenting transactional leadership. The transformational leader instills confidence among team members about their ability to work together to overcome challenges and accomplish team goals. They communicate messages and feedback that convey how team members can go beyond their own self-interests for the sake of the team. Every member is encouraged to contribute to the team's goals, and feedback focuses on the extent to which this is happening.

Feedback in virtual teams is another means of developing mutual trust. The richness of media in collaborative technologies (list-serves, chatrooms, electron bulletin boards, instant messaging, and simple e-mail and conference calls, including teleconferencing) allows for immediate feedback to individuals and to all team members in a variety of ways. Using a variety of cues and channels in the media-rich environment provides ways for the leader and group members to personalize their communications with each other and to have in-depth interactions. The result is a perception of mutual ability, benevolence, and integrity among team members. Avolio et al. (2001) hypothesized that the formation of trust is hindered when media richness is low and facilitated when it is high. However, for early interactions, lean media may help members categorize each other more quickly and understand each team member's potential contribution to the group without the stereotypes from gender, race, or other factors that get in the way in face-to-face groups. As such, initially low media richness may help to prevent stereotypes from getting in the way of group interaction. The group can focus on task-relevant feedback and establish an initial sense of conditional trust. As richer communications media are used and the group develops, unconditional trust will emerge. Avolio et al. (2001) emphasized that these hypotheses are as yet untested. Research is needed to link media richness with virtual team interactions and interpersonal perceptions. Also, research is needed to examine the effects of leadership style (e.g., transactional and transformational), team composition, and media richness on members' communication patterns and the productivity of virtual teams.

In summary, given advancing communications and computer technologies, virtual teams are increasingly prevalent in organizations. They provide a means of using talent regardless where people are located. Early in the team's history, the virtual team can benefit from using just one or two media channels. Simple media and clear communication can help team members categorize each other more quickly, understand each team member's potential contribution to the group, and provide feedback without the stereotypes getting in the way. As trust develops, richer media can be beneficial in promoting the group's development and productivity.

THE ROLE OF FEEDBACK IN NEGOTIATION PROCESSES

The goal in groups is to cooperate in a way that will generate an effective product. Consider another type of interaction in which individuals or groups are attempting to resolve conflict with one or more other individuals or groups. (This section was adapted from London, 1995a, chapter 8). Negotiation or bargaining sessions are good examples. During negotiation sessions, opposing parties gather information to test the viability or acceptability of their own positions. Good scenario planning, trial runs, and feedback become mechanisms for making good decisions in negotiations (Neale & Bazerman, 1991). Negotiators use feedback to adjust their behavior and offers. But this feedback is not likely to be straightforward. More likely, it is biased or ambiguous. Opposing parties do not readily reveal their strategies and reactions to others. They may even try to mislead the opposing negotiator. Also, negotiators are likely to be biased in how they perceive the opposing party's reactions. Even experienced negotiators may misjudge cues from the opposing party.

In traditional positional bargaining, good feedback between groups is avoided. One group does not want to divulge what it has learned. Therefore, negotiators do not exchange information about their interests during the negotiation process (Thompson, 1991). However, feedback is important to avoid faulty judgments in conflict and negotiation situations (Thompson & Hastie, 1990). Feedback has a self-correcting function that allows negotiators to compare their current strategy with a more favorable ideal (Thompson & DeHarpport, 1994). Outcome feedback is knowledge of the results from a decision, whereas cognitive feedback is information about relations in the environment, such as information about the task as well as one's own and others' thought processes (e.g., weights people give to different dimensions of possible outcomes) (Balzer, Doherty, & O'Connor, 1989).

Good feedback is important in principled negotiations wherein negotiators have a common understanding that they can (and want to) reach a win-win settlement. This requires an understanding of the interests of one's opponent. Feedback may come from experience. However, it may help to have information about the opponent. To test this, Thompson and DeHarpport (1994) compared negotiators who were given information about their opponents (such as they may have gained in a principled negotiation) with those who did not have this information (a typical positional negotiation). After an initial negotiation, the negotiators in the cognitive feedback condition were given information about their opponent's payoff schedule for different possible outcomes, whereas the other negotiators were given only information about the payoff resulting from the negotiation. The negotiators who received the cognitive and outcome feedback made more accurate judgments about their opponent's interests, and subsequently negotiated outcomes that were better for both parties. The feedback allowed the negotiators to develop an effective strategic conceptualization of the negotiations. This suggests the value of building such feedback into ongoing, principled negotiations such that both parties are briefed about the emerging interests of each other, perhaps by an independent mediator or a consultants hired separately by each side.

Before negotiation, members of each party's bargaining team often consult with each other and plan effective strategies. After a bargaining session, they are likely to give each other feedback, processing their perceptions of the opposing team's reactions (Ury, Brett, & Goldberg, 1988). They may also discuss the negotiation process with the opposing team. Although this may be unlikely, it would be a chance to raise points of misunderstanding and clarify points of difference between opposing parties. Establishing a regular forum for discussion so opposing parties can consider issues arising in disputes that cut across other aspects of relationships between the parties is a good idea. An example would be the union and management representatives meeting together regularly in "common interest forums" (London, 1988).

In summary, feedback is a contributor to better performing teams. Members give each other advice before the negotiations begin and feedback afterward, thereby sharpening their perceptions of the opposing team. Discussions with the opposition may clarify points of differences and identify commonalities that may foster faster agreements and higher gains for both parties than might have occurred without these discussions.

I now expand this discussion to examine cultural influences on performance judgments in cross-cultural teams and organizations.

PERFORMANCE APPRAISAL IN MULTINATIONAL COMPANIES

Berson, Erez, and Adler (2002) discussed the importance of performance appraisal in multinational companies. Performance appraisal is a way that organizations tie their strategies and goals to individual goals, actions, and rewards. In a multinational company, a common performance appraisal process communicates the key performance dimensions across units of the company. This should be of value in helping teams and individuals recognize common objectives, which in turn should facilitate collaboration within and between organizational units (Evans, Pucik, & Barsoux, 2002; Galunic & Eisenhardt, 2001).

Berson et al. (2002) indicated that whereas there generally are two major leadership competencies, task and employee orientation, managers in multinational companies need to have competencies that allow them to be independent and entrepreneurial, taking advantage of local business opportunities instead of being guided solely by corporate planners who are removed from the marketplace (Bartlett & Ghoshal, 1997). They also need competencies that allow them to develop interdependent connections with other subsidiaries and headquarters. They need to focus on the task, establish effective interpersonal relationships, and build trust. Furthermore, Berson et al. (2002) suggested that multisource feedback can be valuable to expatriates in multinational companies who are not familiar with their host culture. The feedback can help them understand the expectations of the different feedback sources and be more realistic in setting performance goals.

Of course, the acceptance of feedback may be influenced by cultural differences (e.g., "face" and hesitation about saying negatives about people in far Eastern cultures). Multisource feedback captures the high complexity of the global work environment, and this may help managers adapt to their new environment. Although to some extent multinational subsidiaries adapt to the culture of the company's headquarters, establishing a common corporate culture across the multinational organization, there is also the possibility that differences in cultural values may affect the importance of performance dimensions. As a result, some dimensions of performance may be more important in one national culture than another.

Berson et al. (2002) examined the structure of leadership dimensions of managers in multinational cultures, testing for similarities and differences in the performance dimensions across cultures. They collected 360-degree feedback data from 23 sites of a single high-tech organization over a period of 2 years. The performance survey included 31 items. Self, subordinate, peer, customer, and supervisor ratings were obtained for 408 midlevel managers. Factor analysis of the items across all ratings showed four dimensions of performance: task-oriented leadership, people-oriented leadership, strategy development and planning, and change and innovation management.

Next, Berson et al. (2002) examined differences in the favorability of the ratings of the factors between managers in different countries. Task-focused leadership did not vary between countries, perhaps because of the individualism of Western cultures and the high uncertainty avoidance of Eastern cultures (Hofstede, 2001). Managers in the United States were significantly higher than managers in other countries in people-focused leadership. Berson et al. (2002) interpreted this as a result of the high power equalization that typifies management in the United States. Managers in Far Eastern countries were higher than Anglo, Nordic, Latin, and U.S. managers in strategic planning (a dimension that would be important to global strategy). The reason for this may be that Far Eastern countries emphasize the development of new markets (Hofstede, 2001). Also, managers from the United States and Far Eastern countries were significantly higher in the change and innovation dimension than managers from other countries, perhaps because of the competitive spirit in the United States and the need to harmonize and adjust in the Far East. In addition, Berson et al. (2002) found that managers from countries characterized as individualistic, particularly the United States, tended to rate themselves higher than other sources rated them.

Gillespie (2002) took a further step in analyzing cultural factors affecting ratings. She reasoned that examining mean differences in performance ratings across cultures is not sufficient for examining the effects of culture. Managers from different cultures may perceive performance-related behaviors and traits differently, and as a result, the relations among the items and the factors underlying these relations may differ between cultures. This would call into question the ease of "internationalizing" a rating instrument, even when the translations are done carefully to ensure common understanding of the items. (This translation process usually entails translating the items to another language and then translating them back to the original. After several iterations of translation and back-translation by different linguists, equivalence can be determined. This can be a painstaking process, especially when the survey is translated into several different languages.) Without examining the equivalence of factor structure across cultures, mean differences may result in misguided or inaccurate conclusions because the items mean different things in different cultures. This may occur when people from different cultures use different categories of thinking or different constructs to define and interpret behavior (Hofstede, 2001).

Gillespie (2002) obtained subordinate performance ratings for managers in a United States–based transportation company. The managers were Americans working in U.S. operations as well as in-country nationals working in corporate offices in Great Britain, Hong Kong, and Japan. In terms of cultural values, the United States and Great Britain are higher in individualism and lower in power distance than Hong Kong and Japan. Although data were available for thousands of mangers, there were large differences in the numbers of managers between the different locations. As a result, Gillespie (2002) randomly selected 214 direct report surveys for 214 different managers. Ratings on 40 behavioral items were factor analyzed across the sample, resulting in two major leadership dimensions that reflected task and interpersonal orientation. However, this factor structure was not equivalent across cultures.

The inability to demonstrate a consistent factor structure calls into question the ability to ignore cultural differences in reporting performance results. Although different results might be obtained if other rater sources were used (and this is an area for future research), organizations should not assume that country culture is irrelevant. At the very least, within-country norms (e.g., mean levels of performance on items) should be presented to the managers to help them interpret their results (Gillespie, 2002). Feedback workshops should discuss cultural factors that may influence the results. Also, country differences should be considered in an understanding of performance results across the company and the need for training.

Some companies may wish to implement a communications campaign across subsidiaries to develop a common understanding of performance dimensions. Other companies may wish to recognize these differences and determine how they can be advantageous to the firm instead of training to eliminate them. Thus, for instance, a company may select and train managers for transfer on the cultural differences so they can adapt and develop effective working relationships more quickly. Also, understanding these differences will help managers work with other firms (partners and customers) within the culture. It also will facilitate collaboration in joint ventures between cultures.

Cultural Differences in Self-Evaluations

Although leniency in self-ratings is common, it is not universal. However, this may stem from a bias in favor of individualism in Western culture and in other societies. For instance, a study of Taiwanese workers found a "modesty bias" in self-ratings such that self-ratings were lower than ratings obtained from supervisors (Farh, Dobbins, & Cheng, 1991). This may be attributable to a collectivism bias coupled with high deference to authority in the Taiwanese culture. However, a study of blue collar workers in Nanjing, China (the People's Republic) found a leniency bias in self-ratings, as compared with peer and supervisor ratings (Yu & Murphy, 1993). This suggests that culture is not homogeneous and may be differentiated by many factors (country, industry, mode of operations and organization, and so forth). The findings suggest that self–other differences in perceptions may be influenced by cultural factors, and that such factors should be examined and taken into account when results are interpreted. This is especially important given the increasing diversity of employees' backgrounds within global and domestic organizations.

CROSS-CULTURAL TRAINING

Multinational firms must prepare managers to operate effectively in other cultures. As might be expected, cultural insensitivity leads to failure of expatriates. Cultural awareness helps people to recognize their own values, analyze contrasts with other cultures, and apply the insights gained to improved interpersonal effectiveness. Cross-cultural training may apply a number of different methods (Park & Harrison, 1993). For instance, the training may describe the target culture through lectures, readings, videos, and other media. Simulations and role plays may be used to give managers practice functioning in the new culture. Self-assessments may be used to build self-awareness, increasing managers' understanding and acceptance of themselves, thereby giving them greater ability to adjust in another culture.

A popular method of cultural awareness training uses role-playing encounters between a U.S. citizen and a person from another culture with contrasting values (Harris & Moran, 1987). This method highlights awareness of differences, but not necessarily skills for enhancing sensitivity.

Performance of people in new cultures is an increasingly important and exciting area for performance diagnosis and improvement. Cultural factors need to be incorporated into performance review programs. Human resource practitioners will need to assess the extent to which culture influences the introduction, use, and effectiveness of different review methods (e.g., the viability of self-assessment in paternalistic cultures). Also, cultural factors will need to be incorporated into performance competencies and standards (i.e., to evaluate the extent to which expatriates are successful in developing cross-cultural business relationships).

FEEDBACK IN A GLOBAL COMPANY: A CASE STUDY

The following case describes Astro International. (Details of the firm are disguised to maintain its anonymity.) The company manufactures and distributes wireless Internet communications equipment such as handheld 3- by 5-inch video screens for paging, e-mail, Internet search, and telephone. They also operate wireless networks throughout the world. Astro has a manufacturing division, a marketing and sales arm with equipment sales and service through third-party vendors and direct sales to corporate clients, a service division, a consultation division (for Web design), and a large research and development division. In addition, the company is starting a new video-on-demand and television satellite-like program distribution division. Astro employs 50,000 people worldwide, and the firm is growing by 15% to 25% in personnel per year. It is headquartered in Melbourne Australia and has manufacturing in Thailand and India, programmers in India and Israel, billing and computer processing operations in Ireland and Australia, sales offices in Great Britain, Spain, France, the United States Israel, Japan, and Equador, and research and development in Australia and India. Given this rapid growth, the company needs to develop a large cadre of managers who can assume leadership positions quickly.

Astro's human resources department administers a company-wide 360-degree feedback survey. The goal of the survey is to communicate dimensions of importance that are critical throughout the organization and that are the hallmark of the Astro corporate culture. Groups of items give special attention to customer service, rapid delivery and installation, customized network services to corporate clients, and partnerships with telecommunications providers, which are difficult corporate relationships because these are also competitors in some markets. Items also evaluate cross-cultural sensitivity, particularly the manager's understanding of local markets and customs. Items reflect comfort with different cultures, accurately recognizing cultural differences and influences, empathizing with other cultures, valuing cultural differences, seeking new information and clarifying explanations, avoiding culture-bound behaviors, and being flexible (items were derived from London and Sessa's [1999] conceptualization of cultural sensitivity).

The 360-degree feedback survey was administered to 365 top executives across the globe. Surveys were completed by these executives' immediate subordinates, peers, supervisors, and customers. Many respondents worked in cities and countries other than their executive's home base. Data were collected electronically. An e-mail message requested participation and pointed raters to a Web site for confidential entry of ratings. The ratings were submitted through the Web site and automatically scored. Although the company managers generally spoke English, this was not necessarily the case for customers, so the surveys were available in English, Spanish, and Japanese. Careful translation and retranslation procedures were followed to ensure equivalence of meaning. Also, focus groups of lower level managers reviewed the surveys and discussed the meaning of each item to be sure that the item was clear and understood in the same way across cultures. The e-mail and Web site came up in English, offering the respondent a choice of languages for the instructions and actual survey.

Coaches were given the survey reports and asked to review the results, then prepare for in-person, one-on-one feedback sessions with the executives. The coaches, selected by the human resource departments in key offices around the world, were consultants in private practice and consulting firms and had considerable cross-cultural experiences in business and counseling. They were sent to a workshop in Australia to familiarize them with the company, cultural differences that emerge in Astro's business, the pressures executives face—with an emphasis on the difficulties of cross-cultural interactions, and the contents of the 360-degree feedback survey itself. The coaches flew into the home country of the executive for the initial one-on-one meeting. Then they maintained contact with the executives by e-mail and telephone. The headquarters of the human resources department paid for 2 hours of preparation, the initial 2-hour meeting, and three 1-hour follow-ups. The goal of the feedback and coaching was for executives to establish a development plan. Executives who chose to do so could continue the coaching relationship by paying the coach from their own budget.

There were several challenges in this coaching process: matching executives to coaches on the basis of experiences, age, and cultural understanding; ensuring that development plans were formulated by the executive with the coache's support (the coach should not do the work for the executive); ensuring that the coaches did not use their own favorite methods (e.g., asking the executive to complete a particular personality instrument) but stuck to the script of working with the 360-degree feedback data and helping the executive establish a career development plan; warning the coaches not to get enmeshed in the executive's immediate business problems; and getting the coaches out to the field soon after the results were available; the company was evolving so rapidly that if several months elapsed, the organization would have changed and the issues confronting the executive could have been different.

To determine the effectiveness of the feedback and coaching, executives completed a follow-up survey asking about the feedback and the help they received from their coach. The reactions were generally very positive. Also,

20% of the executives contracted with the coach for additional time. The company planned to track changes in 360-degree feedback survey results over the next 2 years to determine whether improvements were achieved and maintained by the executives.

Overall, the human resource department concluded from the initial favorable reaction that the process was favorably received. The cost was equivalent to the cost of sending the executives to a training session that may have lasted several days. However, the customized feedback and personal attention was greater than would have occurred at a typical training session, unless the training had incorporated feedback and coaching, which some executive development programs do—at greater cost, of course. Further follow-up evaluation was needed to evaluate the program's cost effectiveness. An added benefit was that the performance evaluations could be used to identify top executives for future growth. This was not done in the first administration. The executives were assured that the data and coaching would be used solely for their development, not for decision making about them.

The process was not without problems. Some executives were too reliant on their coaches. They called them often, explained their business problems, and asked for advice. Interestingly, executives in Japan and Israel did not welcome their coaches. The coaches had trouble setting up appointments and found the interactions brief and perfunctory. Executives in Japan found the coaching process intrusive and embarrassing. Those in Israel felt they did not need a coach who intruded on their independence. Coaches in Thailand and Japan reported that the feedback results were not very useful because all the ratings were generally positive, whereas the executives rated themselves uniformly low. Were they being overly modest, whereas the raters were overly lenient and there were few differences in different dimensions of performance. Some coaches took too long to get ready and be deployed. Travel expenses were high, as much as the cost of coaching in some cases (e.g., $4,000 for the coach and another $2,000 for travel was not unusual). Where possible, the same coach was assigned to more than one executive in an area, and trips were coordinated so the coach could see several executives at a time. However, this was not always possible because of executives' availability. Also, executives in the same city or country were not always good matches for the same coach. Some executives asked the coach to continue work in their departments, which involved meeting separately with a number of the executives' subordinates to identify ways for them to enhance their teamwork. In this way, coaching expanded from attention to the individual executive's needs for performance improvement to organization development.

Astro intended to extend the process to lower level managers. They developed a 360-degree feedback survey for 2,500 middle managers and translated it into six different languages. Instead of serving as external coaches, executives and managers were asked to serve in the coaching role for their immediate subordinates. Managers were sent reports of their results by e-mail with a message encouraging them to review the results with their supervisor or regional human resource manager.

This larger survey feedback initiative was not without problems. Some executives not ready to be coaches were not receptive to managers' requests for guidance. Also, some managers, particularly in Japan and China, were reluctant to share their results with their boss. Another problem was movement of personnel because of corporate growth. By the time the results were in, the manager or the manager's boss had changed assignments, so continuity of the process was difficult in the context of rapid corporate change. Consequently, Astro refined the process to emphasize self-development even more, and to encourage managers to take responsibility for their own development, with the 360-degree feedback survey results as a support tool.

CONCLUSION

This chapter first reviews how feedback can enhance team performance. Feedback can prompt a team's examination of its strengths and weaknesses and areas for improvement, just as it does for individuals. Team feedback provides members with information about the team as a whole and the behavior of individual members. Feedback is important for an accurate understanding of the expectations members have for each other, the goals of the group, and how the members work together to get work done. The key conclusions of this chapter can be summarized as follows:

1. Group feedback is valuable in informing group members about the performance of the group as a whole. This is appropriate when there is information about the group's performance and group members are interdependent. Group goals should be established during group discussion. With sufficient care, the group setting can be useful for giving feedback to individuals. This works well during developmental programs in which group members can give each other constructive feedback in a nonthreatening environment.

2. Team effectiveness depends on team members developing shared mental models that facilitate coordination. Shared mental models include expectations about behaviors and skill levels, awareness of team members' knowledge and skills, and a shared understanding of the task and goals. Explicit communication about expectations and goals at the outset promote the development of shared mental models. Feedback about behaviors and performance during the task enhance the development of these models and facilitate coordination and task accomplishment. Inaccurate expectations and feedback thwart shared understanding and the capability of the group to coordinate.

3. Feedback is as important in virtual teams as it is in face-to-face teams. The use of feedback in virtual teams may depend on the richness of the

communications media and the leaders' style of management. Transactional leadership focuses on goal-centered feedback that builds conditional trust. Transformational leadership focuses on developing a common understanding of feedback and its meaning for team development that builds unconditional trust. During the initial stages of group development, low media richness and transactional leadership may help to jump start trust building. As the team progresses, increased media richness and transformational leadership may facilitate group development.

4. Feedback is important in negotiating teams to provide insights into the opposition and bargaining situation that individual members may not have alone, and to communicate perceptions between opposing parties as a way of reaching more rapid resolution and higher gains on both sides. There is a growing literature on the effects of cultural differences between employees in domestic and multinational organizations. This chapter discusses a few recent studies that address the effects of culture on performance ratings, particularly in the use of multisource feedback. Cultural issues are likely to be increasingly important in understanding how people rate others and use feedback to set goals for development and improve their performance. Far more research is needed in this area. Meanwhile, the following conclusions are draw from the material discussed in this chapter:

5. Multisource feedback can be a useful way for expatriate managers to understand cultural differences in performance expectations. Cultural differences may influence how people are rated in performance evaluations. For instance, U.S. managers tend to be more people-focused than managers in other cultures. Far Eastern managers tend to be higher in strategic planning. Managers in the United States and the Far East tend to be higher than managers in other countries on change and innovation. Managers from the United States tend to rate themselves more leniently than managers from other cultures (Berson et al., 2002). Relations among performance dimensions (the factor structure) may not be the same in all cultures (Gillespie, 2002). Moreover, culture may affect the level (e.g., leniency) of performance ratings (Farh et al., 1991).

6. People in different cultures may interpret the elements of performance and how they work together differently, and they may vary in rating tendencies or biases. Given this possibility, which needs to be substantiated by further research, feedback to managers should include in-country norms to help managers understand their results within the context of their own culture. Also, the company's performance management program should explain the meaning of performance dimensions used in appraisal methods and multisource surveys, and managers should have a chance to discuss the meaning of these dimensions before they are asked to rate others and before they receive feedback on their own performance.

7. Managers who rate and provide feedback to employees in different cultures may benefit from information and training on sensitivity to cultural

differences. Items in a performance evaluation survey can reflect the company's needs for cross-cultural understanding.

8. Measures of cross-cultural sensitivity can be the basis for selecting managers for development and rapid advancement in fast-growing global enterprises.

9. In implementing feedback and coaching in a multinational firm, care must be taken to ensure that the measures and process are perceived in the same way in different cultures. Also, there may be cultural differences in the value of the feedback and willingness to share results with coaches or their supervisors.

Next, I turn to other trends: how technology is changing performance evaluation and development, and how the changing nature of jobs needs to be reflected in performance measurement, feedback, and development systems.

14

Changing Technologies and Jobs: Toward Feedback-Oriented, Continuous Learning Environments

This concluding chapter continues to examine new horizons for the importance and use of performance feedback. I consider how technology is used in generating and communicating feedback, and in integrating feedback into employee development programs, for instance, in Web-based feedback surveys and online coaching. I examine how changing jobs are changing performance requirements and measurement. Finally, I address how organizations are creating feedback-oriented corporate cultures. In the process, I describe ways that organizations are using feedback to encourage continuous, self-directed learning and show how factors such as age and negative personality characteristics may influence feedback and learning.

TECHNOLOGY AND FEEDBACK

Advanced technology allows the collection of abundant information, which can occur at the expense of individual privacy. It also opens learning to widely accessible information, including performance feedback and self-paced learning.

Electronic Performance Monitoring

Advanced computer technologies allow close tracking and scrutiny of employees' behaviors. In 1990, more than 10 million employees were subject to electronic performance monitoring (9 to 5, Working Women Education Fund, 1990, cited in Aiello & Kolb, 1995). Most of these were clerical workers, but electronic monitoring can also apply to management, technical, and professional employees. For example, for truck drivers, remote monitoring can track location, speed, on-time deliveries, and even elements of the condition of the truck (tire pressure) and possibly driver (i.e., heart rate, response time, and attentiveness). For hospital personnel, detailed patient recording systems can determine the amount and type of patient contact for each health care provider. For factory workers, workstation monitoring can determine quality (accuracy) and quantity (pace) of output. For educators, student test scores can be tracked and summarized by the teacher, controlling for initial student abilities. For attorneys and management consultants, time tracking systems are important for billing, and also for indicating the type and amount of work performed.

Whereas this book has emphasized when and how feedback can be valuable, an open question is how monitoring, especially electronic monitoring, affects the employee's productivity and feelings of stress. Several studies have found that electronic monitoring makes jobs seem more stressful (Gallatin, 1989; Irving, Higgins, & Safayeni, 1986). This may happen not because of the monitoring per se, but because of other changes that accompany the introduction of the new observation method. Such changes may include increased workload and loss of control over the way employees do their jobs (Smith, Carayon, Sanders, Lim, & LeGrande, 1992). However, monitoring may improve the individual performance of people who are highly skilled because such people tend to perform better when they are observed. This is called the "social facilitation" effect (Zajonc, 1965). People who work in groups may not feel this stress if the group as a whole is monitored and the group is cohesive enough to provide members with social support. This was found in a study of students working on a data entry task alone, as members of a noninteracting group, or as members of a cohesive group (Aiello & Kolb, 1995). In the cohesive group, students spent some time getting to know each other before the task, and were told that a test they had taken indicated that they were highly compatible. High-skilled participants performed better when they were monitored than when they were not. Low-skilled participants performed more poorly when they were monitored than when they were not, supporting the concept of social facilitation. The participants reported feeling the least stress when they were not monitored or when they were members of cohesive groups.

Learner-Controlled Instruction

Self-paced or "open" learning, also called self-directed learning, refers to people working on their own to learn new skills and acquire knowledge. Assessment and feedback are generally built into the process to help people determine what they should learn and whether they have learned it. Self-paced material may be presented in written form, through a computer with CD-ROM, in audio tapes or video tapes, or by an interactive video system (Warr & Bunce, 1995). Open learners have autonomy to decide what they will study and how, when, where, and at what pace (Stewart & Winter, 1992). Learners control the time spent on material, the amount of review of explanatory material and feedback, the revision of responses, and the way they explore and test new concepts.

As an example, a British firm incorporated open learning into training programs for junior managers on such topics as communications, problem solving, budgeting, hiring, and health and safety (Warr & Bunce, 1995). The topics were selected after extensive needs analyses for first-line managers in many different organizations. The trainees participated in the program during a 4-month period. They attended a 3-day introductory session, a 2-day workshop at the halfway point, and a 2-day review at the end. The rest of the time, trainees studied on their own, including study during 5 hours of paid time each week. Each module contained a workbook, an audiocassette, and exercises to be completed along with self-testing questions and quizzes. Exercises and assignments were submitted to an assigned tutor for assessment and feedback.

Despite the self-paced design, this was a fairly structured program. Participants were given the modules, and they merely had to go through them on their own. Tutors provided guidance and oversight. Other programs are less directive. They require the participant to select topics for study on the basis of their own interests, views of their capabilities and knowledge, and assessment of career opportunities.

Online Career Planning and Development. Computers provide avenues for individuals to direct their own development. One such program, called "Smart Software," has five components (James, 1994):

Career Review: asks questions about career progress and key learning experiences that occurred on the job.

Motivation to Develop and Career Aspirations: asks questions that promote the respondents' understanding of their future career direction, not specific jobs, but the creation of a alternatives for where and how they could apply their skills.

Competence-Based Job Analysis: asks respondents to rate certain behavioral competencies in terms of their importance to their current role. This results in a weighted competence framework, which allows the respondent to compare his or her assessment with his or her immediate supervisor's assessment.

Competence-Based Self-Assessment: uses "insight" questionnaires to evaluate strengths and weaknesses in areas identified as important in the prior job analysis.

Development Strategies: asks respondents to identify the three main areas they wish to develop. The software then offers appropriate literature that provides key principles in such areas as strategic thinking, problem solving, interpersonal communications, and motivating others.

Overall, self-paced learning, often using computer technology, is a cost-effective, flexible method. It can be accessed by the individual whenever he or she has the time and inclination. Feedback is provided from automatic scoring as the individual progresses. Also, it is applicable to small and large firms alike, because excellent software programs, videos, audiotapes, and written material are increasingly available.

Online Performance Management

In addition to using Web technology to administer multisource feedback surveys, companies are using the technology to offer self-assessment, e-learning, informal learning guides, online and telephone coaching, and career development workshops. For instance, companies can purchase subscriptions to TalentAlliance.com for their employees. This site offers assessments and leadership 360-degree feedback, career coaching, links to distance learning opportunities, career information, and job opportunities. The latter is especially useful to companies in the process of downsizing. The assessments module contains a leadership 360-degree feedback process and self-diagnostic instruments to help employees gain feedback and understand their strengths, work preferences, and career goals. The career coaching module provides telephone contact with a coach for one-on-one career consulting services. The available services are customized to the needs of the company, and Talent Alliance advertises that by using these virtual solutions, clients can experience the same quality career coaching services as those provided in face-to-face meetings. The Web site offers a "coach's corner" that offers a range of practical tips, exercises, and suggestions for helping managers to prepare for performance reviews and coaching sessions with subordinates.

Recognizing the value of feedback and self-assessment through online technology, the consulting branch of the accounting firm Deloitte & Touche developed a Web site to support their consultant's skill development including their team leadership, sales, and responsiveness to clients. Tied to a 360-degree feedback survey and in-person coaching, the Web site provides self-assessments, guidelines for informal learning, and directions for development planning and follow-up. The professionals proceed through each site at their own pace, contacting their coach to discuss assessment results and development plans as they progress.

Overall, the Web provides tools to help managers and professionals take more responsibility for their own career development, including obtaining feedback, seeking help to understand and use it, and recognizing that learning is a continuous process. The Web sites can be customized to enhance their value to the company and the individuals using them. The materials and assessments can reflect corporate strategies and competency requirements. Individuals can use the materials at their convenience and in relation to their needs and goals. The Web site can be related to the company's other performance management tools and training, such as the annual performance appraisal process and courses or workshops provided by the corporate training department. Informal learning guides encourage managers to take advantage of the opportunities for skill development available during their normal course of work, urging them to seek informal feedback instead of waiting for multisource survey results or their annual performance review with their supervisor.

Just-in-Time Multisource Feedback

E-mail and Internet technology open the possibility of collecting performance ratings electronically, making feedback more "real time." This has been used successfully for 360-degree feedback. Indeed, managers actually can construct their own survey, send an invitation for a response and the Web site link by e-mail, collect the data on the Web, and receive the results on the Web relatively quickly. This is called "just-in-time" feedback because managers can start the process when they feel they have a need for feedback.

Here is how online multisource feedback can work. Consider a manager who is responsible for leading a large project with team members spread across the country or the globe. She may want periodic feedback about team conditions, perhaps at key junctures of the project, maybe because there was a problem (e.g., a deadline was missed) or she simply has a sense that things could be going better and wants some idea of how she can improve the situation. (In virtual teams, evaluations of management skills may be less relevant to a supervisor than information about processing and other team issues.) She logs on to a team performance management link on the company's human resource Web site and then clicks a link entitled "Create Your Own 360-Degree Feedback Survey." The Web site guides her through the initial steps in the process. She selects survey items from a list of possibilities categorized by area such as Clarity of Communication, Task Orientation, Interpersonal Relationships, Customer Contact, and Strategy Setting. She clicks the questions she wants to include in the survey. Then she selects raters. The system asks her to select a minimum of 3 to a maximum of 10 raters per group (peers, subordinates, supervisors, or customers). She types in their names and e-mail addresses, or the system ties to the company's human resource database so all she has to do is type in their names. The system then creates the customized survey and automatically sends an e-mail to the designated recipients telling them the purpose of the survey, who requested it, and how they can respond online. The Web address to the survey is embedded in the e-mail so the recipient can click on the site at a convenient time.

Recipients complete the survey on the web, and when they are done, click "submit." The system averages the ratings from each source for each item and produces a report. Mean results are not provided for a given item unless a minimum of three people responded to the item. The report includes the mean ratings for each item along with the company norms (the average rating received on the item by a sample of managers at the same organizational level across the company). The report is sent directly to the manager herself and not to her supervisor, coach, or human resource department representative. The manager may decide to share her results with others or not. The purpose of the report is purely developmental. A danger from such convenience is that some managers, especially those who are insecure, may overuse this option or perform it frequently.

The company may use a similar procedure to administer a multisource survey for all managers. In this case, the items, chosen by top executives or a representative group of managers, would be the same for all feedback recipients. The managers would receive an e-mail from the human resources department requesting their participation and asking them to indicate names of respondents. The report might be sent to the managers' supervisors if the intention was to use the results to make administrative decisions about the managers. In general, this becomes a simple, cost-effective means of administering a survey across a large company.

Electronic Feedback and Coaching

With the advent of instant messaging and e-mail, not to mention telephone coupled with the prevalence of geographically dispersed project teams and work groups, people will use less personal means to give feedback and be a coach. What are the likely psychological effects of electronic feedback on the recipient and the sender? When relationships are in the formation stage, we might expect that instant messaging, e-mail, and the telephone would be positive ways to give feedback and provide suggestions for behavior change. E-mail might even be better than telephone. The reason is the simpler and more direct the media, with more attention focused on the clarity of the message itself. Less information is likely to get lost, confused, or misinterpreted than in a media-rich environment (Avolio, Dahai, Dumdum, & Sivasubramaniam, 2001). Also, conveying feedback non–face-to-face may be easier. However, if there are no face-to-face meetings, the coach has only limited information about the coachee based only on virtual performance. Research is needed to determine whether the nature of feedback and coaching change in virtual conditions.

Face-to-face communication, although more personal, is fraught with a multitude of cues that communicate a variety of explicit and implicit messages simultaneously, including words, voice inflections, gestures, and facial expressions. The potential for misreading these cues is great as is the potential for richer and more complete information. Reactions are likely to be a function of existing relationships (e.g., trusting or not). Givers of negative feedback may worry about the receiver's hurt feelings and defensiveness. Givers of positive feedback may worry about how they will be perceived, for instance, as ingratiating or manipulative. Receivers of negative feedback may try to hide their hurt, perhaps inadvertently communicating a cavalier "could not care less" attitude. Receivers of positive feedback may try to be humble, but may convey a haughty attitude by being aloof or taking the information in stride. E-mail can cut through the game playing. However, e-mail also can be a way to mask true feelings by the careful use of words.

When people know each other well, they have an easier time reading each other's nonverbal behavior, and the use of e-mail to deliver weighty information, such as negative feedback, may be perceived as the cowardly way out. Also, coaching by instant messaging or e-mail may not work well unless the parties have excellent typing skills and the time to convey their true thoughts in depth. Of course, in long-distance work relationships, electronic communication media are for sure the next best thing to being there.

Clearly, future research needs to investigate the effects of feedback and coaching via alternative communication media. We do not know much about this now, and it still is an emerging phenomenon. We would want to know the answer to such questions as the following: Do managers feel more comfortable giving feedback in e-mail messages than in person? Is telephone communication of feedback viewed as more personal and appropriate for feedback than e-mail? Do feedback recipients prefer to hear negative feedback in person? Do the answers to these questions depend on whether the feedback is positive or negative? Is the message clearer when it is delivered in person or in writing? Are people more or less defensive when they receive negative feedback in a written message rather than in person? E-mail correspondence creates a record that can be retained and forwarded to others. Do people view this means of communication as less confidential? Is this a problem in managing geographically dispersed team members with whom communication often is by e-mail? Can managers learn how to communicate more effectively by e-mail, especially using it as a way to delivering clear feedback and useful coaching? The answers to these questions would suggest training methods and guidelines for managers to use the various communications media available to the best advantage.

Summary

Technology opens opportunities for obtaining feedback data (e.g., electronic monitoring) and for conducting self-paced learning. Indeed, e-mail and the Web can be used for online performance management, including the collection of multisource feedback ratings and access to a plethora of job information and even customized advice and coaching.

An open question for research concerns the effects of feedback under various organization conditions. The nature of feedback, its importance, its ease of delivery, and likelihood of acceptance may depend on the climate in the organization and the immediate work pressures. Are people more receptive to feedback, and are supervisors more comfortable giving feedback, when the task demands are high, for instance, when there is a work-related crisis of some sort (e.g., a close customer deadline), the competition is stiff, or the organization is in the process of restructuring at a rapid pace? Under these conditions, everyone may have a sense of urgency. After every meeting, people may talk to their colleagues about how it went, how others reacted to them, and what they can do better the next time.

The effects of organizational stress on feedback may interact with aspects of individuals' personalities, such as their self-esteem. Some people facing tough conditions may be more sensitive to criticism than usual. Recognizing the critical nature of their actions and decisions, they may be more self-critical. This does not mean, however, that they will necessarily welcome feedback and be open to coaching. Indeed, they may be more defensive when they hear negative feedback from others. They may avoid conversations about their performance and may not want to hear suggestions from others.

NEW JOBS, ROLES, AND WORK STRUCTURES

Some fields are experiencing rapid changes in jobs, the creation of new positions and roles, and work team reconfigurations. Often, these changes are imposed with minimal formal education or training. As a result, on-the-job training and feedback become critical to success, and existing employees need to learn how to give feedback to make the new employees effective as they all initiate new roles.

A good example is provided by the health care industry. The nursing shortage in the late 1980s and the concern for lowering health care costs in the 1990s and early 2000s led hospitals to begin changing the mix of licensed and unlicensed employees caring for patients. For instance, the Ochner Foundation Hospital in New Orleans developed the position of nursing care technician, and the Presbyterian Medical Center of Philadelphia created the position of patient care associate (King, 1995). These new personnel work with and for registered nurses (RNs) who delegate and supervise their work. After initial training from the hospitals, these unlicensed assistants learn new skills on the job from RNs. The RNs are trained to learn good delegation, communication, and teambuilding skills. Giving ongoing feedback is an essential part of enhancing the assistant's skills. Each assistant works with two or three RNs, who have a chance to develop close working relationships with the assistant while allowing for flexible scheduling. Therefore, the RNs need to be consistent in their expectations and feedback, to engage in ongoing evaluation of the assistants' role, and to revise expectations and relationships as the assistants learn more skills that do not require licensed personnel.

Communicating Changes in Performance Competencies

As suggested in the chapter 3, people judge others on the basis of mental categories. These categories help to place the individual in our minds and help us form a conception of the individual's performance. A person's judgments can be influenced by category descriptions before he or she makes ratings. For instance, people asked to memorize or use either positive or negative personality trait terms subsequently judge another individual as more attractive if they were exposed previously to favorable rather than unfavorable items (Higgins, Bargh, & Lombardi, 1985; Higgins, Rholes, & Jones, 1977). People form distinct groups in their minds (prototypes) of effective and ineffective performers, and ratings of another individual are strongly related to the group the rater resembles (Kinicki, Hom, Trost, & Wade, 1995). This process may produce an accurate prototype, a view of how the organization conceptualizes an effective individual and the benchmark against which people should compare themselves. The risk is that people are less accurate in discriminating actual behaviors when they have access to the prototype. The tendency is to match people to the category. Furthermore, priming a person to think of negative information before rating another may produce a contrast effect such that positive information is evaluated more positively (Banaji, Hardin, & Rothman, 1993). As a result, it may be important for benchmark information to be presented in neutral terms to produce a schema that establishes meaningful performance standards.

The Performance Management Cycle

Understanding changes in job requirements, current performance, and needs for development is an ongoing process. London and Smither (2002) described a performance management cycle as a process that unfolds over time, lasting days, weeks, or months. (The cycle they describe is similar to the appraisal and development cycle outlined in chapter 11.) A cycle starts with a critical event, perhaps reception of formal feedback from one's boss as part of the annual performance appraisal or as a result of a decision, for instance, being passed over for a promotion. Alternatively, a cycle may begin after an event, such as a major presentation or maybe an argument. The event is observed, and feedback is available. Peers may offer their view of their fellow employee's role in the event. One way or the other, the activity of the event precipitates feedback.

Three Stages in the Performance Feedback. The first stage that ensues after the event involves anticipating and receiving feedback. Anticipated feedback may be accompanied by feelings of apprehension and avoidance tendencies (e.g., staying away from one's supervisor). Eventually, feedback is given, although the extent to which the receiver pays attention to it may depend on his or her openness. The feedback triggers initial emotions:

self-satisfaction from positive feedback, relief in hearing that the feedback was not as bad as anticipated, anxiety in not knowing what to do with the feedback, anger against the bearer of the feedback (blame for the messenger), and the like.

The second stage is that of processing the feedback. Mindful or conscious processing is likely to occur the more the feedback is unexpected, has valued consequences, or comes from a respected source. This second stage entails interpreting the feedback, understanding the reason or reasons for it, dealing with accompanying emotions, and ultimately believing the feedback or discounting or denying its validity.

During the third stage, feedback is used to set goals for skill development or knowledge acquisition and for improving performance. The goals provide standards against which to track change in performance and assess degree of performance improvement.

The feedback cycle will be more potent—meaning that the feedback will be treated more seriously and something will be done about it—by individuals high in feedback orientation and in organizations characterized by a strong feedback culture.

Incorporating Multisource Feedback Into the Performance Management Cycle.   The way 360-degree feedback is used and incorporated into the organization's performance management processes may determine its overall benefits to the organization. One study examined ratings of the perceived benefits associated with 360-degree feedback made by human resource vice presidents of 42 global companies (Rogers, Barriere, Kaplan, & Metlay, 2002). The vice presidents rated the extent to which 360-degree feedback was a competitive advantage, worth the resources, generally beneficial to the organization, a help in accomplishing organizational goals, a factor contributing to increased profitability, and generally a cause for improved job performance. Averaging across these different ratings, the researchers divided the companies that were high, moderate, or low in terms of perceived benefit from 360-degree feedback. Then they examined whether the high- and low-benefit groups differed in how they used the feedback process. They found that the high-benefit organizations were more likely to use the 360-degree feedback as a basis for coaching and individual development planning and to encourage managers to share their results with their supervisor than the low-benefit organizations. The high-benefit companies provided more training in the purpose and uses of 360-degree feedback before delivering the feedback. Also, as compared with the low-benefit organizations, the high-benefit organizations were more likely to include customers among the raters. They tended to use specific criteria to select coaches, and then to inform the coaches about the procedures used to develop and collect the 360-degree feedback survey data. Also, the high-benefit companies were more likely to evaluate the 360-degree feedback process than the low-benefit companies. Overall, the results indicated that human resource executives perceived more positive results from using 360-degree feedback when they used it with coaching and, more generally, development, and when they followed up to determine the long-term effects of the feedback in the organization.

Of course, it may be that human resource executives who sponsor extensive performance management practices, (e.g., the use of customers as raters and the use of coaches to help explain the data) are more likely to perceive that multisource feedback has greater value to the organization. Nevertheless, concerted, concentrated performance efforts at least are perceived by human resource executives as enhancing the value of multisource feedback to the organization.

Developing an Integrated Human Performance System

Feedback should be an integral part of a human resource management system. Such a system should include human resource programs that support employee selection, training, job design, placement, appraisal, feedback, compensation, and outplacement. These functions should be integrated in the sense that they should be based on the organization's goals and the employee competencies needed to accomplish these goals. Personnel recruitment and selection criteria, development options and training modules, career planning programs, appraisal processes, and compensation should be targeted to the same set of organization objectives. These are "support" programs in that managers and employees make a human performance system work. They are responsible for using the system to manage their performance and enhance that of their subordinates and coworkers.

Summary

New jobs, roles, and structures give rise to new competencies and standards that must be understood and assessed. Performance measurement and feedback provide opportunities for managers to discuss changing competency requirements with employees, highlighting implications for development. Feedback should be thought of as part of an integrated human performance system that includes assessing changing performance needs.

CREATING A FEEDBACK-ORIENTED, CONTINUOUS LEARNING ORGANIZATIONAL CULTURE

In the past, organizations often took responsibility for employees' development, with supervisors deciding, for instance, which employees got what training and when. Although today's organizations provide the enabling resources, such as career planning programs and training courses of all types, they do not necessarily assign people to these programs and courses unless there is an immediate business need (e.g., the requirement for employees to learn new software system). Instead, the organization makes resources available, and employees can decide for themselves whether to take advantage of these resources.

Clardy (2000) examined the extent to which organizational factors are related to self-directed learning (e.g., taking a course). Interviewing 56 employees of five organizations in such positions as technically and mechanically skilled jobs and unskilled labor, he discovered that organizational factors can require or encourage self-directed learning. Although some people engage in self-directed learning without any precipitating organizational or job changes, new organizational conditions can ignite an employee's readiness to act and learn. Clardy (2000) called this "synergistic voluntary self-directed learning." Organizational factors that required self-directed learning included explicit performance standards, an assignment to work on a new task, or an event that showed an imbalance between job expectations and performance capabilities (i.e., performing a task poorly). Synergistic voluntary self-directed learning resulted from motivation to act and learn combined with the spark of an organizational change, such as a promotion to a new job.

London and Smither (1999) outlined the components of an organization environment that empowers self-development. This is an environment that promotes feedback (a feedback-oriented corporate culture). Managers may participate in assessment centers or multisource feedback surveys that give them feedback on their abilities and potential to advance to higher organizational levels. The organization can make available information about organizational goals and business directions and the implications of anticipated changes for performance expectations and promotional opportunities. There may be a call to action, for instance, asking for volunteers to be considered for a new subsidiary or work abroad. Here, the opportunity is presented, and you, the employee, must decide what to do: engage in development that prepares you for the opportunity or ignore the opportunity.

The employee's immediate supervisor can create a supportive climate by conveying information about opportunities, offering coaching, and providing resources for development, such as time away from the office along with tuition and travel expenses to attend training. The supervisor also may hold their subordinates accountable for their continuous learning. Employees need to understand what they need to know to be valuable to the organization. If they do not keep up, may suffer the consequences: poorer performance and lower than average salary increases, or possibly layoff during a downsizing initiative.

Organizations that empower self-development expect employees to recognize their development needs and take responsibility for their own learning. Employees can do this by actively seeking performance feedback, not waiting for it to arrive. They can compare their self-assessments with the perspectives of others and with predictions of future performance standards and job requirements. That is, they need to determine whether they will be ready to meet the needs of the organization today and tomorrow. They should then use these assessments to set development goals and investigate opportunities for development, and then take part in development activities. Empowered self-development is a continuous process. As progress is evaluated, goals are adjusted. New goals are set as old ones are accomplished.

Developing a Feedback Culture

A feedback-oriented culture is one in which managers and employees are comfortable giving and receiving feedback, and feedback is an integral part of the performance management process. The organization develops a feedback culture in a number of different ways (London & Smither, 2002): For instance, it can support nonthreatening feedback by instituting multisource feedback surveys for use in development but not in decision making. It can train supervisors to be better coaches to their employees, ready to help their employees interpret feedback results and use the data to set goals for development. Also, the organization can strengthen the link between performance improvement resulting from development and valued outcomes, such as pay increases or promotion. That is, in developmentally oriented feedback cultures, people are rewarded for performance improvement, and goal setting, participation in development activities, and continued performance review are encouraged.

Generally, organizations develop a feedback culture by enhancing the quality of feedback, emphasizing the importance of feedback in the organization, and providing support for using feedback (London & Smither, 2002). The quality of feedback can be increased by training managers in how to provide feedback that is constructive (helpful in pinpointing behaviors that will enhance performance, and not judgmental or critical of personal characteristics). It also can be increased by ensuring that there are clear performance standards, goals, expectations, and measurements of performance. The quality of feedback also can be improved by providing time to review and clarify the feedback results, for instance, encouraging employees to ask questions when their supervisor gives them feedback or encouraging managers to share their feedback survey results with their peers and subordinates and to discuss the meaning of the results.

The organization can highlight the importance of feedback by having top executives participate in and model a multisource process, asking their subordinate managers to rate them, then receiving a feedback report and participating in development activities. As such, the executives can become role models for the feedback process. Research is needed to determine the extent to which this actually happens. All managers should ensure that

everyone receives feedback. Moreover, they should encourage the importance of informal feedback and give feedback to others "in the moment",
immediately after a critical event during which they observed the behavior of a subordinate, peers, or even a supervisor. Also, as stated earlier, the
importance of feedback is enhanced when improvement in performance
is rewarded through pay raises, promotions, valued assignments, and other
forms of recognition.

Support for feedback may include providing skilled facilitators or coaches
to help feedback recipients interpret the meaning of the feedback, set goals
for development, and collect data to track changes in their performance over
time. Coaching is a central management responsibility in corporate cultures
that value feedback. Managers are rewarded for devoting time and energy to
coaching their subordinates. The amount of time they spend coaching and
the quality of that time can be measured by asking employees about their
supervisor's coaching behavior in attitude and multisource feedback surveys.
In addition, organizations support feedback by providing opportunities for
development. In other words, the organization needs to support not only
the delivery and discussion of feedback and developmental goal setting, but
also the availability of training programs, special job assignments, and other
ways to enhance development.

Feedback Orientation.   A feedback culture is enhanced when individuals in the organization develop stronger feedback orientations. Some people
have high growth and curiosity traits. They welcome feedback naturally.
They have a sufficiently thick skin (high self-esteem) to seek feedback regardless of its favorability. To be more specific, London and Smither (2002)
described the components of feedback orientation. People high in feedback
orientation like feedback. They do not fear being evaluated. They seek out
feedback and process it carefully and deeply. They want to know what it
means and why people feel the way they do about their performance. People
high in feedback orientation are sensitive to how others view them, and
they care what other people think of them (i.e., they are self-monitors, as
described in chapter 4). They believe that feedback offers insights that may
help them become more effective. In other words, they believe that feedback is, indeed, useful. Moreover, they feel accountable to use the feedback
because their colleagues or customers bothered to provide it and because
the company clearly wants them to take advantage of feedback as a guide
for improving their performance.

Steelman, Levy, and Snell (2002; see also Steelman & Levy, 2001) developed the Feedback Environment Scale to measure the extent to which
the workplace supports the use of feedback. The feedback environment
goes beyond the formal presentation of the annual performance appraisal to
include the daily interactions between members of the organization in terms
of how performance feedback is mentioned and discussed. Steelman et al.
(2002; reported in Norris-Watts & Levy, 2002) identified the following

seven factors that reflect how supervisors and coworkers deal with feedback:

1. *Source credibility:* the feedback source's expertise and trustworthiness as a provider of feedback (e.g., "My supervisor (coworker) is generally familiar with my performance on the job").
2. *Feedback quality:* the consistency and usefulness of the feedback (e.g., "My supervisor (coworker) gives me useful feedback about my job performance").
3. *Feedback delivery:* how considerate the feedback provider is of the recipient's feelings (e.g., "My supervisor (coworker) is supportive when giving me feedback about my job performance").
4. *Favorable feedback:* the frequency with which positive feedback is provided and is consistent with the recipient's self-perceptions (e.g., "My supervisor (coworker) generally lets me know when I do a good job at work").
5. *Unfavorable feedback:* the frequency with which negative feedback is provided and is consistent with the recipient's self-perceptions (e.g., "My supervisor (coworker) tells me when my work performance does not meet organizational standards").
6. *Source availability:* the amount of contact the recipient has with the feedback source and the effort the recipient needs to expend to receive the feedback (e.g., "My supervisor (coworker) is usually available when I want performance information").
7. *Promotion of feedback seeking:* the supportiveness of the supervisor or coworker in encouraging a response to feedback seeking (e.g., "My supervisor (coworker) encourages me to ask for feedback whenever I am uncertain about my job performance").

Norris-Watts and Levy (2002) found that the stronger the feedback environment perceived by student employees, the higher employees' organization citizenship behavior (e.g., altruism and courtesy, as rated by their supervisors) and the lower their absenteeism, especially in the case of individuals committed to the organization (i.e., they identify with, are involved in, and are emotionally attached to the organization). That is, favorable feedback environments affected behaviors that go beyond performance improvement to influence how people relate to each other as they contribute to the organization. The authors concluded that if supervisors understand how their daily interactions with subordinates influence subordinate work behaviors, then supervisors may be able to generate more favorable work behaviors and improve cooperation and team work. Supervisors may need to be reminded that they should consistently encourage their subordinates to seek feedback, and that this will increase employees' favorable perceptions of the feedback environment. In turn, this should limit absenteeism and increase employees' citizenship behavior.

AREAS FOR FUTURE RESEARCH ON GIVING AND RECEIVING FEEDBACK

The following topics are ideas for future investigation. There has been little or no research on these topics.

Age Differential

Investigations are needed to determine the effects of age and age differences on giving and receiving feedback. The ease of giving feedback may depend on the ages and roles of the feedback provider and recipient. Supervisors who are considerably older (say 15 years or more) than their subordinates may have an easier time delivering negative feedback because they can assume a parental or mentoring role more easily than supervisors who are closer in age to their subordinates. Similarly, subordinates may be less threatened by negative feedback from managers who are more senior in age or level in the organization. Negative information may be more difficult to discount or ignore when it comes from a more senior, and presumably more respected, manager. Perhaps the subordinate's respect for the manager is more important than age or position effects. Managers who are highly respected for their accomplishment may find that their subordinates are more receptive to their feedback than managers who are less revered by their subordinates. On the other hand, managers who understand and value the esteem in which others hold them may be reluctant to risk this status by being critical.

Style of Leadership and Feedback

A leader's style of leadership may influence, or be evident, in how he or she delivers and receives feedback. Leaders strong in task structure are likely to deliver clear and cogent feedback. They may be less likely to praise accomplishments and more likely to focus on areas for improvement. Leaders strong in building interpersonal relationships are likely to be empathetic and considerate of others' feelings. As such, they would be diplomatic or tactful in delivering negative feedback and effusive in recognizing accomplishments. These are hypotheses, at this point, however. Research is needed for understanding how leadership style influences the way feedback is delivered and received.

The Dark Side of Feedback: Effects of Personality on Feedback

The personality of managers is related to how others rate their managerial performance (Fleming, & Holland, 2002 a,b; McDaniel, Pezzina, Bedon, & Kortick, 2002; Smither, London, & Richmond, 2002). There are many ways in which personality may influence managerial style. We know that raters may manipulate their ratings to convey certain impressions, for instance, evaluating their supervisor leniently because they think their supervisor will repay them in kind, even though the ratings are anonymous (Kozlowski, Chao, & Morrison, 1998). An open question is whether the personality of managers influences how they rate others' performance. Are vindictive people likely to use their feelings to get back at others, essentially undermining the manager they are rating and simultaneously sabotaging the performance evaluation system? Do they use their ratings to ingratiate themselves with the people they are rating? How does the rater's personality relate to the quality of the ratings or written responses to open-ended questions? Do some raters deliberately provide wrong, no, or incomplete information?

Research is needed to determine the prevalence of ratings that are systematically biased by the personality of the rater. To the extent that this occurs, human resource practitioners will be challenged to develop ways to guard against such inaccurate and misleading ratings. One advantage of multisource ratings is that performance evaluations are averaged across raters. Thus, if one rater has a personal agenda, the ratings will at least be averaged with others who hopefully are not similarly biased and the bias effects will be minimized. Ratings can be examined for systematic biases, for instance, identifying raters with uniformly negative ratings that do not differentiate between different dimensions of performance. These ratings could then be removed from the calculation of the results.

The effects of negative personality influencing feedback are more problematic when it comes to in-person feedback. That is, controlling how and what a bitter, angry, or vindictive supervisor may say or do is more difficult than identifying and removing biased survey ratings. However, subordinate ratings may be useful in identifying leaders with performance problems likely to be caused by negative personality traits. Higher level management can monitor the performance of these individuals with particular attention to how they treat their subordinates and the decisions they make about their subordinates. The fairness and accuracy of their decisions can be evaluated and, if necessary, called into question. Training, or ultimately, disciplinary action, may be needed. This is how leaders with personality deficiencies eventually are unmasked and derailed (McCall & Lombardo, 1983).

Raters are sensitive to their ratees' personalities. Research has found that ratings of job performance are related positively to characteristics that promote the ability to get ahead in life such as conscientiousness, emotional stability, and integrity (John, 1990; Ones, Viswesvaran, & Schmidt, 1993). Performance appraisal results and multisource performance ratings may reflect dysfunctional managerial behavior. Because most managers achieve results through other people, interpersonal ability is a key element of successful leadership. Coaches and supervisors should be alert to these signs and be ready to address them in feedback and coaching sessions. Dysfunctional interpersonal behavior suggests poor management and probably also defensiveness in dealing with feedback.

Fleming and Holland (2002a) asked the question, "Do flawed interpersonal strategies negatively affect job performance?" Summarizing the results of six independent studies involving more than 800 people, they found that lower performance ratings across a variety of jobs were associated with people characterized as micromanagers, aloof, cautious, and high-strung. Such flawed interpersonal strategies may arise from a person's distorted beliefs about others. Interestingly, people viewed as colorful (i.e., engaging yet distractible) tended to receive positive ratings. Another study correlated 360-degree feedback ratings with personality measures in a sample of 39 managers (Fleming & Holland, 2002b). The 360-degree feedback survey involved bosses, peers, and direct reports to rate managers' technical, interpersonal, and behavioral competencies. The study found lower performance ratings from all rater sources for managers who were perceived as mistrustful, arrogant, manipulative, melodramatic, and eccentric.

Human resource researchers at Bristol-Myers Squibb examined the relation between 360-degree feedback and executives' evaluations of managers' career potential. The executives evaluating potential were two organizational levels above the managers they rated. Only 5% of the 1,086 managers rated were evaluated by the executives as on the verge of derailing (meaning it was time to let them know that further career advancement was unlikely, or that they may have been in danger of losing their jobs), as compared with 94% who were judged to have high potential for further promotion or to be key contributors to the organization. Ratings on the 20-item 360-degree feedback survey were positively related to executives' prediction of derailment. Ratings from immediate supervisors were correlated most highly with derailment ($r = 4.33$; $p < .05$). The relation between peer ratings and executive evaluation of derailment also was significant ($r = .22$; $p < .05$). However, subordinates' ratings were not significantly related to executives' evaluations of derailment, suggesting that subordinates do not have the same understanding as peers and immediate supervisors about a manager's potential for advancement. Successful leaders were evaluated higher than derailed leaders on behaviors of accepting accountability, achieving results, setting priorities and allocating resources, driving innovation, and creating a vision.

In summary, there is a dark side to performance ratings and feedback. They may identify people with negative personality characteristics that portend derailing. This may be good in pinpointing people in need of development, but probably the least likely to be responsive to the feedback. These people actually may undermine establishment of a feedback, development-oriented culture, or at least they may make the establishment of such a culture more difficult, especially if they head large departments.

Creating a Learning Organization

Some organizations work hard to develop employees' performance capabilities continually. These "learning organizations" (Senge, 1990) emphasize *generative learning:* "an emphasis on continuous experimentation and feedback in an ongoing examination of the very way organizations go about defining and solving problems" (McGill, Slocum, & Lei, 1992, p. 5).

Self-Denying Prophecies

Unfavorable feedback is likely to lower motivation, particularly for people low in self-esteem and ready to believe negative prophecies about themselves (Brockner, Derr, & Laing, 1987). However, employees can shift their behavior to avoid a negative prophecy (Hurley, 1993). A self-denying prophecy happens when a person sets a goal to void a negative expectation.

Performance Enhancement Spirals.   A positive, cyclic relation between beliefs about one's effectiveness and one's performance can build upon itself (Lindsley, Brass, & Thomas, 1995). Coaches and athletes are aware of the cognitive aspects of physical performance. A positive frame of mind can have a similar effect on business performance. Three types of spirals are possible: A *self-correcting spiral* occurs when a decrease in performance and self-efficacy is followed by an increase in performance. The person adjusts future efforts, reversing the prior decrease in performance. An *upward spiral* occurs when positive changes in efficacy and performance build on each other, creating confirmation of ability and performance that is reflected in subsequent effort. A *downward spiral* occurs when negative changes in efficacy and performance build on each other, limiting subsequent effort, thereby reinforcing the negative trend.

The *Galatea effect* (enhancement of motivation by expectation of achieving higher goals) has been induced experimentally by simply explaining to a trainee that test scores indicate that he or she has high potential for success (Eden & Ravid, 1982). Thus, using feedback to raise self-expectations can build on subordinates' capacity to mobilize their own resources to perform better (Eden, 1992).

Eden and Aviram (1993) showed that building self-esteem was important to improved reemployment prospects of unemployed workers. As part of an 8-day workshop, which met every other work day for $2\frac{1}{2}$ weeks, a behavior modeling process was used to increase job search skills. The process started with short videos demonstrating successful job search behavior followed by brief discussion of the behavior, and then by role playing in small groups. This latter step allowed each participant to practice the behavior and receive feedback from the others. The treatment resulted in increased general self-esteem and job search behavior. Reemployment increased more for those people who were initially low in self-esteem.

The Role of Feedback in Creating Positive Performance Cycles.   Feedback is the key to self-correcting adjustment in effort and performance and avoiding downward spirals (Lindsley, Brass, & Thomas, 1995). Knowing whether one succeeded or failed is not enough. Feedback must provide accurate, timely, and specific information about how one's behavior led to performance improvement. Inaccurate or delayed feedback may cause one to use inappropriate performance strategies in the future. That is, the person must understand the cause–effect relation between his or her behavior and subsequent performance. This is why negative feedback should be provided without threatening the person's self-image. Similarly, positive feedback should be given in a way that fosters attention to the effort–behavior–performance linkages rather than general flattery. Breaking tasks into small components can be an effective way to obtain manageable information and experiment with new behaviors without undue risk. Small losses can be analyzed carefully and new behaviors tried. Small wins can be repeated and followed by incrementally more complex actions.

Learning to Use Feedback

Negative feedback alone will not necessarily lead to a constructive response. Instead, it may lead people to be defensive or merely to ignore the information. Negative feedback will not have much effect on people who are low in self-awareness. These individuals are likely to tune out unfavorable information about their performance. However, people with low performance who are guided through the feedback in a way that makes them pay attention to and reflect on the performance data are likely to avoid the same mistakes later (Heatherton, Polivy, Herman, & Baumeister, 1993). When confronted with unfavorable feedback, subordinates are likely to be defensive, deny the problem, or blame situational factors beyond their control, including the supervisor's unrealistic expectations and demands (Meyer, 1991). Interventions can encourage people to consider feedback more carefully (the topics of chapters 11 and 12).

Summary

This section describes the concepts involved in developing a corporate culture that encourages feedback and enhances employees' favorable disposition toward feedback. Rather than deny, ignore, or withhold feedback, employees and managers seek, provide, and discuss performance feedback and learning needs on an ongoing basis, creating positive performance cycles. However, negative feedback can become a self-fulfilling prophesy, and some people's negative personality characteristics are likely to thwart the value of feedback. Organizations need to work hard to create environments that support learning, and feedback, goal setting, and development are keys to successful learning.

CONCLUSION

This chapter concludes the section on new horizons in feedback started in the preceding chapter's discussion of feedback in teams and cross-cultural organizations. Here, I discuss how emerging technologies facilitate providing feedback, coaching, and opportunities for self-determined learning. I describe how feedback, embedded in an integrated human performance system, can create positive performance improvement cycles. In general, organizations can establish environments that use feedback effectively to promote continuous learning that matches the organization's need for change. Here are some final conclusions:

1. We can expect abundant feedback from objective, technology-based sources of information. This poses some threat and raises the challenge to develop useful computer-based modes for involving people in self-management for continuous performance improvement.

2. People are increasingly responsible for their own assessment of their skills, evaluation of opportunities and needs, and acquisition of the skills and knowledge required for continued success. Self-paced learners have autonomy to decide what they study as well as how, when, where, and at what pace. This raises exciting opportunities for cost-effective ways to deliver education effectively. However, these methods must take into account the need to motivate self-paged learners to evaluate their own strengths and weaknesses, learn on their own, set performance goals, and track their performance.

3. Jobs, roles, and work group structures are being transformed to impose new demands on employees. These changes emphasize work processes that cross functions, departments, and organization levels. People need to learn new competencies to work in these environments. They must learn how to design new positions and support the feedback and development of employees in the new and evolving positions.

4. Performance review and feedback processes should be part of an integrated human performance system that supports organizational goals. The system should include human resource policies and programs that support the same set of performance standards and objectives. Ensuring this linkage is not solely the responsibility of human resource professionals. A key component of every supervisor's job is human resource management. Therefore, all supervisors should recognize and be accountable for ongoing performance review and constructive feedback aimed at employees' development and continuous performance improvement.

5. An organization environment that empowers self-development promotes the collection and use of feedback (e.g., through a multisource feedback survey and the availability of coaches). Also, the organization can make available information about organizational goals and business directions and

the implications of anticipated changes for performance expectations and promotional opportunities.

6. A feedback-friendly, or feedback-oriented, corporate culture is one in which managers and employees are comfortable with giving and receiving feedback, and in which feedback is an integral part of the performance management process. A feedback-oriented culture can be developed by enhancing the quality of feedback, emphasizing the importance of feedback in the organization, and providing support for using feedback.

7. Employees high in feedback orientation like feedback, do not mind being evaluated, and actually seek feedback. They are sensitive to how others view them, and they care what other people think of them. Feedback-oriented corporate cultures promote employees' feedback orientation.

8. Reactions to feedback may depend on the ages, leadership style, and personality of the feedback provider and receiver. Performance ratings generally are highly related to the personality of the person rated, indicating that ratings are a way to identify people with dysfunctional characteristics. Also, these characteristics may negatively influence the validity of these managers' ratings of others.

9. As people learn to use feedback, they can set goals to avoid negative results and establish positive cycles of reinforcement for performance improvement.

References

9 to 5, Working Women Education Fund (1990). *Stories of mistrust and manipulation: The electronic monitoring of the American workforce.* Cleveland, OH: Author.

Abelson, R. P. (1976). Script processing, attitude formation and decision making. In J. S. Carroll & J. W. Payne (Eds.), *Cognition and social behavior* (pp. 33–46). Hillsdale, NJ: Lawrence Erlbaum Associates.

Aiello, J. R., & Kolb. K. J. (1995). Electronic performance monitoring and social context: Impact on productivity and stress. *Journal of Applied Psychology, 80,* 339–353.

Altman, I., & Taylor, D. A. (1973). *Social penetration: The development of interpersonal relationships.* New York: Holt, Rinehart and Winston.

Anderson, L. R. (1990). Toward a two-track model of leadership training: Suggestions from self-monitoring theory. *Small Group Research, 21*(2), 147–167.

Anderson, L. R., & Thacker, J. (1985). Self-monitoring and sex as related to assessment center ratings and job performance. *Basic and Applied Psychology, 6,* 345–361.

Antonioni, D. (1994). The effects of feedback accountability on upward appraisal ratings. *Personnel Psychology, 47,* 349–356.

Antonioni, D. (1996). Designing an effective 360-degree appraisal feedback process. *Organizational Dynamics, 25,* 24–38.

Ashford, S. J. (1986). Feedback seeking in individual adaptation: A resource perspective. *Academy of Management Journal, 29,* 465–487.

Ashford, S. J. (1989). Self-assessments in organizations: A literature review and integrative model. *Research in Organizational Behavior, 11,* 133–174.

Ashford, S. J., & Cummings, L. L. (1983). Feedback as an individual resource: Personal strategies of creating information. *Organizational Behavior and Human Performance, 32,* 370–398.

Ashford, S. J., & Northcraft, G. B. (1992). Conveying more (or less) than we realize: The role of impression management in feedback-seeking. *Organizational Behavior and Human Decision Processes, 53,* 310–334.

Ashford, S. J., & Tsui, A. S. (1991). Self-regulation for managerial effectiveness: The role of active feedback seeking. *Academy of Management Journal, 34*(2), 251–280.

Atwater, L. E., Brett, J. F., Waldman, D., & Yammarino, F. (2000). *Predictors and outcomes of upward feedback.* Unpublished manuscript, Arizona State University West.

Atwater, L. E., Ostroff, C., Yammarino, F. J., & Fleenor, J. W. (1998). Self–other agreement: Does it really matter. *Personnel Psychology, 51,* 577–598.

Atwater, L., Roush, P., & Fischthal, A. (1992). *The impact of feedback on leaders' performance and self-evaluations.* SUNY-Binghamton, School of Management, Working Paper 92–220.

Atwater, L. E., Roush, P., & Fischthal, A. (1995). The influence of upward feedback on self and follower ratings of leadership. *Personnel Psychology, 48*, 34–60.

Atwater, L. E., Waldman, D., Atwater, D., & Cartier, P. (2000). An upward feedback field experiment: Supervisors' cynicism, follow-up, and commitment to subordidnates. *Personnel Psychology, 53*, 275–297.

Atwater, L. E., Waldman, D. A., & Brett, J. F. (2002). Understanding and optimizing multisource feedback. *Human Resource Management Journal, 41*(2), 193–208.

Avolio, B. J., Kahai, S., Dumdum, R., & Sivasubramaniam, N. (2001). Virtual teams: Implications for e-leadership and team development. In M. London (Ed.), *How people evaluate others in organizations* (pp. 337–358). Mahwah, NJ: Lawrence Erlbaum Associates.

Babad, E. Y., Inbar, J., & Rosenthal, R. (1982). Pygmalion, Galatea, and the Golem: Investigations of biased and unbiased teachers. *Journal of Educational Psychology, 74*, 459–474.

Bailey, B. A. (1990). Developing self-awareness through simulation gaming. *Journal of Management Development, 9*(2), 38–42.

Bales, R. F. (1950). *Interaction process analysis: A method for the study of small groups*. Cambridge, MA: Addison-Wesley.

Bales, R. F. (1988). A new overview of the SYMLOG system: Measuring and changing behavior in groups. In R. B. Polley, A. P. Hare, & P. J. Stone (Eds.), *The SYMLOG practitioner: Applications of small group research* (pp. 319–344). New York: Praeger.

Balzer, W., Doherty, M., & O'Connor, R., Jr. (1989). Effects of cognitive feedback on performance. *Psychological Bulletin, 106*, 410–433.

Banaji, M., Hardin, C., & Rothman, A. (1993). Implicit stereotyping in person judgment. *Journal of Personality and Social Psychology, 65*, 272–281.

Bandura, A. (1982). Self-efficacy mechanisms in human agency. *American Psychologist, 37*, 122–147.

Bandura, A. (1986). *Social foundations of thought and action: A social-cognitive view*. Englewood Cliffs, NJ: Prentice-Hall.

Bandura, A. (1997). *Self-efficacy: The exercise of control*. New York, NY: Freeman.

Barnes-Farrell, J. L. (2001). Performance appraisal: Person perception processes and challenges. In M. London (Ed.), *How people evaluate others in organizations* (pp. 135–153). Mahwah, NJ: Lawrence Erlbaum Associates.

Baron, R. A. (1988). Negative effects of destructive criticism: Impact on conflict, self-efficacy, and task performance. *Journal of Applied Psychology, 73*, 199–207.

Barrick, M. R., & Mount, M. K. (1991). The Big Five personality dimensions and performance: A meta-analyses. *Personnel Psychology, 44*, 1–26.

Barrick, M. R., Stewart, G. L., & Piotrowski, M. (2002). Personality and job performance: Test of the mediating effects of motivation among sales representatives. *Journal of Applied Psychology, 87*(1), 43–51.

Bartlett, C. A., & Ghoshal, S. (1997). The myth of the general manager. *California Management Review, 40*, 92–116.

Bass, B. M., & Yammarino, F. J. (1991). Congruence of self and others' leadership ratings of naval officers for understanding successful performance. *Applied Psychology: An International Review, 40*, 437–454.

Bassman, E. S. (1992). *Abuse in the workplace: Management remedies and bottom line impact*. Westport, CT: Quorum Books.

Bateman, T. S., & Organ, D. W. (1983). Job satisfaction and the good soldier: The relationship between affect and employee "citizenship." *Academy of Management Journal, 26*, 587–595.

Baumeister, R. F. (1982). A self-presentational view of social phenomena. *Psychological Bulletin, 91*, 3–26.

Beach, L. R. (1990). *Image theory: Decision making in personal and organizational contexts*. New York: Wiley.

Beach, L. R., & Mitchell, T. R. (1978). A contingency model for the selection of decision strategies. *Academy of Management Review, 3*, 439–449.

Benedict, M. E., & Levine, E. L. (1988). Delay and distortion: Tacit influences on performance appraisal effectiveness. *Journal of Applied Psychology, 73*, 507–514.

Bernardin, H. J., Hagan, C., Ross, S., & Kane, J. S. (1995, May). *The effects of a 360–degree appraisal system on managerial performance.* Paper presented in a symposium titled "Upward feedback: The ups and downs of it" (Chair: W. W. Tornow) at the Tenth Annual Conference of the Society for Industrial and Organizational Psychology, Orlando, FL.

Berson, Y. R., Erez, M., & Adler, S. (2002, April). *360-degree feedback on managerial performance across cultures.* Paper presented at the 17th Annual Meeting of the Society of Industrial and Organizational Psychology, Toronto, Ontario, Canada.

Blakely, G. L. (1993). The effects of performance rating discrepancies on supervisors and sub- ordinates. *Organizational Behavior and Human Decision Processes, 54*, 57–80.

Boice, R. (1983). Observational skills. *Psychological Bulletin, 93*, 3–29.

Borman, W. C. (1979). Format and traiing effects on rating accuracy and rater errors. *Journal of Applied Psychology, 64*, 410–421.

Borman, W. C., Buck, D. E., Hanson, M. A., Motowidlo, S. J., Stark, S., & Drasgow, F. (2001). An examination of the comparative reliability, validity, and accuracy of performance rat- ings made using computerized adaptive rating scales. *Journal of Applied Psychology, 86*(5), 965–973.

Botwood, L. (2002, April). Feelings about feedback: *Predicting affective reactions from work goal orientation.* Paper presented at the 17th Annual Meeting of the Society for Industrial and Organizational Psychology, Toronto, Ontario, Canada.

Bracken, D. W. (1996). Multisource (360–degree) feedback: Surveys for individual and organi- zational development. In A. I. Kraut (Ed.), *Organizational surveys: Tools for assessment and change* (pp. 117–143). San Francisco: Jossey-Bass.

Brett, J. F., & Atwater, L. E. (2001). 360° feedback: Accuracy, reactions, and perceptions of usefulness. *Journal of Applied Psychology, 86*, 930–942.

Brink, K. E. (2002, April). *Self-efficacy and goal change in the absence of external feedback: Pre- dicting executive performance with multirater surveys: Who you ask matters.* Paper presented at the 17th Annual Meeting of the Society for Industrial and Organizational Psychology, Toronto, Ontario, Canada.

Brockner, J., Derr, W. R., & Laing, W. N. (1987). Self- esteem and reactions to negative feedback: Toward greater generalizability. *Journal of Research in Personality, 21*, 318–333.

Brooks, P. W., Jr. (1998). Contextual trait measurement of leadership effectiveness: A field study of the retail industry. *Dissertation Abstracts International: Section B: The Sciences & Engineering, 58*(12-B), 6852.

Brown, D. J., & Lord, R. G. (2001). Leadership and perceiver cognition: Moving beyond first order constructs. In M. London (Ed.), *How people evaluate others in organization* (pp. 181– 202). Mahwah, NJ: Lawrence Erlbaum Associates.

Brown, S. P., Ganesan, S., & Challagalla, G. (2001). Self-efficacy as a moderator of information- seeking effectiveness. *Journal of Applied Psychology, 86*(5), 1043–1051.

Buss, D. M. (1991). Evolutionary personality psychology. In M. R. Rosenzweig, & L. W. Porter (Eds.), *Annual review of psychology* (pp. 459–492). Palo Alto, CA: Annual Reviews.

Carnevale, P. J. D. (1985). Accountability of group representatives and intergroup relations. *Advances in Group Processes, 2*, 227–246.

Carver, C. S., & Scheier, M. F. (1981). *Attention and self-regulation: A control theory of human behavior.* New York: Springer-Verlag.

Carver, C. S., & Scheier, M. F. (1982). Control theory: A useful conceptual framework for personality-social, clinical, and health psychology. *Psychological Bulletin, 92*, 111–135.

Cascio, W. F. (1986). *Managing human resources.* New York: McGraw-Hill.

244 REFERENCES

Cascio, W. F., & Silbey, V. (1979). Utility of the assessment center as a selection device. *Journal of Applied Psychology, 64*, 107–118.

Casey, J. T., London, M., & Chatterjee, S. (1995, May). *Anticipated reactions to mixed performance feedback: Self-enhancement and loss aversion.* Paper presented at the Annual Meeting of the Society for Industrial and Organizational Psychology, Orlando, FL.

Church, A. H. (2000). Do higher performing managers actually receive better ratings? A validation of multirater assessment methodology. *Consulting Psychology Journal: Practice and Research, 52*, 99–116.

Cialdini, R. (1989). Indirect tactics of image management: Beyond basking. In R. A. Giacalone & P. Rosenfeld (Eds.), *Impression management in the organization* (pp. 45–56). Hillsdale, NJ: Lawrence Erlbaum Associates.

Clardy, A. (2000). Learning on their own: Vocationally oriented self-directed learning projects. *Human Resource Development Quarterly, 11*(2), 105–125.

Cohen, R., Bianco, A. T., Cairo, P., & Geczy, C. (2002, April). *Leadership performance as a function of multisource survey feedback.* Paper presented at the 17th Annual Meeting of the Society for Industrial and Organizational Psychology, Toronto, Ontario, Canada.

Colquitt, J. A., LePine, J. A., & Noe, R. A. (2000). Toward an integrative theory of training motivation: A meta-analytic path analysis of 20 years of research. *Journal of Applied Psychology, 85*(5), 678–707.

Conway, J. M., & Huffcutt, A. I. (1997). Psychometric properties of multisource performance ratings: A meta-analysis of subordinate, supervisor, peer, and self-ratings. *Human Performance, 10*(4), 331–360.

Conway, R. L. (1999). *The impact of coaching midlevel managers utilizing multirater feedback.* Doctoral dissertation, University of La Verne, La Verne, CA.

Copeland, J. T. (1993). Motivational approaches to expectancy confirmation. *Current Directions in Psychological Science, 2*, 117–121.

Cortina, J. M., Goldstein, N. B., Payne, S. C., Davison, H. K., & Gilliland, S. W. (2000). The incremental validity of interview scores over and above cognitive ability and conscientiousness scores. *Personnel Psychology, 53*, 325–352.

Dalton, M., & Wilson, M. (2000). The relationship of the Five-Factor model of personality to job performance for a group of Middle Eastern expatriate managers. *Journal of Cross-Cultural Psychology, 31*(2), 250–258.

Dalton, M. A., & Hollenbeck, G. P. (2001). After feedback: How to facilitate change in behavior. In D. W. Bracken, C. W. Timmreck, & A. H. Church (Eds.), *The handbook of multisource feedback* (pp. 352–367). San Francisco, CA: Jossey-Bass.

Dalessio, A. T. (1998). Using multisource feedback for employee development and personnel decisions. In J. W. Smither (Ed.), *Performance appraisal: State of the art in parctice* (pp. 278–330). San Francisco: Jossey-Bass.

DeNisi, A. S., & Kluger, A. N. (2000). Feedback effectiveness: Can 360-degree appraisals be improved. *Academy of Management Executive, 14*(1), 129–139.

Deutch, M., & Gerard, H. B. (1955). Study of normative and informational influence upon individual judgment. *Journal of Abnormal and Social Psychology, 51*, 629–636.

Dobbins, G. N., & Russell, J. M. (1986). The biasing effects of subordinate likaideness on leaders' response to poor perfumes: A laboratory and a field study. *Personnel Psychology, 39*, 759–777.

Drasgow, F., Olson, J. B., Keenan, P. A., Moberg, P., & Mead, A. D. (1993). Computerized assessment. *Research in Personnel and Human Resources Management, 11*, 163–206.

Drew, S. A. W., & Davidson, A. (1993). Simulation-based leadership development and team learning. *The Journal of Management Development, 12*(8), 39–352.

Dweck, C. S. (1986). Motivational processes affecting learning. *American Psychologist, 41*, 1040–1048.

Dweck, C. S., & Legget, E. L. (1988). A social-cognitive approach to motivation and personality. *Psychological Review, 95*, 256–273.

Edelstein, B. C., & Armstrong, D. J. (1993). A model for executive development. *Human Resource Planning, 16*(4), 51–64.

Eden, D. (1992). Leadership and expectations: Pygmalion effects and other self-fulfilling prophecies in organizations. *Leadership Quarterly, 3*, 271–305.

Eden, D., & Aviram, A. (1993). Self-efficacy training to speed reemployment: Helping people to help themselves. *Journal of Applied Psychology, 78*, 352–360.

Eden, D., & Ravid, G. (1982). Pygmalion vs. self-expectancy: Effects of instructor- and self-expectancy on trainee performance. *Organizational Behavior and Human Performance, 30*, 351–364.

Elliot, A. J., & Harackiewicz, J. M. (1996). Approach and avoidance achievement goals and intrinsic motivation: A mediational analysis. *Journal of Personality and Social Psychology, 70*, 461–475.

Evans, P., Pucik, V., & Barsoux, J. L. (2002). *The global challenge.* New York: McGraw Hill.

Facteau, C. L., Facteau, J. D., Schoel, L. C., Russell, J. E. A., & Poteet, M. L. (1998). Reactions of leaders to 360-degree feedback from subordinates and peers. *Leadership Quarterly, 9*(4), 427–448.

Fandt, P. M., & Ferris, G. R. (1990). The management of information and impressions: When employees behave opportunistically. *Organizational Behavior and Human Decision Processes, 45*, 140–158.

Farh, J. L., Dobbins, G. H., & Cheng, B. S. (1991). Cultural relativity in action: A comparison of self-ratings made by Chinese and U.S. workers. *Personnel Psychology, 44*, 129–147.

Fedor, D. B., Buckley, M. R., & Eder, R. W. (1990). Measuring subordinate perceptions of supervisor feedback intentions: Some unsettling results. *Educational and Psychological Measurement, 50*, 73–89.

Fedor, D. B., Rensvold, R. B., & Adams, S. M. (1992). An investigation of factors expected to affect feedback seeking: A longitudinal field study. *Personnel Psychology, 45*, 779–805.

Feldman, J. M. (1981). Beyond attribution theory. Cognitive processes in performance appraisal. *Journal of Applied Psychology, 66*, 127–148.

Fenigstein, A., & Abrams, D. (1993). Self-attention and the egocentric assumption of shared perspectives. *Journal of Experimental Social Psychology, 29*, 287–303.

Ferris, G. R., Judge, T. A., Rowland, K. M., & Fitzgibbons, D. E. (1994), Subordinate influence and performance evaluation process: Test of a model. *Organizational Behavior and Human Decision Processes, 58*, 101–135.

Festinger, L. (1954). A theory of social comparison processes. *Human Relations, 7*, 117–140.

Fiore, S. M., Salas, E., & Cannon-Bowers, J. A. (2001). Group dynamics and shared mental model development. In M. London (Ed.), *How people evaluate others in organizations* (pp. 309–336). Mahwah, NJ: Lawrence Erlbaum Associates.

Fisher, C. D. (1979). Transmission of positive and negative feedback to subordinates: A laboratory investigation. *Journal of Applied Psychology, 64*, 533–540.

Fiske, S. T., Xu, J., Cuddy, A. J. C., & Glick, P. (1999). (Dis)respecting versus (dis)liking: Status and interdependence predict ambivalent stereotypes of competence and warmth. *Journal of Social Issues, 55*(3), 473–489.

Fleenor, J., McCauley, C., & Brutus, S. (1996). Self–other rating agreement and leader effectiveness. *Leadership Quarterly, 7*, 487–506.

Fleming, B., & Holland, B. (2002a, April). *How dark side personality factors impact performance ratings: A meta-analysis.* Paper presented at the 17th Annual Meeting of the Society for Industrial and Organizational Psychology, Toronto, Ontario, Canada.

Fleming, B., & Holland, B. (2002b, April). *Flawed interpersonal strategies and multisource feedback.* Paper presented at the 17th Annual Meeting of the Society for Industrial and Organizational Psychology, Toronto, Ontario, Canada.

Fleming, J. B. (1979). *Stopping wife abuse*. New York: Anchor Books.

Ford, J. K., & Weldon, E. (1981). Forewarning and accountability: Effects on memory-based interpersonal judgments. *Personality and Social Psychology Bulletin, 7*, 264–268.

Forgas, J. P. (1995). Mood and judgment: The affect infusion model (AIM). *Psychological Bulletin, 117*, 39–66.

Fournies, F. F. (1999). *Coaching for improved work performance* (3rd ed.). New York: McGraw-Hill.

Fried, Y., Tiegs, R. B., & Bellamy, A. R. (1992). Personal and interpersonal predictors of supervisors' avoidance of evaluating subordinates. *Journal of Applied Psychology, 77*, 462–468.

Funder, D. C. (1987). Errors and mistakes. Evaluating the accuracy of social judgment. *Psychological Bulletin, 101*, 75–90.

Fusilier, M. R. (1980). The effects of anonymity and outcome contingencies on rater beliefs and behavior in a performance appraisal situation. *Proceedings of the 40th Annual Meeting of the Academy of Management*, pp. 273–277.

Gabarro, J. J. (1990). The development of working relationships. In J. Galegher, R. E. Kraut, & C. Egido (Eds.), *Intellectual teamwork: Social and technological foundations of cooperative work* (pp. 79–110). Hillsdale, NJ: Lawrence Erlbaum Associates.

Gallatin, L. (1989). *Electronic monitoring in the workplace: Supervision or surveillance?* Boston: Massachusetts Coalition on New Office Technology.

Galunic, D. C., & Eisenhardt, K. M. (2001). Architectural innovation and modular corporate forms. *Academy of Management Journal, 44*, 1229–1249.

Gangestad, S., & Snyder, M. (1985). To carve nature at its joints: On the existence of discrete classes of personality. *Psychological Review, 92*, 317–349

Gardner, W. L., III. (1991, April). *The impact of impression management on the performance appraisal process*. Paper presented at the Sixth Annual Meeting of the Society for Industrial and Organizational Psychology, St. Louis, MO.

Gardner, W. L, III. (1992). Lessons in organizational dramaturgy: The art of impression management *Organizational Dynamics, 21*(1), 33–46.

Geen, R. G. (1991). Social motivation. *Annual Review of Psychology, 42*, 377–399.

Gersick, C. (1988). Time and transition in work teams: Toward a new model of group development. *Academy of Management Journal, 31*, 9–41.

Gersick, C. J. G. (1989). Marking time: Predictable transitions in task groups. *Academy of Management Journal, 32*, 274–309.

Gersick, C. J. G., & Hackman, J. R. (1990). Habitual routines in task-performing groups. *Organizational Behavior and Human Decision Processes, 47*, 65–97.

Ghorpade, J. (2000). Managing five paradoxes of 360-degree feedback. *Academy of Management Executive, 14*(1), 140–150.

Gifford, R. (1994). A lens-mapping framework for understanding the encoding and decoding of interpersonal dispositions in nonverbal behavior. *Journal of Personality and Social Psychology, 66*, 398–412.

Gillespie, T. L. (2002, April). Global 360: *Balancing consistency across cultures*. Paper presented at the 17th Annual Meeting of the Society of Industrial and Organizational Psychology, Toronto, Ontario, Canada.

Goffin, R. D., & Anderson, D. W. (2002, April). *Differences in self- and superior ratings of performance: Personality provides clues*. Paper presented at the 17th Annual Meeting of the Society for Industrial and Organizational Psychology, Toronto, Ontario, Canada.

Goldberg, L. R. (1990). An alternative "description of personality": The big five factor structure. *Journal of Personality and Social Psychology, 59*, 1216–1229.

Goldberg L. R. (1992). The development of markers for the big five factor structure. *Psychological Assessment, 4*, 26–42.

Goldstein, A. P., & Sorcher, M. (1974). *Changing supervisory behavior*. Elmsford, NY: Pergamon Press.

Goodstone, M. S., & Diamante, T. (1998). Organizational use of therapeutic change: Strengthening multisource feedback systems through interdisciplinary coaching. *Consulting Psychology Journal: Practice and Research, 50*(3), 152–163.

Gordon, S., Mian, M. Z., & Gabel, L. (2002, April). *An exploratory analysis of the validity of multirater feedback and assessment center ratings.* Presented at the 17th Annual Meeting of the Society for Industrial and Organizational Psychology, Toronto, Ontario, Canada.

Graddick, M. M., & Lane, P. (1998). Evaluating executive performance. In J. W. Smither (Ed.), *Performance appraisal: State-of-the-art in practice* (pp. 370–403). San Francisco: Jossey-Bass.

Greenberg, J. (1990). Organizational justice: Yesterday, today, and tomorrow. *Journal of Management, 16,* 401–434.

Hackman, J. R. (Ed.).(1990). *Groups that work (and those that don't): Creating conditions for effective teamwork.* San Francisco: Jossey-Bass.

Hall, D. T., Otazo, K. L., & Hollenbeck, G. P. (1999). Behind closed doors: What really happens in executive coaching. *Organizational Dynamics, 27*(3), 39–52.

Hallam, G. (2001). Multisource feedback for teams. In D. W. Bracken, C. W. Timmreck, & A. H. Church (Eds.), *The handbook of multisource feedback* (pp. 289–300). San Francisco, CA: Jossey-Bass.

Halverson, S., Tonidandel, S., Barlow, C., & Dipboye, R. L. (2002, April). *Self–other agreement on a 360-degree leadership evaluation.* Paper presented at the 17th Annual Meeting of the Society for Industrial and Organizational Psychology, Toronto, Ontario, Canada.

Hardin, C. D., & Higgins, E. T. (1996). Shared reality: How social verification makes the subjective objective. In R. M. Sorrentino & E. T. Higgins (Eds.), *Handbook of motivation and cognition: The interpersonal context* (Vol. 3, pp. 28–84). New York: Guilford Press.

Harris, M. (1999). Practice network: Look, it's an I-O psychologist . . . No, it's a trainer . . . No, it's an executive coach! *The Industrial-Organizational Psychologist, 36*(3), 38–42.

Harris, M. M., & Schaubroeck, J. (1988). A meta-nalysis of self–manager, self–peer, and peer–manager ratings. *Personnel Psychology, 41,* 43–62.

Harris, P. R., & Moran, R. T. (1987). *Managing cultural difference.* Houston: Gulf.

Hatten, J. T., Glaman, J. M., Houston, J., & Cochran, C. C. (2002, April). *Do assessment center scores predict 360 evaluations?* Presented at the 17th Annual Meting of the Society for Industrial and Organizational Psychology, Toronto, Ontario, Canada.

Hazucha, J. F., Hezlett, S. A., & Schneider, R. J. (1993). The impact of 360-degree feedback on management skills development. *Human Resource Management, 32,* 325–351.

Heath, C., & Jourden, F. (1997). Illusion, disillusion, and the buffering effect of groups. *Organizational Behavior and Human Decision Processes, 69*(2), 103–116.

Heatherton, T. F., Polivy, J., Herman, C. P., & Baumeister, R. F. (1993). Self-awareness, task failure, and disinhibition: How attentional focus affects eating. *Journal of Personality, 61,* 49–59.

Hegarty, W. H. (1974). Using subordinate ratings to elicit behavioral changes in managers. *Journal of Applied Psychology, 59,* 764–766.

Herriot, P. (1989). Attribution theory and interview decisions. In R. W. Eder & G. R. Ferris (Eds.), *The employment interview: Theory, research, and practice* (pp. 97–110). Newbury Park, CA: Sage.

Heslin, P. A., & Latham, G. P. (2001, April). *The effect of upward feedback on managerial behavior.* Paper presented at the Sixteenth Annual Conference of the Society for Industrial and Organizational Psychology, San Diego, CA.

Higgins, E. T. (1987). Self-discrepancy: A theory relating self and affect. *Psychological Review, 94,* 319–340.

Higgins, T., Bargh, J., & Lombardi, W. (1985). Nature of priming effects on categorization. *Journal of Experimental Psychology: Learning, Memory, and Cognition, 11,* 59–69.

Higgins, T., Rholes, W., & Jones, C. (1977). Category accessibility and impression formation. *Journal of Experimental Social Psychology, 13,* 141–154.

Hill, C. E., & Corbett, M. M. (1993). A perspective on the history of process and outcome research in counseling psychology. *Journal of Counseling Psychology, 40*, 3–24.

Hillman, L. W., Schwandt, D. R., & Bartz, D. E. (1990). Enhancing staff members' performance through feedback and coaching. *The Journal of Management Development, 9*(3), 20–27.

Hofstede, G. (2001). *Culture's consequences* (2nd ed.). Thousand Oaks: Sage.

Hogan, R., Hogan J., & Roberts B. W. (1996). Personality measurement and employment decisions: Questions and answers. *American Psychologist, 51*, 469–477.

Hollenbeck, G. P., & McCall, M. W. (1999). Leadership development: Contemporary practices. In A. I. Kraut and A. K. Korman (Eds.), *Evolving practices in human resource management.* (pp. 172–200). San Francisco: Jossey-Bass.

Holt, K., Noe, R. A., & Cavanaugh, M. (1995). *Managers' developmental responses to 360-degree feedback.* Working paper, Department of Management, Michigan State University.

Howard, A. (1997). A reassessment of assessment centers: Challenges for the 21st century. *Journal of Social Behavior and Personality, 12*(5), 13–52.

Hurley, A. E. (1993). *The effects of self-esteem and source credibility on self-denying prophecies.* Unpublished manuscript, Harriman School for Management and Policy, SUNY-Stony Brook.

Ilgen, D. R., Barnes-Farrell, J. L., & McKellin, D. B. (1993). Performance appraisal process research in the 1980s: What has it contributed to appraisals in use?*Organizational Behavior and Human Decision Processes, 54*, 321–368.

Ilgen, D. R., Fisher, C. D., & Taylor, M. S. (1979). Consequences of individual feedback on behavior in organizations. *Journal of Applied Psychology, 64*, 349–371.

Ilgen, D. R., & Knowlton, W. A. (1980). Performance attribution effects on feedback from supervisors. *Organizational Behavior and Human Performance, 25*, 441– 456.

Irving, R. H., Higgins, C. A., & Safayeni, F. R. (1986). Computerized performance monitoring systems: Use and abuse. *Communications of the ACM, 29*, 794–801.

Jackson, D. N. (1997). *Jackson Personality Inventory—Revised: Manual.* Port Huron, MI: Sigma Assessment Systems.

Jacobson, N. S., & Margolin, G. (1979). *Marital therapy: Strategies based on social learning and behavior exchange principles.* New York: Brunner/Mazel.

James, S. (1994). Recent advances in management development: Self-directed, continuous development through "Smart Software." *The Journal of Management Development, 13*(7), 35–39.

Jawahar, I. M. (2001). Attitudes, self-monitoring, and appraisal behavior. *Journal of Applied Psychology, 86*(5), 875–883.

Jawahar, I. M., & Stone, T. H. (1997). Appraisal purpose versus perceived consequences: The effects of appraisal purpose, perceived consequences, and rater self-monitoring on lenience of ratings and decisions. *Research and Practice in Human Resource Management, 5*, 33–54.

Jawahar, I. M., & Williams, C. R. (1997). Where all the children are above average: The performance appraisal purpose effect. *Personnel Psychology, 50*, 905–925.

John, O. (1990). The "Big-Five" factor taxonomy: Dimensions of personality in the natural language and in questionnaires. In L. A. Pervin (Ed.), *Handbook of personality theory and research* (pp. 66–100). New York: Guilford.

Johnson, J. W. (2001). The relative importance of task and contextual performance dimensions to supervisor judgments of overall performance. *Journal of Applied Psychology, 86*(5), 984–996.

Johnson, J. W., & Ferstl, K. L. (1999). The effects of interrater and self–other agreement on performance improvement following upward feedback. *Personnel Psychology, 52*(2), 271–303.

Johnson, K. M., & Johnson, J. W. (2001, April). *The influence of self–other agreement on performance improvement following feedback from multiple sources.* Paper presented at a symposium titled "If I could put time in a model: Understanding constructs longitudinally" (Chair, F. L. Oswald) at the Sixteenth Annual Conference of the Society for Industrial and Organizational Psychology, San Diego, CA.

Johnston, S. (1986). How one organization uses "The Looking Glass, Inc." *The Journal of Management Development, 5*(4), 46–50.

Jones, E. E. (1964). *Ingratiation: A social psychological analysis*. New York: Appleton-Century-Crofts.

Jones, E. E., & Berglas, S. (1978). Control of attributions about the self through self-handicapping strategies: The appeal of alcohol and the role of underachievement. *Personality and Social Psychology Bulletin, 4,* 200–206.

Jones, R. G., & Whitmore, M. D. (1995). Evaluating developmental assessment centers as interventions. *Personnel Psychology, 48,* 377–388.

Jourden, F., & Heath, C. (1996). The evaluation gap in performance perceptions: Illusory perceptions of groups and individuals. *Journal of Applied Psychology, 81,* 369–379.

Judge, T. A., & Bono, J. E. (2001). Relationship of core self-evaluation traits—self-esteem, generalized self-efficacy, locus of control, and emotional stability—with job satisfaction and job performance: A meta-analysis. *Journal of Applied Psychology, 86,* 80–92.

Judge, T. A., & Ferris, G. R. (1993). Social context of performance evaluation decisions. *Academy of Management Journal, 36,* 80–105.

Kahn, W. A. (1993). Caring for caregivers: Patterns of organizational care giving. *Administrative Science Quarterly, 38,* 546.

Kanter, R. M. (1977). *Men and women of the corporation*. New York: Basic Books.

Kaplan, R. E. (1986). What one manager learned in "The Looking Glass" and how he learned it. *The Journal of Management Development, 5*(4), 36–45.

Kaplan, R. E. (1993). 360-degree Feedback PLUS: Boosting the power of coworker ratings for executives. *Human Resource Management, 32,* 299–314.

Karl, K. A., & Kopf, J. M. (1993, August). *Will individuals who need to improve their performance the most, volunteer to receive videotaped feedback?* Presented at the Annual Meeting of the Academy of Management, Atlanta, GA.

Kelley, H. H. (1972). Attribution theory in social interaction. In E. Jones, D. E. Kanouse, H. H. Kelley, R. E. Nisbett, S. Valins, & B. Weinere (Eds.), *Attribution: Perceiving the causes of behavior*. Morristown, NJ: General Learning Press.

Kelly, J. R., & McGrath, J. E. (1985). Effects of time limits and task types on task performance and interaction of four-person groups. *Journal of Personality and Social Psychology, 49,* 395–407.

Kenny, D. A., & DePaulo, B. M. (1993). Do people know how others view them? An empirical and theoretical account. *Psychological Bulletin, 114,* 145–161.

Keys, J. B. (Ed.). (1994). Practice fields for the learning organization. *The Journal of Management Development, 13*(8), 1–56.

Kilburg, R. R. (1996). Toward a conceptual understanding and definition of executive coaching. *Consulting Psychology Journal: Practice and Research, 48*(2), 134–144.

Kilburg, R. R. (1997). Coaching and executive character: Core problems and basic approaches. *Consulting Psychology Journal: Practice & Research, 49*(4), 281–299.

King, B. A. (1995). Working with a new staff mix. *RN,* June, 38–41.

Kinicki, A. J., Hom, P. W., Trost, M. R., & Wade, K. J. (1995). Effects of category prototypes on performance-rating accuracy. *Journal of Applied Psychology, 80,* 354–370.

Klimoski, R., & Inks, L. (1990). Accountability forces in performance appraisal. *Organizational Behavior and Human Decision Processes, 45,* 194–208.

Klimoski, R. J., & Donahue, L. M. (2001). Person perception in organizations: An overview of the field. In M. London (Ed.), *How people evaluate others in organizations* (pp. 5–43). Mahwah, NJ: Lawrence Erlbaum Associates.

Kluger, A. N., & DeNisi, A. (1996). Effects of feedback interventions on performance: A historical review, a meta-analysis, and preliminary feedback intervention theory. *Psychological Bulletin, 119,* 254–284.

Kluger, A. N., & DeNisi, A. (1998). Feedback interventions: Toward the understanding of a double-edged sword. *Current Directions in Psychological Scinece, 7*(3), 67–72.

Kopelman, R. E. (1986). *Managing productivity in organizations: A practical, people-oriented perspective*. New York: McGraw-Hill.

Korsgaard, M. A., Meglino, B. M., & Lester, S. W. (1997). Beyond helping: Do other-oriented values have broader implications in organizations? *Journal of Applied Psychology, 82,* 160–177.

Kozlowski, S. W. J., Chao, G. T., & Morrison, R. F. (1998). Games raters play: Politics, strategies, and impression management in performance appraisal. In J. W. Smither (Ed.), *Performance appraisal: State of the art in parctice* (pp. 163–205). San Francisco: Jossey-Bass.

Kozlowski, S. W. J., DeShon, R. P., Schmidt, A. M., & Chambers, B. A. (2002, April). *Effects of feedback and goal orientation on individual and team regulation, learning, and performance.* Paper presented at the 17th Annual Meeting of the Society for Industrial and Organizational Psychology, Toronto, Ontario, Canada.

Kumar, K., & Beyerlein, M. (1991). Construction and validation of an instrument for measuring ingratiatory behaviors in organizational settings. *Journal of Applied Psychology, 76,* 619–627.

Langer, E. J. (1992). Matters of mind: Mindfulness/mindlessness in perspective. *Consciousness & Cognition: An International Journal, 1,* 289–305.

Larson, J. R., Jr. (1984). The performance feedback process: A preliminary model. *Organizational Behavior and Human Performance, 33,* 42–76.

Larson, J. R., Jr. (1986). Supervisors' performance feedback to subordinates: The impact of subordinate performance valence and outcome dependence. *Organizational Behavior and Human Performance, 37,* 391–408.

Larson, J. R., Jr. (1988). The dynamic interplay between employees' feedback-seeking strategies and supervisors' delivery of performance feedback. *Academy of Management Review, 14,* 408–422.

Latham, G. P., & Wexley, K. N. (1981). *Increasing productivity through performance appraisal.* Reading, MA: Addison-Wesley.

Lawler, E. E., III. (1999). *Rewarding excellence.* New York: Wiley.

Leary, M. R. (1983). *Understanding social anxiety.* Beverly Hills, CA: Sage.

Lennox, R., & Wolfe, R. (1984). Revision of the self-monitoring scale. *Journal of Personality and Social Psychology, 46,* 1349–1364.

Leonard, E., & Williams, J. R. (2001). *An empirical examination of accountability perceptions within a multisource feedback system.* Presented at the 16th Annual Meeting of the Society for Industrial and Organizational Psychology, San Diego, CA.

Levy, P. E. (1991). *Self-appraisal and attributional judgments.* Paper presented at the Sixth Annual Meeting of the Society for Industrial and Organizational Psychology, St. Louis, MO.

Lindsley, D. H., Brass, D. J., & Thomas, J. B. (1995). Efficacy-performance spirals: A multilevel perspective. *Academy of Management Review, 20*(3), 645–678.

Locke, E. A., & Latham, G. P. (1990). *A theory of goal setting and task performance.* Englewood Cliffs, NJ: Prentice-Hall.

Locke, E. A., & Latham, G. P. (1992). Comments on McLeod, Liker, and Lobel. *Journal of Applied Behavioral Science, 28,* 42–45.

Logue, A. W. (1995). *Self-control: Waiting until tomorrow for what you want today.* Englewood Cliffs, NJ: Prentice-Hall.

London, M. (1985). *Developing managers.* San Francisco: Jossey-Bass.

London, M. (1988). *Change agents: New roles and innovation strategies for human resource professionals.* San Francisco, CA: Jossey-Bass.

London, M. (1995a). *Self and interpersonal insight: How people learn about themselves and others in organizations.* New York: Oxford University Press.

London, M. (1995b). *Achieving excellence in university administration.* Westport, CT: Praeger.

London, M. (1995c). Giving feedback: Source-centered antecedents and consequences of constructive and destructive feedback. *Human Resource Management Review, 5*(3), 159–188.

London, M. (2001). The great debate: Should multisource feedback be used for administration or development only? In D. W. Bracken, C. W. Timmreck, & A. H. Church (Eds.), *The handbook of multisource feedback: The comprehensive resource for designing and implementing MSF processes* (pp. 368–385). San Francisco: Jossey-Bass.

London, M., & London, M. (1996). Tight coupling in high performing ensembles. *Human Resource Management Review, 6*(1), 1–24.

London, M., & Mone, E. M. (1987). *Career management and survival in the workplace.* San Francisco: Jossey-Bass.

London, M., & Mone, E. M. (1993). Managing marginal performance in an organization striving for excellence. In A. K. Korman (Ed.), *Human resources dilemmas in work organizations: Strategies for resolution* (pp. 95–124). New York: Guilford.

London, M., & Sessa, V. I. (1999). *Selecting international executives: A suggested framework and annotated bibliography.* Greensboro, NC: Center for Creative Leadership.

London, M., & Smither, J. W. (1995). Can multisource feedback change self-awareness and behavior? Theoretical applications and directions for research. *Personnel Psychology, 48,* 803–840.

London, M., & Smither, J. W. (1999). Empowered self-development and continuous learning. *Human Resource Management, 38*(1), 3–16.

London, M., & Smither, J. W. (2002). Feedback orientation, feedback culture, and the longitudinal performance management process. *Human Resource Management Review, 12*(1), 81–101.

London, M., Smither, J. W., & Adsit, D. J. (1996). Accountability: The Achilles Heal of multisource feedback. *Group and Organization Management, 22,* 162–184.

London, M., & Tornow, W. W. (1998). Introduction: 360-degree feedback–More than a tool! In W. W. Tornow and M. London (Eds.), *Maximizing the value of 360-degree feedback: A process for successful individual and organizational development* (pp. 1–8). San Francisco: Jossey-Bass.

London, M., Wohlers, A. J., & Gallagher, P. (1990). 360-degree feedback surveys: A source of feedback to guide management development. *Journal of Management Development, 9,* 17–31.

Lord, R., & Hanges, P. (1987). A control system model of organizational motivation. *Behavioral Science, 32,* 161–178.

Luft, J. (1970). *Group processes: An introduction to group dynamics.* Palo Alto, CA: National Press Books.

Mabe, P. A., & West, S. G. (1982). Validity of self-evaluation of ability: A review and meta-analysis. *Journal of Applied Psychology, 67,* 280–296.

Martocchio, J. J., & Dulebohn, J. (1994). Performance feedback effects in training: The role of perceived controllability. *Personnel Psychology, 47,* 357–373.

Maurer, T. J., Mitchell, R. D., & Barbeite, F. G. (2002). Predictors of attitudes toward a 360-degree feedback system and involvement in postfeedback management development activity. *Journal of Occupational and Organizational Psychology, 75,* 87–107.

Maurer, T. J., & Tarulli, B. A. (1994). *Acceptance of peer and upward performance appraisal systems: Considerations from employee development, job analysis, and leadership.* Unpublished manuscript, Georgia Institute of Technology.

McAfee, R. B., & Champagne, P. J. (1993). Performance management: A strategy for improving employee performance and productivity. *Journal of Managerial Psychology, 8*(5), 24–32.

McCall, M., & Lombardo, M. (1983). *Off the track: Why and how successful executives get derailed.* Technical Report # 21. Greensboro, NC: Center for Creative Leadership.

McCauley, C., & Lombardo, M. (1990). Benchmarks: An instrument for diagnosing managerial strengths and weaknesses. In K. E. Clark & M. B. Clark (Eds.), *Measures of leadership* (pp. 535–545). West Orange, NJ: Leadership Library of America.

McClelland, D. C. (1965). Achievement motivation can be developed. *Harvard Business Review, 43*(6), 6–14, 178.

McCrae, R. R., & John, O. P. (1992). An introduction to the five-factor model and its applications. *Journal of Personality, 60,* 175–216.

McDaniel, S., Pezzina, C., Bedon, B., & Kortick, S. (2002, April). *Multisource feedback and derailment: Predicting the dark side of leadership.* Paper presented at the 17th Annual Meeting of the Society for Industrial and Organizational Psychology, Toronto, Ontario, Canada.

McGill, M. E., Slocum, J. W., Jr., & Lei, D. (1992). Management practices in learning organizations. *Organizational Dynamics, 21*(1), 5.

McGovern, J., Lindemann, M., Vergara, M., Murphy, S., Barker, L., & Warrenfeltz, R. (2001). Maximizing the impact of executive coaching: Behavioral change, organizational outcomes, and return on investment. *The Manchester Review, 6*(1), 1–9.

McLeod, P. L., Liker, J. K., & Lobel, S. (1992). Process feedback in task groups: An application of goal setting. *Journal of Applied Behavioral Science, 28,* 15–41.

McManus, M. A., & Kelly, M. L. (1999). Personality measures and biodata: Evidence regarding their incremental predictive value in the life insurance industry. *Personnel Psychology, 52,* 137–148.

Mero, N. P., & Motowidlo, S. J. (1995). Effects of rater accountability on the accuracy and the favorability of performance ratings. *Journal of Applied Psychology, 80,* 517–524.

Meyer, H. H. (1991). A solution to the performance appraisal feedback enigma. *Academy of Management Executive. 5*(1), 68–76.

Mitchell, T. R., & Wood, R. E. (1980). Supervisor responses to subordinate poor performance: A test of an attributional model. *Organizational Behavior and Human Performance, 25,* 123–138.

Mitchell, T. W., & Klimoski, R. (1984). *Accountability bias in performance appraisal.* (Working Paper Series in Industrial/Organizational Psychology). Columbus: The Ohio State University.

Morrison, E. W., & Bies, R. J. (1991). Impression management the feedback-seeking process: A literature review and research agenda. *Academy of Management Review, 16*(3), 522–541.

Morrison, E. W., & Vancouver, J. B. (1993, August). *The effects of source attributes on feedback seeking.* Presented at the Annual Meeting of the Academy of Management. Atlanta, GA.

Motowidlo, S. J., & Van Scotter, J. R. (1994). Evidence that task performance should be distinguished from contextual performance. *Journal of Applied Psychology, 79,* 475–480.

Mount, M. K., & Barrick, M. R. (1998). Five reasons why the "Big Five" article has been frequently cited. *Personnel Psychology, 51,* 849–857.

Mount, M. K., Barrick, M. R., & Stewart, G. L. (1998). Five-factor model of personality and performance in jobs involving interpersonal interactions. *Human Performance, 11,* 145–165.

Mount, M. K., & Scullen, S. E. (2001). Multisource feedback ratings: What do they really measure. In M. London (Ed.), *How people evaluate others in organizations* (pp. 155–176), Mahwah, NJ: Lawrence Erlbaum Associates.

Munchus, G., III, & McArthur, B. (1991). Revisiting the historical use of the assessment centre in management selection and development. *Journal of Management Development, 10*(1), 5–13.

Murphy, K. R., Balzer, W. K., Kellam, K. L., & Armstrong, J. G. (1984). Effects of the purpose of rating on accuracy in observing teacher behavior and evaluating teaching performance. *Journal of Educational Psychology, 76,* 45–54.

Murphy, K. R., & Cleveland, J. (1995). *Understanding performance appraisal: Social, organizational, and goal-based perspectives.* Thousand Oaks, CA: Sage.

Murphy, K. R., & Cleveland, J. N. (1991). *Performance appraisal: An organizational perspective.* Needham Heights, MA: Allyn & Bacon.

Nadler, D. A. (1977). *Feedback and organization development: Using data-based methods.* Reading, MA: Addison-Wesley.

Nadler, D. A. (1979). The effects of feedback on task group behavior: A review of the experimental research. *Organizational Behavior and Human Performance, 23,* 309–338.

Napier, N. K., & Latham, G. P. (1986). Outcome expectancies of people who conduct performance appraisals. *Personnel Psychology, 39,* 827–837.

Neale, M. A., & Bazerman, M. H. (1991) *Cognition and rationality in negotiation.* New York: The Free Press.

Nemeroff, W. F., & Cosentino, J. (1979). Utilizing feedback and goal setting to increase performance appraisal interviewer skills of managers. *Academy of Management Journal, 22,* 566–576.

Nickerson, R. S. (1999). How we know—and sometimes misjudge—what others know: Imputing one's own knowledge to others. *Psychological Bulletin, 125,* 737–759.

Nisbett, R. E., & Wilson, T. D. (1977). Telling more than we know: Verbal reports on mental processes. *Psychological Review, 84,* 231–259.

Norris-Watts, C., & Levy, P. E. (2002, April). *The feedback environment and work outcome variables.* Paper presented at the 17th Annual Meeting of the Society for Industrial and Organizational Psychology, Toronto, Ontario, Canada.

Olivero, G., Bane, K. D., & Kopelman, R. E. (1997). Executive coaching as a transfer of training took effects on productivity in a public agency. *Public Personnel Management, 26,* 461–469.

Ones, D. S., Viswesvaran, C., & Schmidt, F. L. (1993). Comprehensive meta-analysis of integrity test validities: Findings and implications for personnel selection and theories of job performance. *Journal of Applied Psychology, 78,* 679–703.

Operario, D., & Fiske, S. T. (2001). Causes and consequences of stereotypes in organizations. In M. London (Ed.), *How people evaluate others in organizations* (pp. 45–62), Mahwah, NJ: Lawrence Erlbaum Associates.

Organ, D. W. (1988). *Organizational citizenship behavior: The good soldier syndrome.* Lexington, MA: Lexington Books.

Oz, S., & Eden, D. (1994). Restraining the Golem: Boosting performance by changing the interpretation of low scores. *Journal of Applied Psychology, 79,* 744–754.

Padgett, M. Y., & Ilgen, D. R. (1989). The impact of ratee performance characteristics on rater cognitive processes and alternative measures of rater accuracy. *Organizational Behavior and Human Decision Processes, 44,* 232–260.

Park, H., & Harrison, J. K. (1993). Enhancing managerial cross-cultural awareness and sensitivity: Transactional analysis revisited. *The Journal of Management Development, 12*(3), 20–29.

Perkins, D. N. (1981). *The mind's best work.* Cambridge, MA: Harvard University Press.

Podsakoff, P. M., & Farh, J. L. (1989). Effects of feedback sign and credibility on goal setting and task performance. *Organizational Behavior and Human Decision Processes, 44,* 45–67.

Prochaska, J. M., Prochaska, J. O., & Levesque, D. A. (2001). A transtheoretical approach to changing organizations. *Administration and Policy in Mental Health, 28*(4), 247–261.

Reilly, B. A., & Doherty, M. E. (1989). A note on the assessment of self-insight in judgment research. *Organizational Behavior and Human Decision Processes, 44,* 123–131.

Reilly, B. A., & Doherty, M. E. (1992). The assessment of self-insight in judgment policies. *Organizational Behavior and Human Decision Processes, 53,* 285–309.

Reilly, R. R., Smither, J. W., & Vasilopoulos, N. L. (1996). A longitudinal study of upward feedback. *Personnel Psychology, 49,* 599–612.

Reilly, R. R., Warech, M. A., & Reilly, S. (1993). *The influence of self-monitoring on the reliability and validity of upward feedback.* Paper presented at the Annual Meeting of the Society for Industrial and Organizational Psychology, San Francisco, CA.

Reiter–Palmon, R., & Haley, E. M. (2002, April). 360-feedback evaluation and turnover. Is there a relationship? Paper presented at the 17th annual meeting of The society for Industrial and Organizational Psychology, Toronto, Canada.

Rogers, C. R. (1980). *A way of being.* Boston: Houghton Mifflin.

Rogers, E., Barriere, M. T., Kaplan, I. T., & Metlay, W. (2002, April). *Multisource feedback practices that enhance organizational outcomes.* Paper presented at the 17th Annual Meeting of the Society for Industrial and Organizational Psychology, Toronto, Ontario, Canada.

Rose, D., & Farrell, T. (2002, April). *The use and abuse of comments in 360-degree feedback.* Paper presented at the 17th Annual Meeting of the Society for Industrial and Organizational Psychology, Toronto, Ontario, Canada.

Rosenthal, R. (1991). Teacher expectancy effects: A brief update 25 years after the Pygmalion experiment. *Journal of Research in Education, 1*, 3–12.

Rosenthal, R., & Jacobson, L. (1968). *Pygmalion in the classroom: Teacher expectations and pupils' intellectual development*. New York: Holt, Rinehart & Winston.

Ross, E. M., & Allen, N. J. (2002, April). *Evaluation of task performance: Do groups make a difference?* Paper presented at the 17th Annual Meeting of the Society for Industrial and Organizational Psychology, Toronto, Ontario, Canada.

Rouch, P. E., & Atwater, L. E. (1992). Using the MBTI to understand transformational leadership and self-perception accuracy. *Military Psychology, 4*, 17–34.

Russo, J. E., & Schoemaker, P. J. H. (1992). Managing overconfidence. *Sloan Management Review, 33*(2), 7–17.

Ryan, A. M., Brutus, S., Greguras, G. J., & Hakel, M. D. (2000). Receptivity to assessment-based feedback for management development. *Journal of Management Development, 19*(4), 252–276

Saavedra, R., Earley, P. C., & Van Dyne, L. (1993). Complex interdependence in task-performing groups. *Journal of Applied Psychology, 78*, 61–72.

Sackett, P. R., & Dreher, G. F. (1982). Constructs and assessment center dimensions: Some troubling empirical findings. *Journal of Applied Psychology, 67*(4), 401–410.

Sackett, P. R., & Dreher, G. F. (1984). Situation specificity of behavior and assessment center validation strategies: A rejoinder to Neidig and Neidig. *Journal of Applied Psychology, 69*, 187–190.

Sackett, P. R., & Tuzinski, K. A. (2001). The role of dimensions and exercises in assessment center judgments. In M. London (Ed.), *How people evaluate others in organizations* (pp. 111–129), Mahwah, NJ: Lawrence Erlbaum Associates.

Sala, F., & Dwight, S. (2002, April). *Predicting executive performance with multirater surveys: Who you ask matters.* Paper presented at the 17th Annual Meeting of the Society for Industrial and Organizational Psychology, Toronto, Ontario, Canada.

Salancik, G. R., & Pfeffer, J. A. (1978). A social information processing approach to job attitudes and task design. *Administrative Science Quarterly, 23*, 224–253.

Salvemini, N. J., Reilly, R. R., & Smither, J. W. (1993). The influence of rater motivation on assimilation effects and accuracy in performance ratings. *Organizational Behavior and Human Decision Processes, 55*, 41–60.

Sanders, M. M. (1993). Situational constraints through the cognitive looking glass: A reinterpretation of the relationship between situations and performance judgments. *Human Resource Management Review, 3*, 129–146.

Scherbaum, C. A., & Vancouver, J. B. (2002, April). *Testing two explanations for goal-setting effects: A persistent question.* Paper presented at the 17th Annual Meeting of the Society for Industrial and Organizational Psychology, Toronto, Ontario, Canada.

Schmit, M. J., Kihm, J. A., & Robie, C. (2000). Development of a global measure of personality. *Personnel Psychology, 53*(1), 153–193.

Schmit, M. J., & Ryan, A. M. (1993). The big five in personnel selection: Factor structure in applicant and nonapplicant populations. *Journal of Applied Psychology, 78*, 966–974.

Schrauger, J. S. (1975). Responses to evaluation as a function of initial self-perceptions. *Psychological Bulletin, 82*, 581–596.

Scott, J. C., & London, M. (in press). The evaluation of 360-degree feedback programs. In J. E. Edwards, J. C. Scott, & N. S. Raju (Eds.). *The human resources evaluation handbook*. Thousand Oaks, CA: Sage Publications.

Scullen, S. E., Mount, M. K., & Goff, M. (2000). Understanding the latent structure of job performance ratings. *Journal of Applied Psychology, 85*(6), 956–970.

Senge, P. M. (1990). *The fifth discipline: The art and practice of the learning organization*. New York: Doubleday.

Shrauger, J. S., & Shoeneman, J. (1979). Symbolic interactionist view of self-concept: Through the looking glass darkly. *Psychological Bulletin, 86,* 549–573.

Silverman, S. B. (1991). Individual development through performance appraisal. In K. N. Wexley, (Ed.), *Developing human resources* (pp. 120–151). Washington, D.C.: The Bureau of National Affairs.

Simonson, I., & Nye, P. (1992). The effect of accountability on susceptibility to decision errors. *Organizational Behavior and Human Decision Processes, 51,* 416–446.

Slovic, P., & Lichenstein, S. (1971). Comparison of Bayesian and regression approaches to the study of information processing in judgment. *Organizational Behavior and Human Performance, 6,* 649–744.

Smith, M. J., Carayon, P., Sanders, K. J., Lim, S.-Y., & LeGrande, D. (1992). Employee stress and health complaints in jobs with and without electronic performance monitoring. *Applied Ergonomics, 23,* 17–28.

Smither, W., London, M., Flautt, R., Vargas, Y., & Kucine, I. (2002, April). *Can executive coaches enhance the impact of multisource feedback on behavior change? A quasi-experimental field study.* Paper presented at the Annual Meeting of the Society of Industrial and Organizational Psychology, Toronto, Ontario, Canada.

Smither, J. W., London, M., Flautt, R., Vargas, Y., & Kucine, I. (in press). Can executive coaches enhance the impact of multisource feedback on behavior change? A quasi-experimental field study. *Personnel Psychology.*

Smither, J. W., London, M., & Richmond, K. R. (2002, April). *Relationships between leaders' personality and reactions to, and use of, multisource feedback: A longitudinal study.* Presented at the Annual Meeting of the Society for Industrial and Organizational Psychology. Toronto, Ontario, Canada.

Smither, J. W., London, M., & Richmond, K. R. (in press). Relationships between leaders' personality and reactions to, and use of, multisource feedback: A longitudinal study. *Group and Organization Management.*

Smither, J. W., & Reilly, S. P. (2001). Coaching in organizations. In M. London (Ed.), *How people evaluate others in organizations* (pp. 221–252), Mahwah, NJ: Lawrence Erlbaum Associates.

Smither, J. W., London, M., Vasilopoulos, N. L., Reilly, R. R., Millsap, R. E., & Salvemini, N. (1995). An examination of the effects of an upward feedback program over time. *Personnel Psychology, 48,* 1–34.

Smith-Jentsch, K. A., Campbell, G. E., Milanovich, D. M., & Reynolds, A. M. (2001). Measuring teamwork mental models to support training needs assessment, development, and evaluation: Two empirical studies. *Journal of Organizational Behavior, 22,* 179–194.

Snyder, M. (1974). Self-monitoring of expressive behavior. *Journal of Personality and Social Psychology, 30,* 526–537.

Snyder, M. (1979). Self-monitoring process. *Advances in Experimental Social Psychology, 30,* 526–537.

Snyder, M. (1987). *Public appearances, private realities: The psychology of self-monitoring.* New York: W. H. Freeman.

Snyder, M., & Gangestad, S. (1986). On the nature of self-monitoring: Matters of assessment, matters of validity. *Journal of Personality and Social Psychology, 51,* 125–135.

Spychalski, A. C., Quinones, M., Gaugler, B. B., & Pohley, K. (1997). A survey of assessment center practices in organizations in the United States. *Personnel Psychology, 50*(1), 71–90.

Stajkovic, A. D., & Luthans, F. (1998). Self-efficacy and work-related performance: A meta-analysis. *Psychological Bulletin, 124,* 240–261.

Stamoulis, D. T., & Hauenstein, N. M. A. (1993). Rater training and rating accuracy: Training for dimensional accuracy versus training for ratee differentiation. *Journal of Applied Psychology, 78,* 994–1003.

Steele, C. M., Spencer, S. J., & Lynch, M. (1993). Self-image resilience and dissonance: The role of affirmational resources. *Journal of Personality and Social Psychology, 64,* 885–896.

Steelman, L. A., & Levy, P. E. (2001). *The feedback environment and its potential role in 360-degree feedback.* Paper presented at the 16th Annual Meeting of the Society for Industrial and Organizational Psychology, San Diego, CA.

Steelman, L. A., Levy, P. E., & Snell, A. F. (2002). *The feedback environment scale (FES): Construct definition, measurement, and validation.* Unpublished manuscript, The University of Akron.

Steiner, D. D., Rain, J. S., & Smalley, M. M. (1993). Distributional ratings of performance: Further examination of a new rating format. *Journal of Applied Psychology, 78,* 438.

Steward, B. L., Carson, K. P., & Cardy, R. L. (1996). The joint effect of conscientiousness and self-leadership training on employee self-directed behavior in a service setting. *Personnel Psychology, 49,* 143–164.

Stewart, J., & Winter, R. (1992). Open and distance learning. In S. Truelove (Ed.), *Handbook of training and development* (pp. 197–229). Oxford: Blackwell.

Stinson, L., & Ickes, W. (1992). Empathic accuracy in the interactions of male friends versus male strangers. *Journal of Personality and Social Psychology, 62*(5), 787–797.

Stone, D., & Stone, E. (1985). The effects of feedback consistency and feedback favorability on self-perceived task competence and perceived feedback accuracy. *Organizational Behavior and Human Decision Processes, 36,* 167–185.

Storms, M. D. (1973). Videotape and the attribution process: Reversing actors' and observers' points of view. *Journal of Personality and Social Psychology, 27,* 165–175.

Stowell, S. J. (1988). Coaching: A commitment to leadership. *Training and Development Journal, 42*(6), 34–41.

Stumpf, S. A., & Dutton, J. E. (1990). The dynamics of learning through management simulations: Let's dance. *The Journal of Management Development, 9*(2), 7–15.

Stumpf, S. A., Watson, M. A., & Rustogi, H. (1994). Leadership in a global village: Creating practice fields to develop learning organizations. *Journal of Management Development, 13*(8), 16–25.

Summers, D. A., Taliaferro, J. D., & Fletcher, D. J. (1970). Subjective vs. objective descriptions of judgment policy. *Psychonomic Science, 18,* 249–250.

Sundstrom, E., De Meuse, K. P., & Futrell, D. (1990). Work teams: Applications and effectiveness. *American Psychologist, 45,* 120–133.

Surber, C. F. (1985). Measuring the importance of information in judgment: Individual differences in weighting ability and effort. *Organizational Behavior and Human Decision Processes, 35,* 156–178.

Taylor, S. M., Fisher, C. D., & Ilgen, D. R. (1984). Individuals' reactions to performance feedback in organizations: A control theory perspective. In K. M. Rowland & G. R. Ferris (Eds.), *Research in Personnel and Human Resources Management, 2,* 81–124.

Tetlock, P. E. (1983). Accountability and the perseverance of first impressions. *Social Psychology Quarterly, 46,* 74–83.

Tetlock, P. E. (1985a). Accountability: A social check on the fundamental attribution error. *Social Psychology Quarterly, 48,* 227–236.

Tetlock, P. E. (1985b). Accountability: The neglected social context of judgment and choice. *Research in Organizational Behavior, 7,* 297–332.

Tetlock, P. E., & Kim, J. I. (1992). Accountability and judgment processes in a personality prediction task. *Journal of Personality and Social Psychology, 52,* 700–709.

Tetlock, P. E., Skitka, L., & Boettger, R. (1989). Social and cognitive strategies for coping with accountability: Conformity, complexity, and bolstering. *Journal of Personality and Social Psychology, 57,* 632–640.

Thomas, J. B., Clark, S. M., & Gioia, D. A. (1993). Strategic sensemaking and organizational performance: Linkages among scanning, interpretation, action, and outcomes. *Academy of Management Journal, 36,* 239–270.

Thompson, L. (1991). Information exchange and negotiation. *Journal of Experimental Social Psychology, 27,* 161–179.

Thompson, L., & DeHarpport, T. (1994). Social judgment, feedback, and interpersonal learning in negotiation. *Organizational Behavior and Human Decision Processes, 58,* 327–345.

Thompson, L., & Hastie, R. (1990). Social perception in negotiation. *Organization and Human Decision Processes, 47,* 98–123.

Thornton, G. C., III, & Byham, W. C. (1982). *Assessment centers and managerial performance.* New York: Academic Press.

Thurstone, L. L. (1927). Psychophysical analysis. *American Journal of Psychology, 38,* 368–389.

Tice, D. M., & Baumeister, R. F. (1990). Self-esteem, self-handicapping, and self-presentation: The strategy of inadequate practice. *Journal of Personality, 58,* 443–464.

Timmreck, C. W., & Bracken, D. W. (1997). Multisource feedback: A study of its use in decision making. *Employment Relations Today, 24*(1), 21–27.

Tornow, W. W. (1993). Perceptions or reality: Is multiperspective measurement a means or an end? *Human Resource Management, 32,* 221–230.

Tsui, A. S., & Ohlott, P. (1988). Multiple assessment of managerial effectiveness: Interrater agreement and consensus in effectiveness models. *Personnel Psychology, 41,* 779–803.

Ury, W. I., Brett, J. M., & Goldberg, S. B. ((1988). *Getting disputes resolved.* San Francisco: Jossey- Bass.

VandeWalle, D. (1997). Development and validation of a work domain instrument. *Educational and Psychological Measurement, 57,* 995–1015.

VandeWalle, D., Brown, S. P., Cron, W. L., & Slocum, J. W., Jr. (1999). The influence of goal orientation and self-regulation tactics on sales performance: A longitudinal field test. *Journal of Applied Psychology, 84,* 249–259.

VandeWalle, D. M., & Cummings, L. L. (1997). A test of the influence of goal orientation on the feedback seeking process. *Journal of Applied Psychology, 82,* 390–400.

Van Velsor, E., & Leslie, J. B. (1991). *Feedback to managers: A guide to rating multiater feedback instruments,* Vol. 1. Report 149. Greensboro, NC: Center for Creative Leadership.

Waldman, D. A., & Atwater, L. E. (2001). Attitudinal and behavioral outcomes of an upward feedback process. *Group and Organization Management, 26,* 189–205.

Walker, A. G., & Smither, J. W. (1999). A five-year study of upward feedback: What managers do with their results matters. *Personnel Psychology, 52,* 393–423.

Warr, P., & Bunce, D. (1995). Training characteristics and the outcomes of open learning. *Personnel Psychology, 48,* 347–375.

Wayne, S. J., & Kacmar, K. M. (1991). The effects of impression management on the performance appraisal process. *Organizational Behavior and Human Decision Processes, 48,* 70–88.

Weick, K. E. (1995). *Sensemaking in organizations.* Newbury Park, CA: Sage.

Wells, L., Jr. (1992). Feedback, the group unconscious, and the unstated effects of experimental methods. *Journal of Applied Behavioral Science, 28,* 46–53.

White, J. W., & Gerstein, L. H. (1987). Helping: The influence of anticipated social sanctions and self-monitoring. *Journal of Personality, 55,* 41–54.

Whitney, K. (1994). Improving group task performance: The role of group goals and group efficacy. *Human Performance, 7,* 55–78.

Whitworth, L., Kimsey-House, H., & Sandahl, P. (1998). *Co-active coaching: New skills for coaching people toward success in work and life.* Palo Alto, CA: Consulting Psychologists Press.

Williams, K. J., DeNisi, A. S., Blencoe, A. G., & Cafferty, T. P. (1985). The role of appraisal purpose: Effects of purpose on information acquisition and utilization. *Organizational Behavior and Human Performance, 35,* 314–339.

Witherspoon, R., & White, R. P. (1996). Executive coaching: A continuum of roles. *Consulting Psychology Journal: Practice & Research, 48,* 124–133.

Witherspoon, R., & White, R. P. (1997). *Four essential ways that coaching can help executives.* Greensboro, NC: Center for Creative Leadership.

Witt, L. A., Burke, L. A., Barrick, M. R., & Mount, M. K. (2002). The interactive effects of conscientiousness and agreeableness on job performance. *Journal of Applied Psychology, 87*(1), 164–169.

Woehr, D. J., & Feldman, J. (1993). Processing objective and question order effects on the causal relation between memory and judgment in performance appraisal: The tip of the iceberg. *Journal of Applied Psychology, 78,* 232–241.

Wofford, J. C. (1994). An examination of the cognitive processes used to handle employee job problems. *Academy of Management Journal, 37,* 180–192.

Wohlers, A. J., & London, M. (1989). Ratings of managerial characteristics: Evaluation difficulty, coworker agreement, and self-awareness. *Personnel Psychology, 42,* 235–260.

Yammarino, F. J., & Atwater, L. E. (1993). Understanding self-perception accuracy: Implications for human resources management. *Human Resource Management, 32,* 231–249.

Yammarino, F. J., & Atwater, L. E. (1997). Do managers see themselves as others see them? Implications of self–other ratings agreement for human resources management. *Organization Dynamics, 25*(1), 35–44.

Yammarino, F. J., & Dubinsky, A. J. (1992). Supervisor–subordinate relationships: A multiple level of analysis approach. *Human Relations, 45,* 575–600.

Yu, J., & Murphy, K. R. (1993). Modesty bias in self-ratings of performance: A test of the cultural relativity hypothesis. *Personnel Psychology, 46,* 357–363.

Zajonc, R. B. (1965, July 16). Social facilitation. *Science, 149,* 269–274.

Zalesny, M. D., & Highhouse, S. (1992). Accuracy in performance evaluations. *Organizational Behavior and Human Decision Processes, 51,* 22–50.

Author Index

Subject Index

360-degree feedback, see Multisource feedback

A

Abusive behavior, 18
Accountability, 179–192
    definition, 181
    theory, 185–190
Adaptive performance, 68
Affiliation-dominated relationships, 19
Anonymity, 92
Appraisal and development cycle, 163–165
Assessment centers, 118–119
    and computerized testing, 126
    for development, 119–120
    measurement, 121–126
    multisource ratings, 122–126
Attribution biases, 59
Avon Corporation, 28

B

Behaviorally anchored rating scales, 71
Business games, see Business simulations,
    126–132
Business simulations, 118, 126–132
    computer based, 127
    group simulations, 127–129
    Looking Glass, 129, 131–132

C

Career planning, 221–222
Central tendency, 81
Change processes, see Change stages
Change stages, 138–141

Coaching, 154, 168–171
    elements, 170
    evaluating effects of, 173–175
    on-line, 223, 224–225
    stages, 171–172
    steps for effective coaching, 172–173
Cognitive processing, 57–58
Computerized adaptive rating scales, 72
Computerized testing, 126
Conscientiousness, 41
Constructive feedback, 15–17, 151–152
Corporate culture, 156–158
Cross-cultural organizations, 195
Cross-cultural training, 212–213

D

Decisions
    administrative, 87–88
Design
    survey and program development, 92–93
Destructive feedback, 17–20

E

Electronic performance monitoring,
    219–220
Empathy, 61

F

Feedback
    acceptance, 46–47
    anticipated reactions to, 34

265